How to Draw
Super Cute

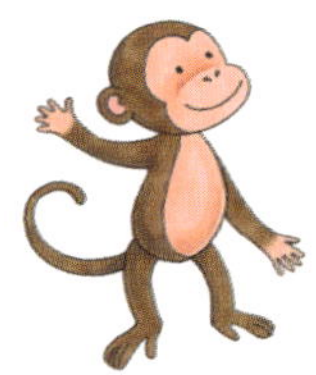

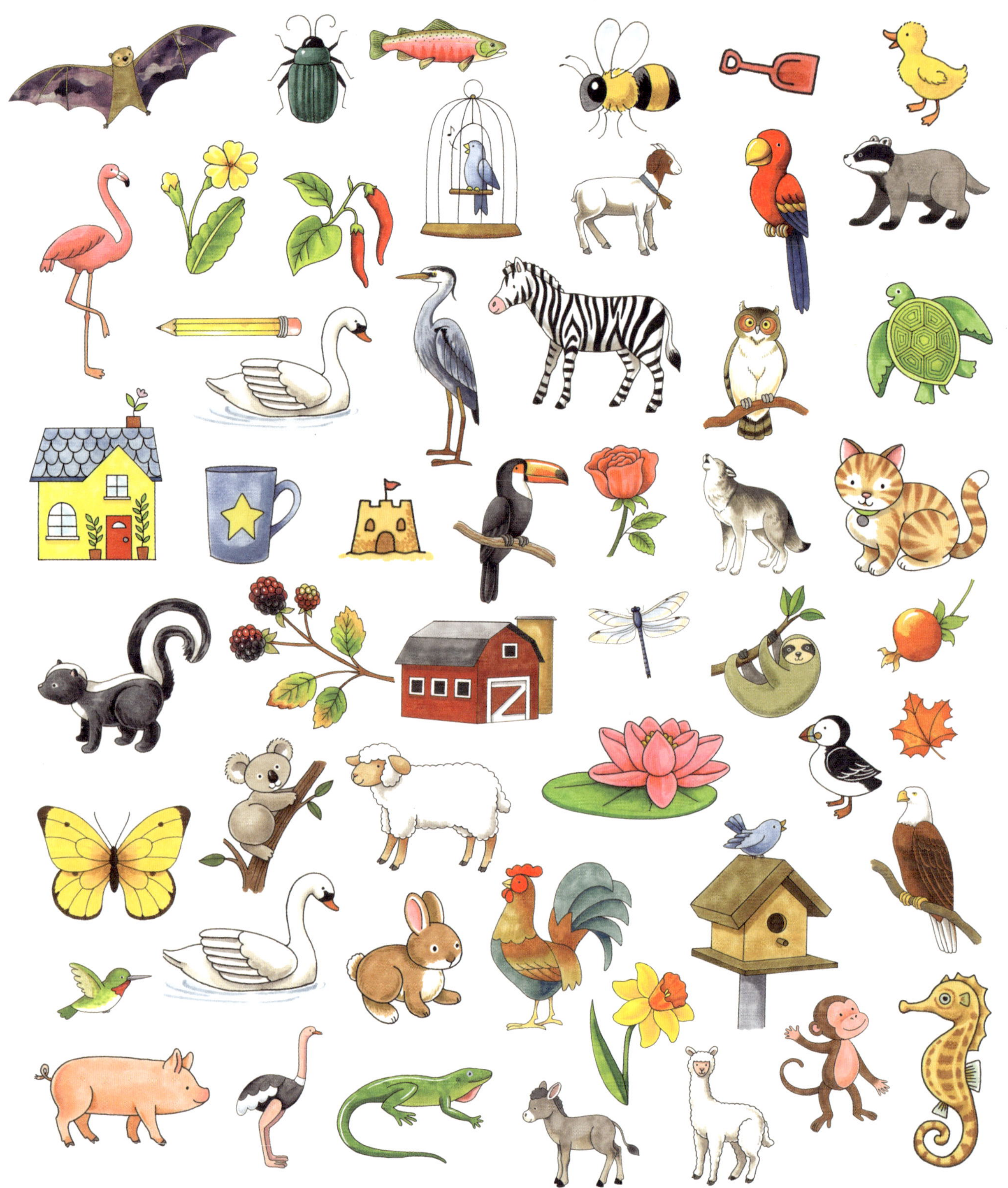

How to Draw
Super Cute

Adorable Doodles
Step by Step

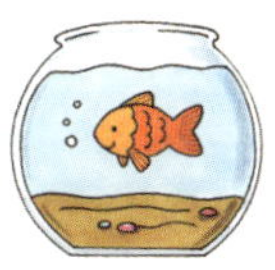

Jane Maday

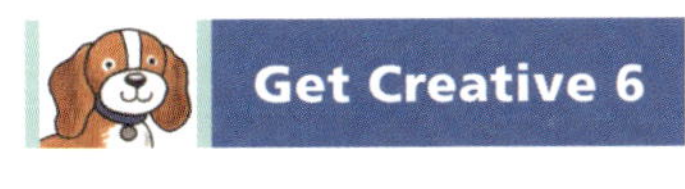

Get Creative 6

NEW YORK

Get Creative 6

An imprint of Mixed Media Resources, LLC
19 West 21st Street, Suite 601
New York, NY 10010

Editor
PAM KINGSLEY

Creative Director
IRENE LEDWITH

Art Director
FRANCESA PACCHINI

Chief Executive Officer
CAROLINE KILMER

President
ART JOINNIDES

Chairman
JAY STEIN

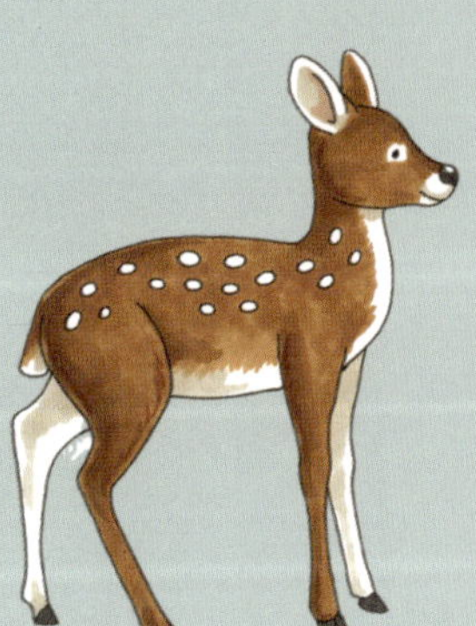

Copyright © 2024 Jane Maday

All rights reserved. No part of this publication may be reproduced or used in any form or by any means—graphic, electronic, or mechanical, including photocopying, recording, or information storage-and-retrieval systems—without permission of the publisher.

The designs in this book are intended for the personal, noncommercial use of the retail purchaser and are under federal copyright laws; they are not to be reproduced in any form for commercial use.

Library of Congress Cataloging-in-Publication Data
Names: Maday, Jane, author.
Title: How to draw super cute : adorable doodles step by step / Jane Maday.
Description: First edition. | New York, NY : Get Creative 6, [2024]
Identifiers: LCCN 2024024441 | ISBN 9781684620807 (paperback)
Subjects: LCSH: Doodles—Technique. | Drawing—Technique.
Classification: LCC NC915.D6 .M33 2024 | DDC 741.2—dc23/eng/20240530
LC record available at https://lccn.loc.gov/2024024441

ISBN: 978-1-68462-080-7

Manufactured in China

3 5 7 9 8 6 4 2

First Edition

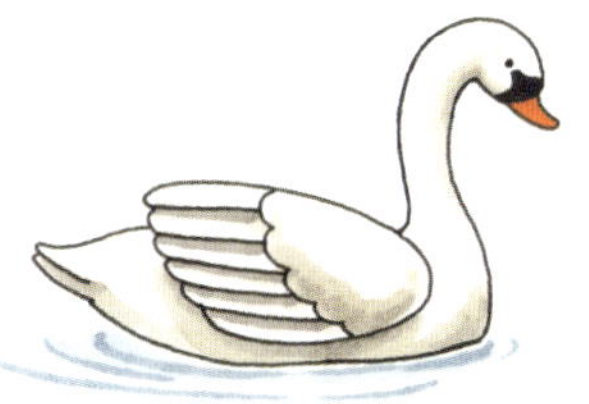

Contents

This book is dedicated to all my new friends
in the creative world.
It is so wonderful to be a part of a
community of kindred spirits.

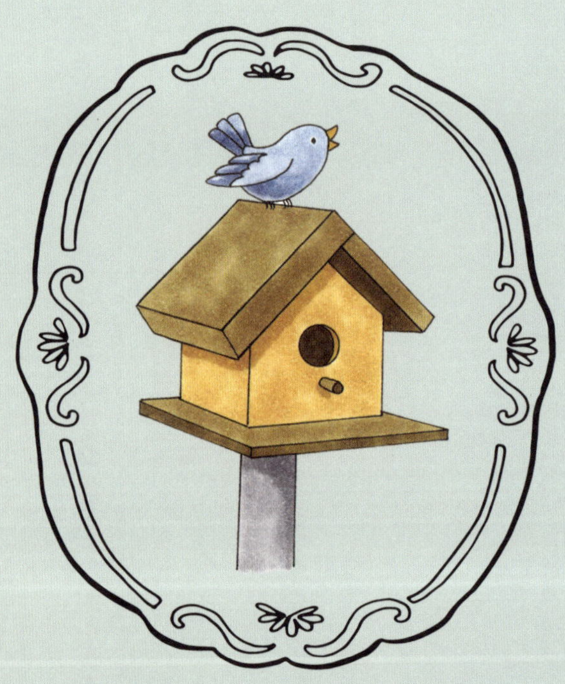

Many thanks to the crew at
Mixed Media Resources and Get Creative 6,
especially Pam, Caroline, and Francesca.

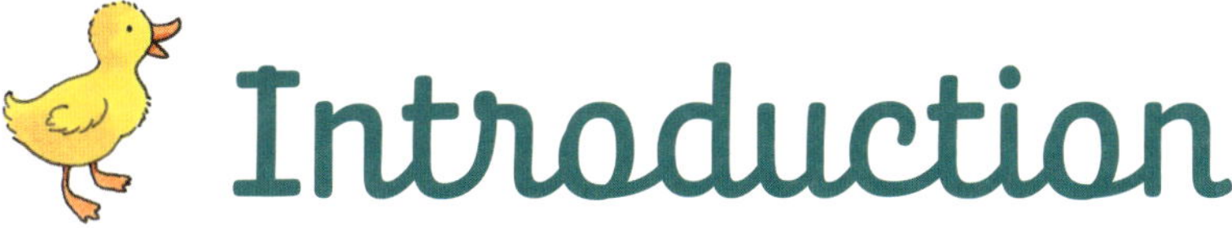 Introduction

Cute drawings appeal to nearly everyone. I love adding them to my journals and sketchbooks. The goal of my art is always to put a smile on the face of everyone who sees it, including me!

In this book, I'm going to teach you my method of drawing cute animals and objects, which is super easy. Art is a learning process that never stops. Everyone has to start somewhere, so let's start here together. And remember, there is no pressure to achieve perfection. Drawing cute is meant to be fun and relaxing. Think of it as an enjoyable and stress-free expression of self-care!

I encourage you to keep a sketchbook handy—I've always got one with me. You never know when inspiration will strike, or when you will find yourself with a few minutes and need something to occupy your mind and hands. Daily drawing is a valuable practice in both mindfulness and advancing your skills. It is also wonderful to be able to look back through your sketchbooks and see your progress.

I hope you enjoy using this book as much as I have enjoyed creating it for you. Your happiness will shine through your drawings and bring joy to those with whom you choose to share them. Relax, grab a pencil and pen, and get ready for some fun!

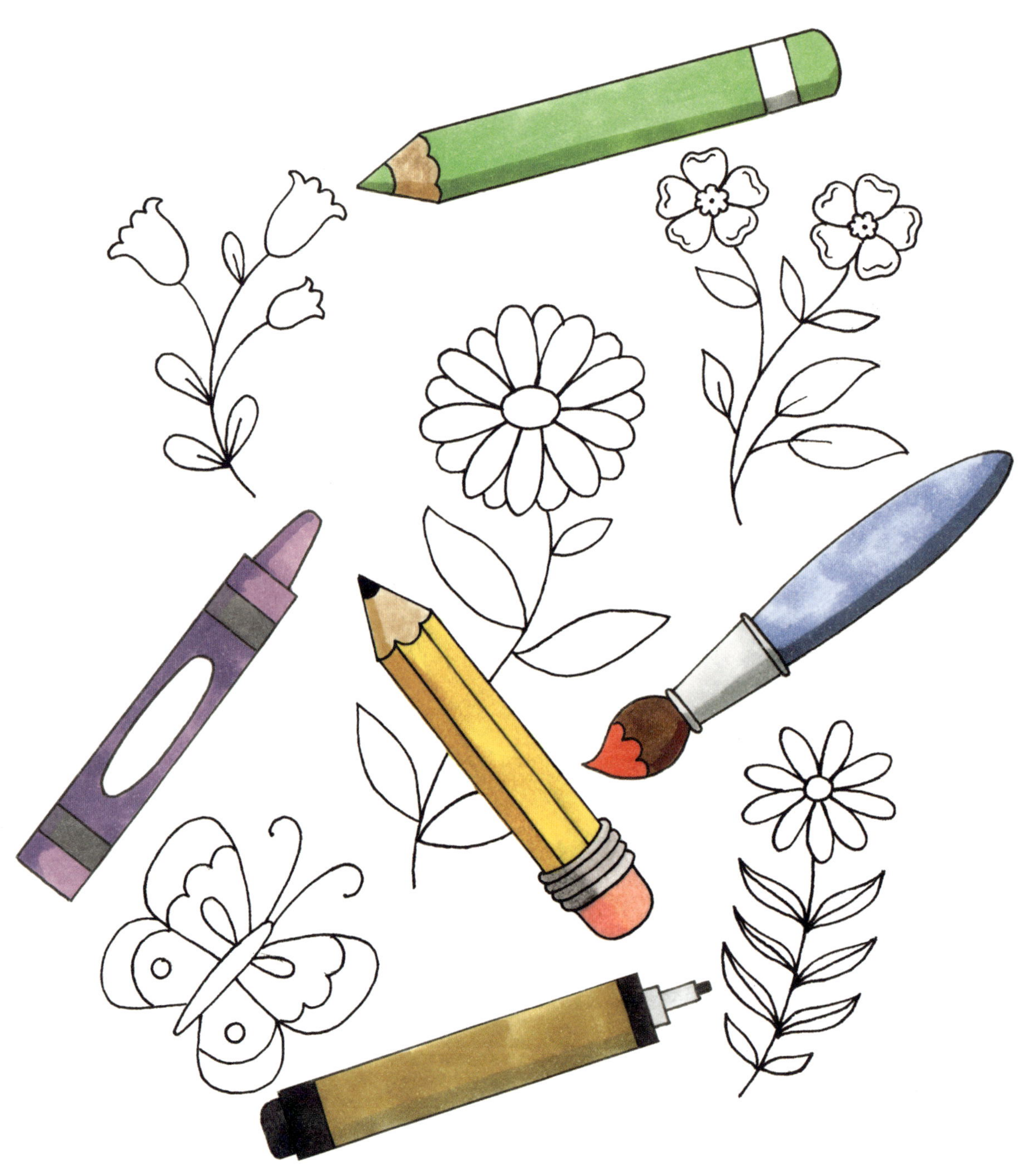

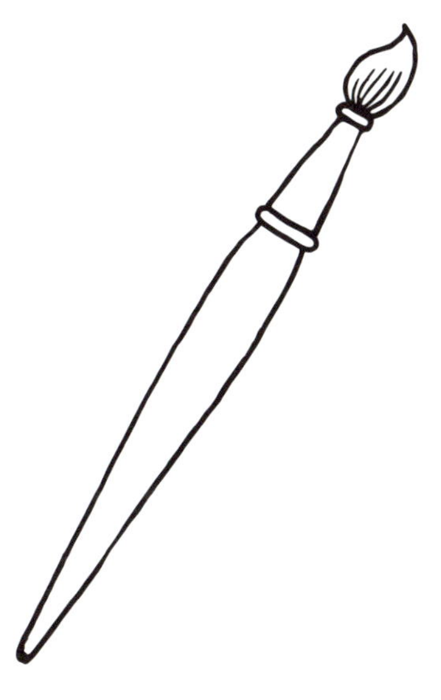

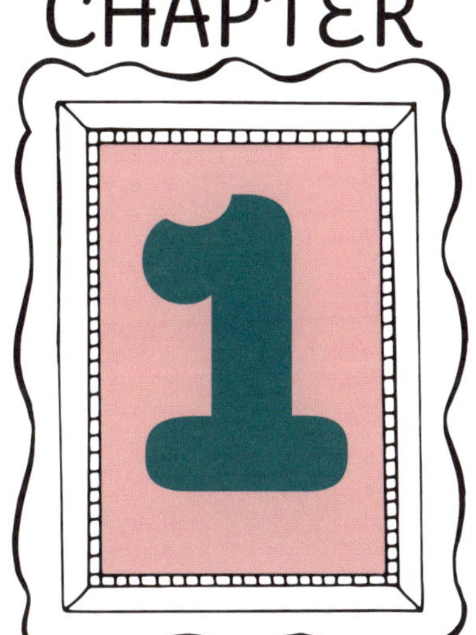

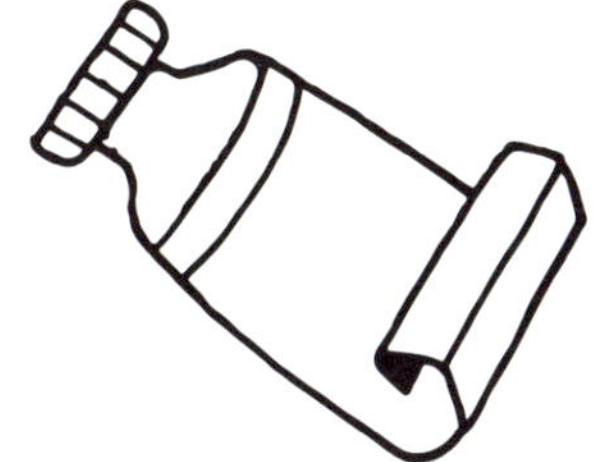

Materials & Techniques

In this chapter I will introduce you to the art supplies you might want to try, as well as basic drawing and coloring techniques. Feel free to play and experiment. Your drawings don't need to be perfect—the goal is to have fun!

Materials

You don't need a lot of fancy equipment to draw—you can start simply, with a pencil and eraser.

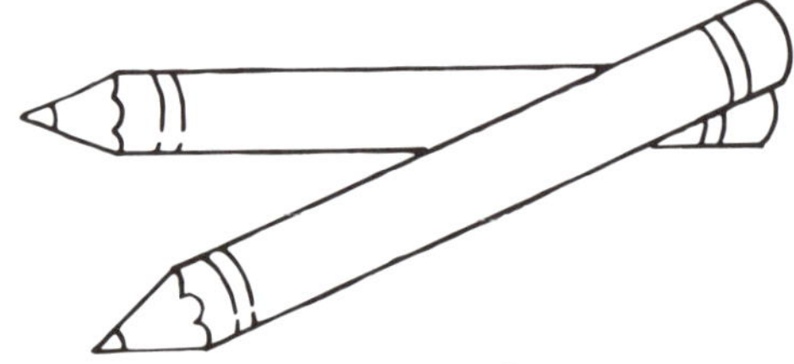

DRAWING TOOLS

I like mechanical pencils because they don't need sharpening, but an ordinary #2 school pencil is something everyone has. You can use the erasers that come with your pencils, but I prefer the white plastic ones, since they seem to remove pencil lines more cleanly. You can buy them either in a pencil or plain rectangular shape.

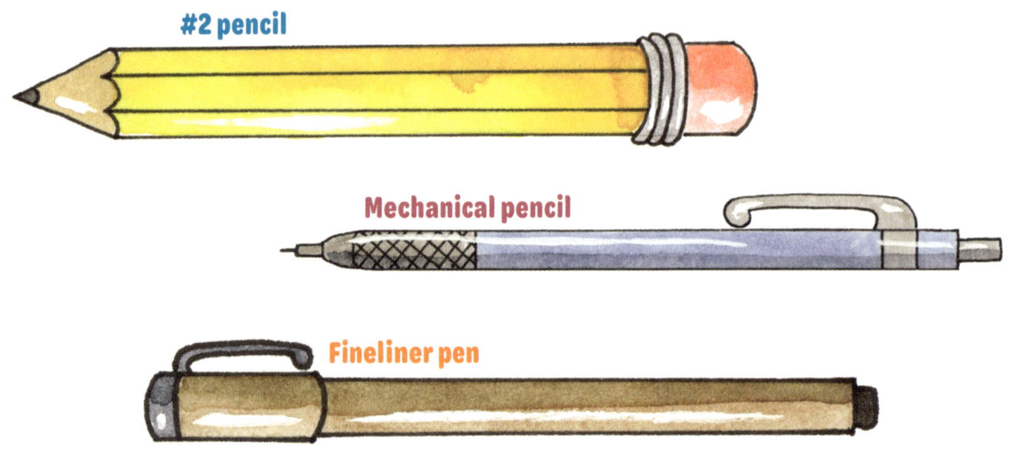

I draw everything with a pencil first, then go over it with a pen. My preference is a fineliner pen, in either black or brown. If you are going to color your drawings with markers or watercolors, make sure to use a waterproof pen or it will smear and ruin your drawing.

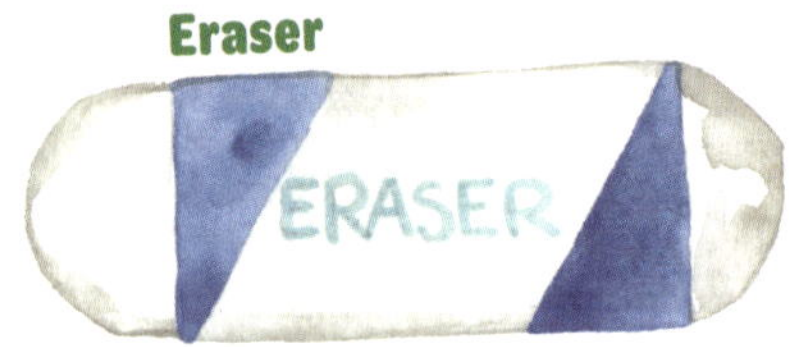

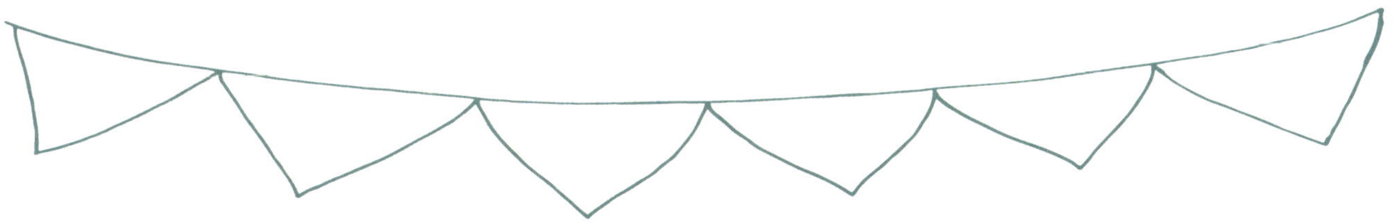

COLORING TOOLS & PAPER

All the drawings in this book have been colored using alcohol markers. I suggest buying a brand that sells them individually, rather than in sets, so that you can just buy the colors you want.

Alcohol markers usually have either a chisel tip and a brush tip, or a fine-point tip and a brush tip. I prefer the brush tip. Some other coloring options include colored pencils, watercolors, and water-based markers.

Always do a test to see how your paper will handle your chosen coloring medium. Alcohol markers will bleed through most papers, so place a protective sheet underneath when you are coloring. If you are using watercolor, you will need a fairly thick paper (at least 160gsm) for the best results. Colored pencils work best on paper that does not have much texture.

Alcohol marker with dual tips

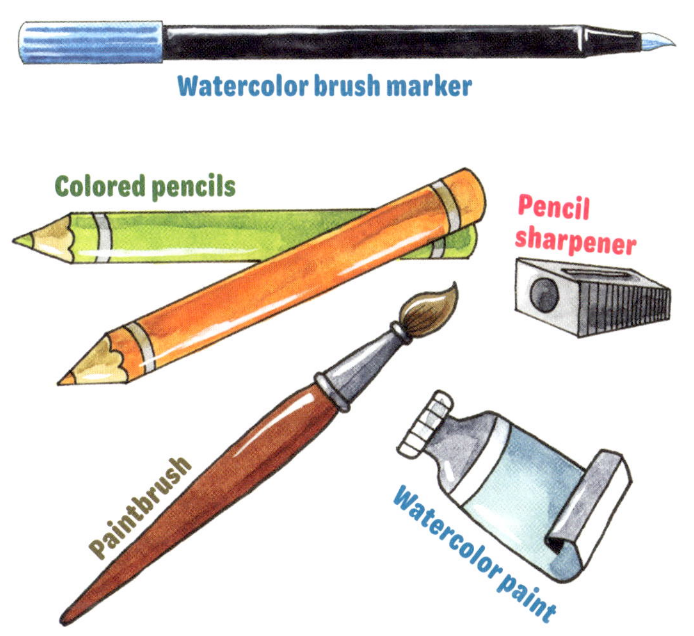

I like **alcohol markers** because I find it is easier to create a smooth blend with them. Watercolor brush markers might leave streaks on the paper, although that effect can sometimes be attractive if you are going for a sketchier look.

Lines & Values

Different tools create lines of different widths and result in differences in the depth of color, or values.

Pencils are generally graded from 6B (the softest) to 6H (the hardest). Softer pencils make darker marks that are harder to erase.

Here you can see the gradation in tone from a 6B pencil to a 6H pencil.

6B　　　　　　　　　　　　　　　　　　　　　　　　　　　　　**6H**

Fineliner pens make a solid line, and are great for outlining. They are good to use with a ruler, and they come in different widths. Brush pens give you a line that will vary in thickness, depending on how much pressure you apply. The greater the pressure, the thicker the line. They make a more expressive line than a fineliner pen or pencil.

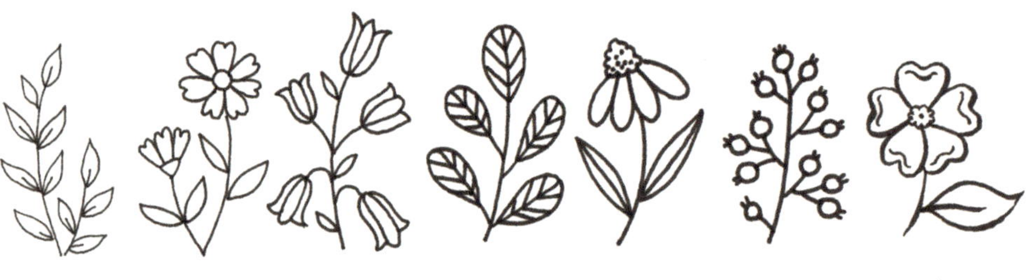

These sketches give examples of fineliner widths.

Whether you are working in pencil or in color, **value** refers to the range from dark to light. Your drawing will be more pleasing if it has contrast, meaning both lighter and darker areas, rather than all one value of color or tone.

Layer your color to achieve a blend from light to dark.

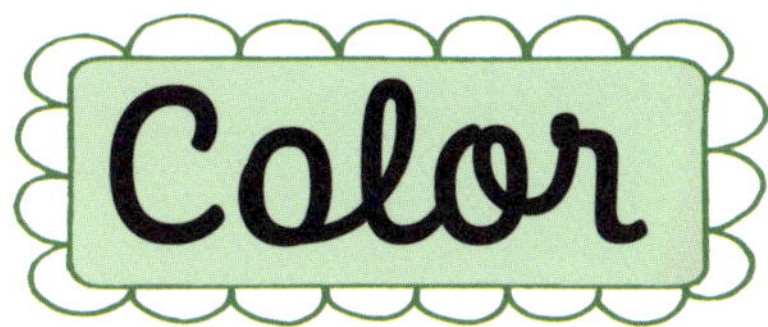

Color

Color is one of the most fun aspects of drawing! Here are a few basic guidelines.

Primary colors are red, blue, and yellow.

Secondary colors are the colors that can be made by adding different primary colors together: orange (red + yellow), green (blue + yellow), and violet (blue + red).

Tertiary colors are created by blending different secondary colors together: yellow-green, yellow-orange, and red-violet.

Complementary colors are colors that are opposite one another on the color wheel (red and green, blue and orange, yellow and violet).

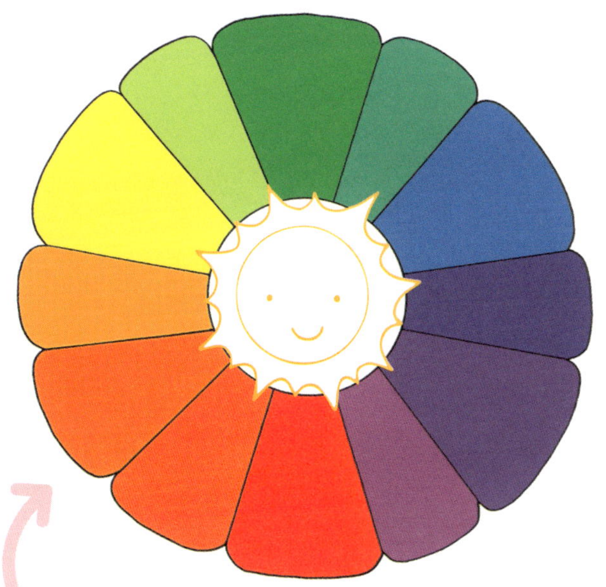

The **color wheel** shows how colors relate to one another. Familiarity with it will help you create harmonious color palettes for your drawings.

CHOOSING COLORS FOR YOUR DRAWING

When deciding which colors to use, look at the color wheel to see which ones will go well together, whether they are blended into one another or simply together in the composition. An effective way to draw the eye to an object is to use a complementary color for it. For example, red berries will pop in a composition of green leaves.

When you want to blend colors, a good rule of thumb is to choose colors next to each other on the color wheel since they blend well. Complementary colors, on the other hand, end up looking muddy when blended together.

Complementary colors green and red blend into an unattractive muddy brown.

Next to each other on the color wheel, violet and blue make a lovely blend.

The Super Easy Way to Draw Super Cute

My super cute method is so easy that most of the tutorials in the book don't even have any written directions—just look at the examples and copy!

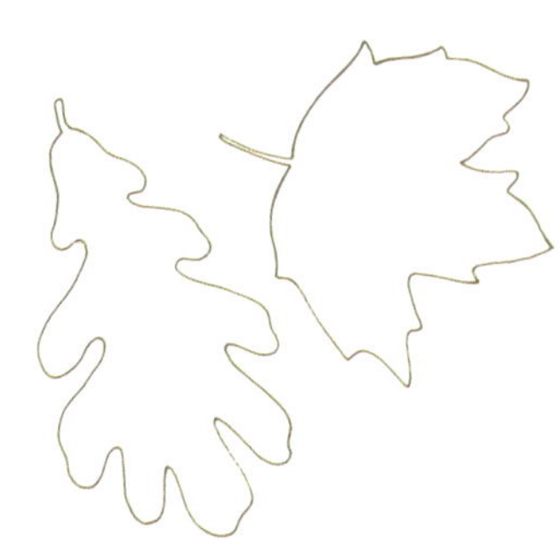

But for this first tutorial, drawing an adorable moose, I'll take you through each step in detail. I suggest making a rough pencil sketch first. Try to draw lightly so the lines can be easily erased. When you're happy with it, go over the pencil lines with a pen, and then color!

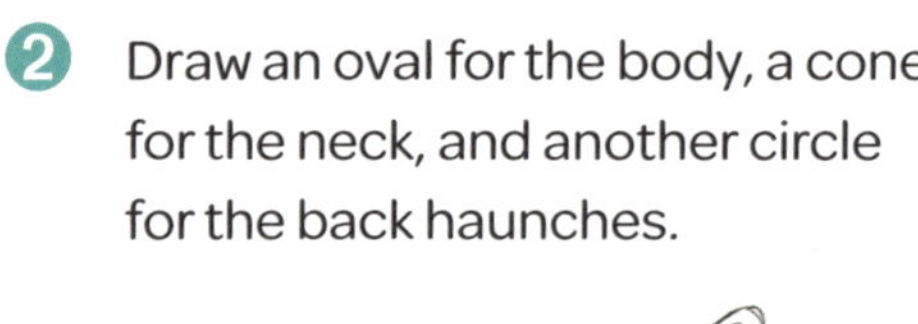

2 Draw an oval for the body, a cone for the neck, and another circle for the back haunches.

1 Most every drawing starts with a circle (or other simple shape) for the head.

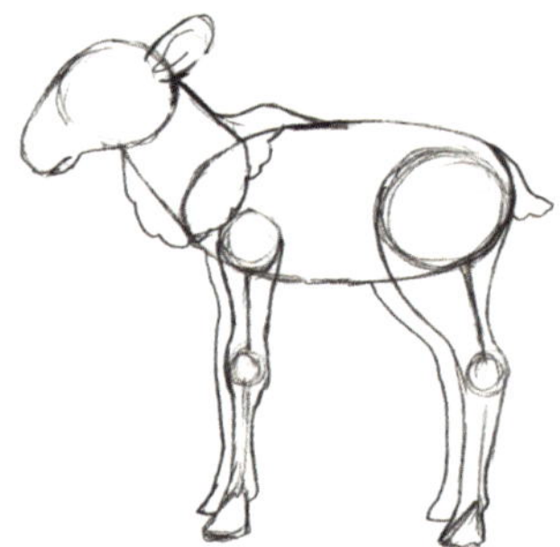

4 Start adding details, filling in around the neck and adding the tail. Draw in the legs, using the lines as guidelines.

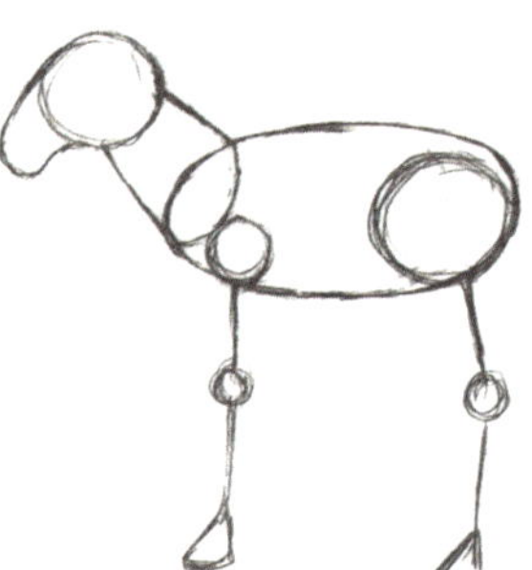

3 Add the outline of the muzzle and straight lines for legs, with small circles to represent the knees and triangles for the hooves.

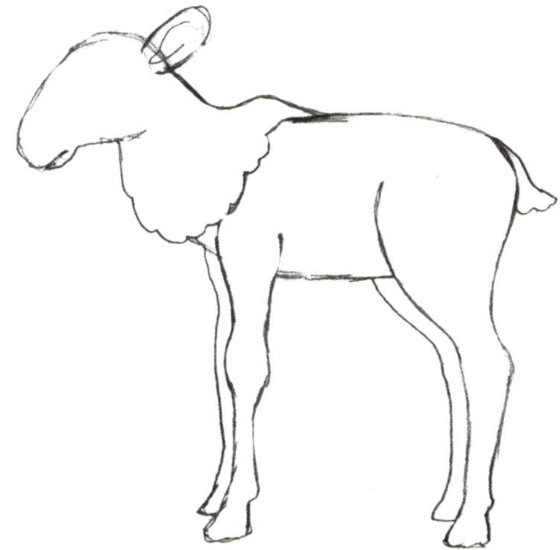

5. The drawing really starts to take shape when you erase any guidelines you no longer need.

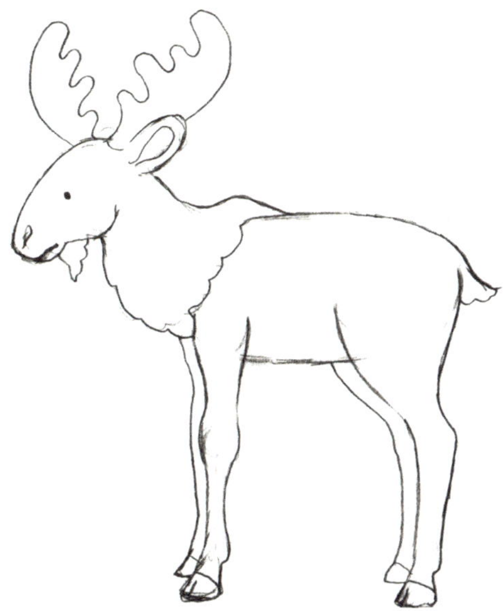

6. Continue to refine the drawing by adding more details.

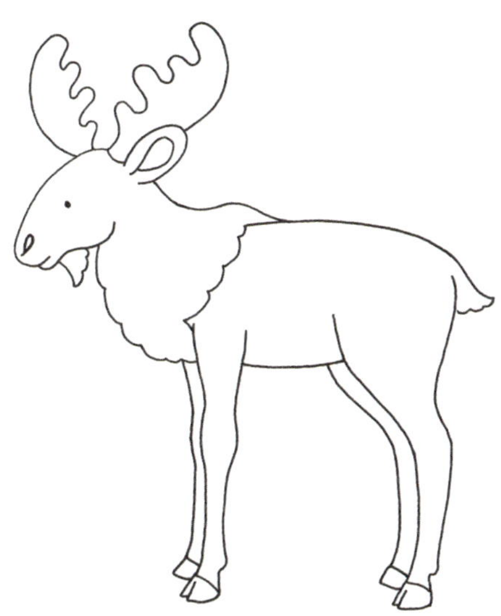

7. Once you have it the way you want it, go over the pencil lines with a pen. Then erase the pencil marks.

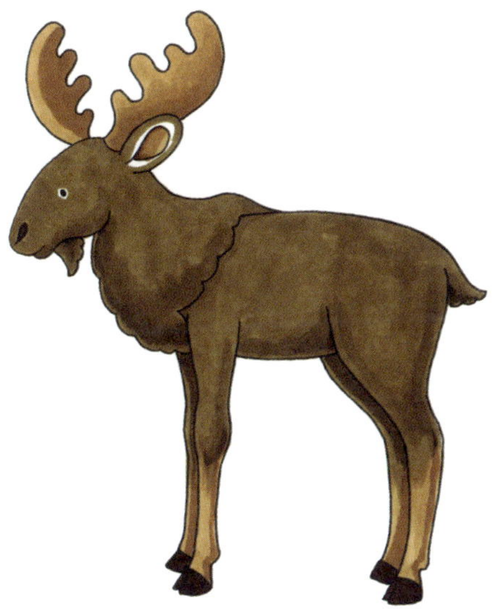

8. Add color using your favorite tools. (For this book, I used alcohol markers.)

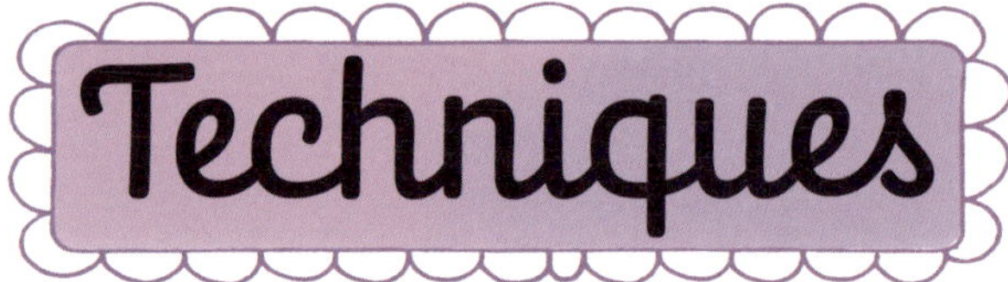

Techniques

If you want to leave your drawings as simple linework, that's fine! But when you are ready to add more depth and form to your drawings, shading is key. These are the different methods I use.

SHADING

Shading is what turns a flat circle into a rounded sphere, as shown below. If you want your drawings to have depth rather than look like flat cutouts, you will need to add shading.

Hatching is made with parallel straight lines. The closer together the lines are, the darker the shading.

Cross-hatching is the same as hatching, with the addition of another set of lines at a 90-degree angle.

Stippling is simple—just make dots! As with hatching, the closer your dots, the darker the shading.

Scumbling is made by overlapping scribbled circles. It's a great way to build up layers of shading. It works best with pencils. If you do it with markers, it can damage the surface of the paper.

Blended pencil shading uses a tool like a blending stump to smudge your pencil marks to create shading and shadow.

Colored shading is best achieved by building up layers of increasingly darker hues of the same color.

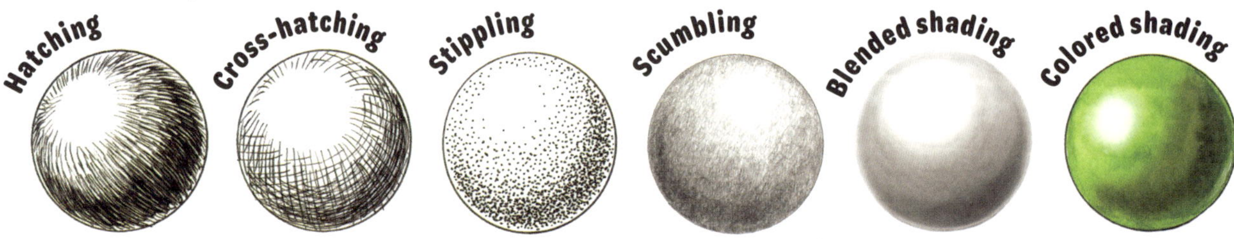

SHADING WITH A WATERCOLOR BRUSH MARKER

You can use shading techniques like hatching with watercolor brush markers but the method below will yield a smoother result.

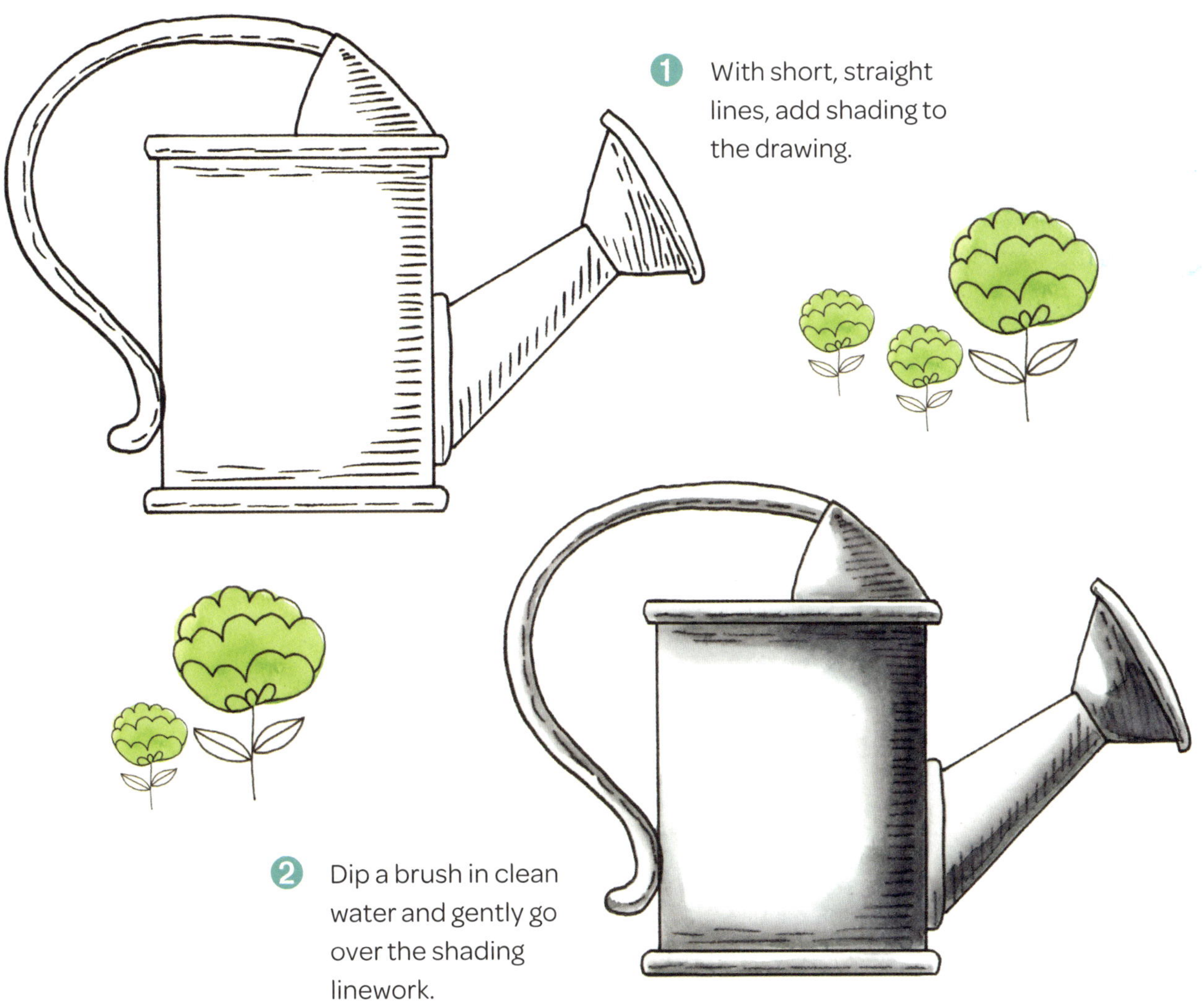

1. With short, straight lines, add shading to the drawing.

2. Dip a brush in clean water and gently go over the shading linework.

SHADING AND BLENDING WITH ALCOHOL MARKERS

When coloring in, blending is important so that you don't end up with a patchwork of colors. This kind of color layering can also be used to add shading for greater depth.

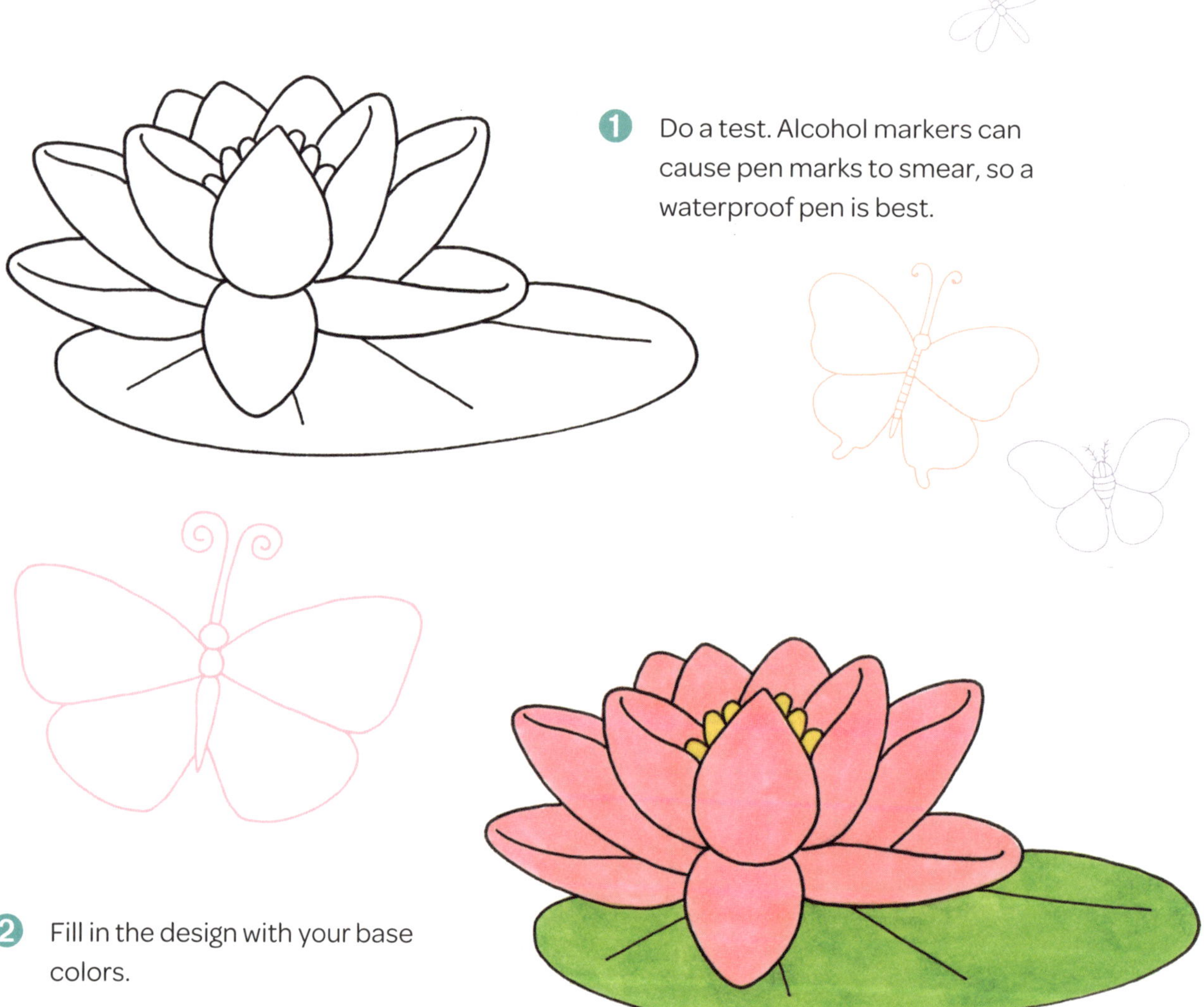

1 Do a test. Alcohol markers can cause pen marks to smear, so a waterproof pen is best.

2 Fill in the design with your base colors.

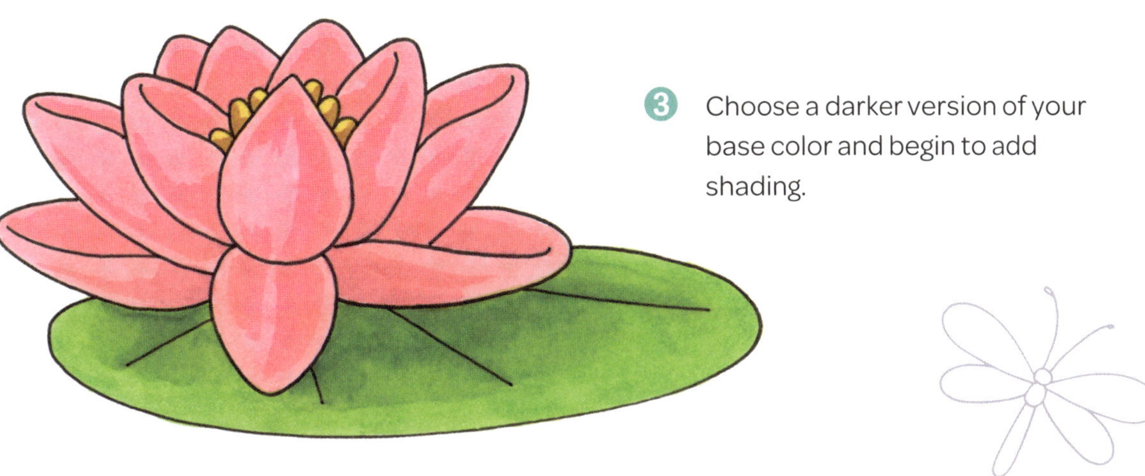

3 Choose a darker version of your base color and begin to add shading.

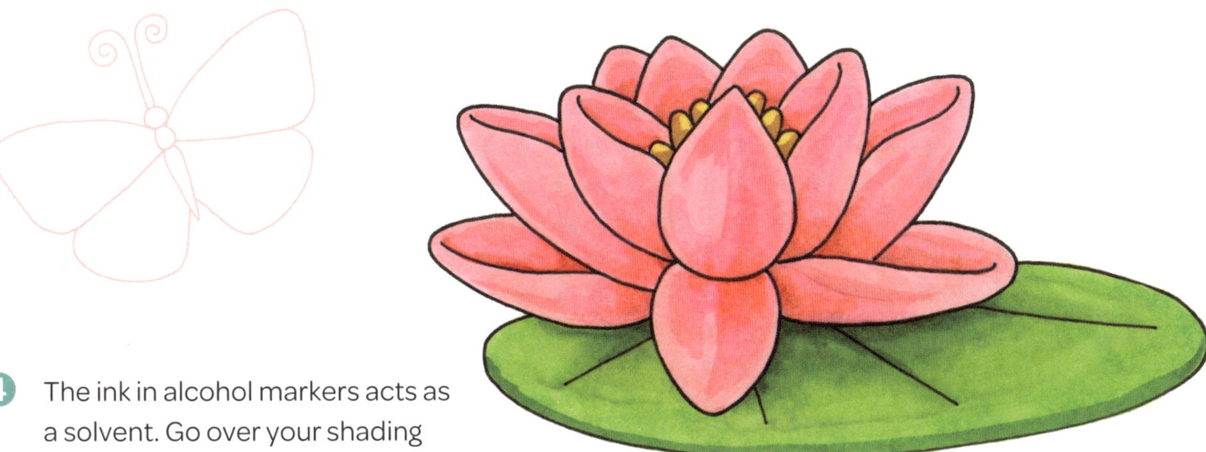

4 The ink in alcohol markers acts as a solvent. Go over your shading with the original base color and it will blend it. Alternate between the darker and lighter colors until you have the coloring you prefer.

COLORING FUR

This is so easy to do and will give your animal drawings lots of personality. For this demo, I used alcohol markers, but colored pencils and watercolors work, too. My palette for this wolf was four warm grays, from light to dark.

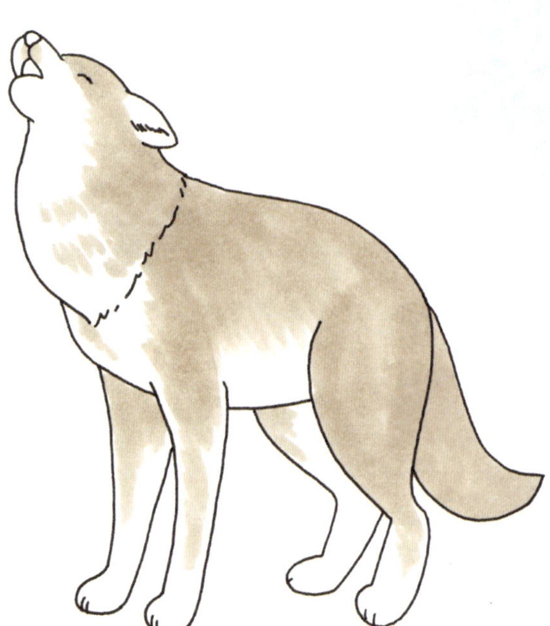

1 Begin to color with the lightest shade, lifting your marker, pencil, or brush at the end of each stroke so that it gets thinner at the end. Your strokes should follow the direction fur would grow in.

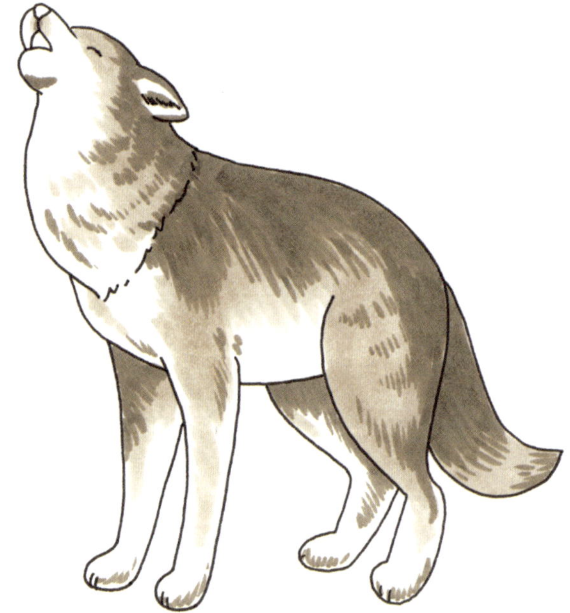

2 Switch to a midtone hue and use the same tapering stroke but do not completely cover the first layer of color or fill in too solidly.

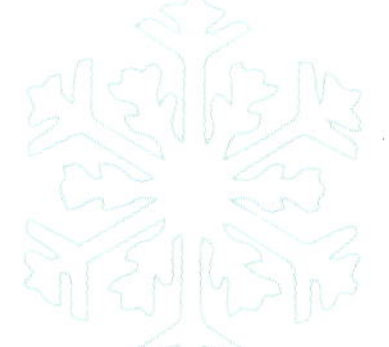

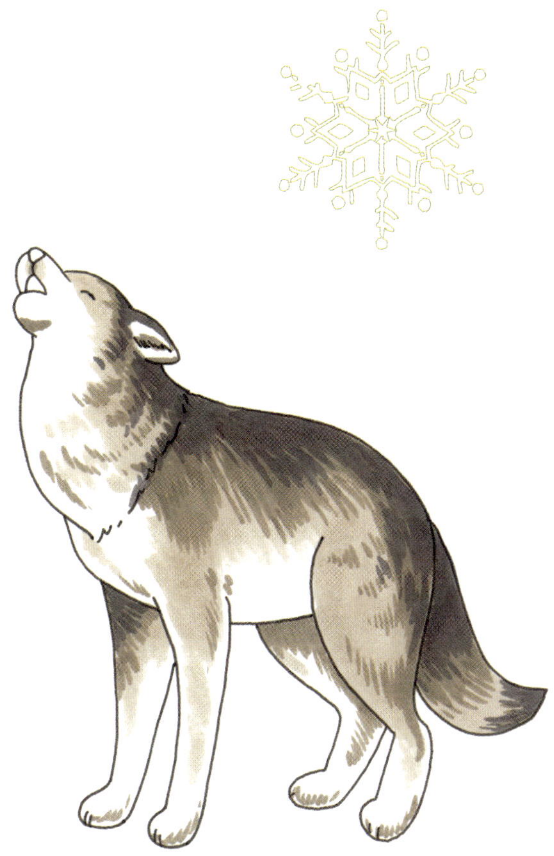

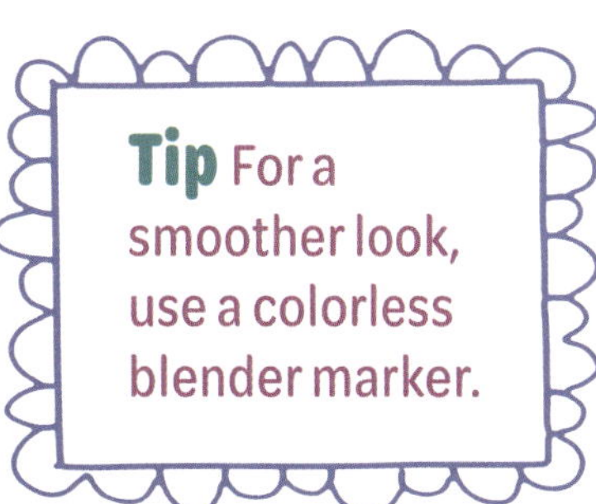

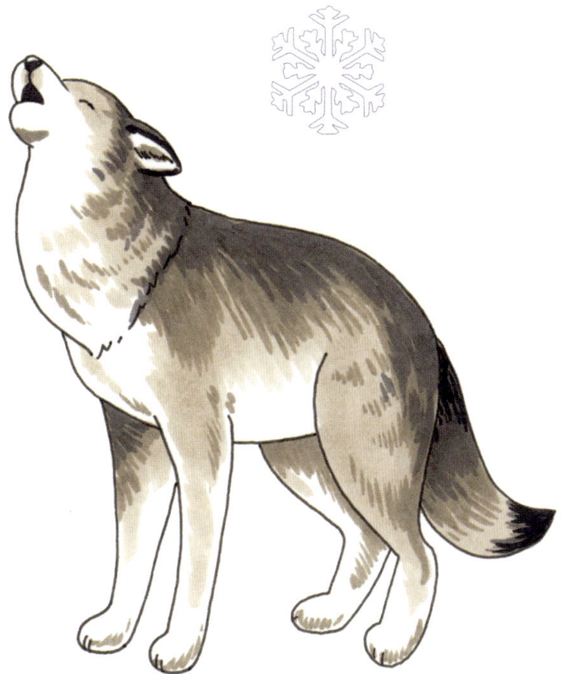

3 Use the same method to add a layer of the next darkest color; again, don't entirely cover your second layer.

4 Finally, add details with the darkest color. Use this color sparingly, so it stands out.

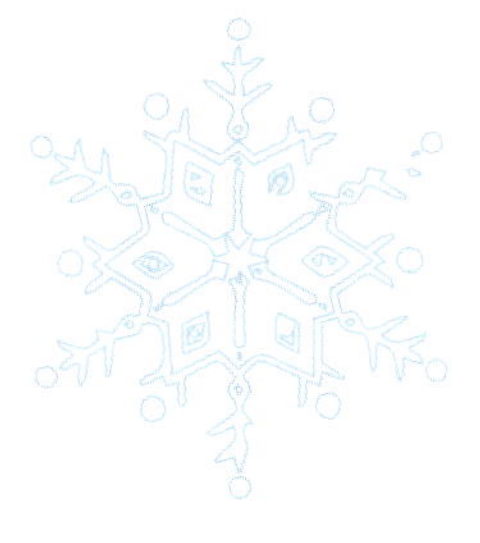

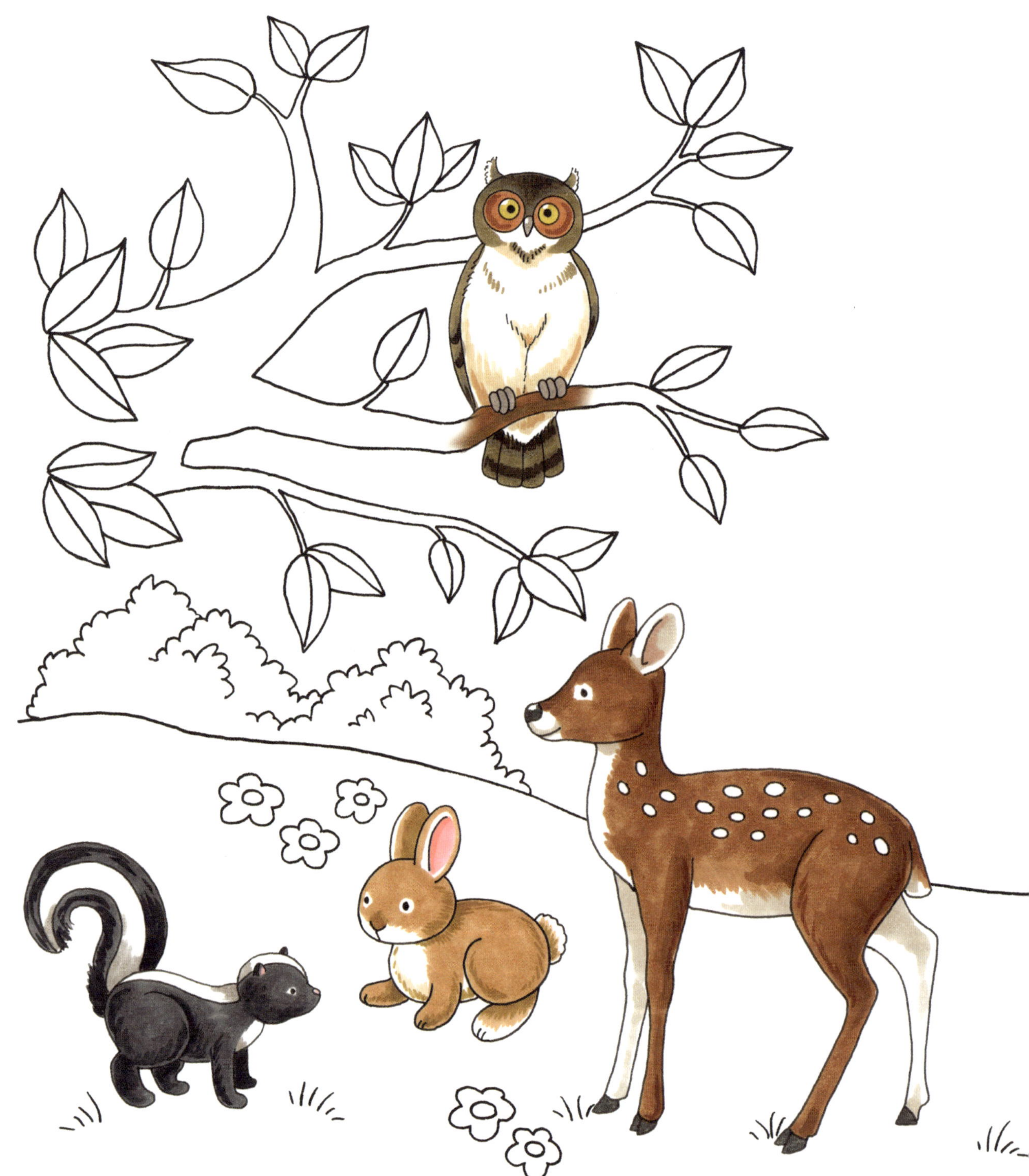

Woodland Wonders

Drawing is a great way to relax and record the world around you. There are lots of opportunities to observe nature close to home. Try exploring your local park or walking trails—even your backyard! In this chapter I will show you how to draw the fauna and flora you might see.

Owl

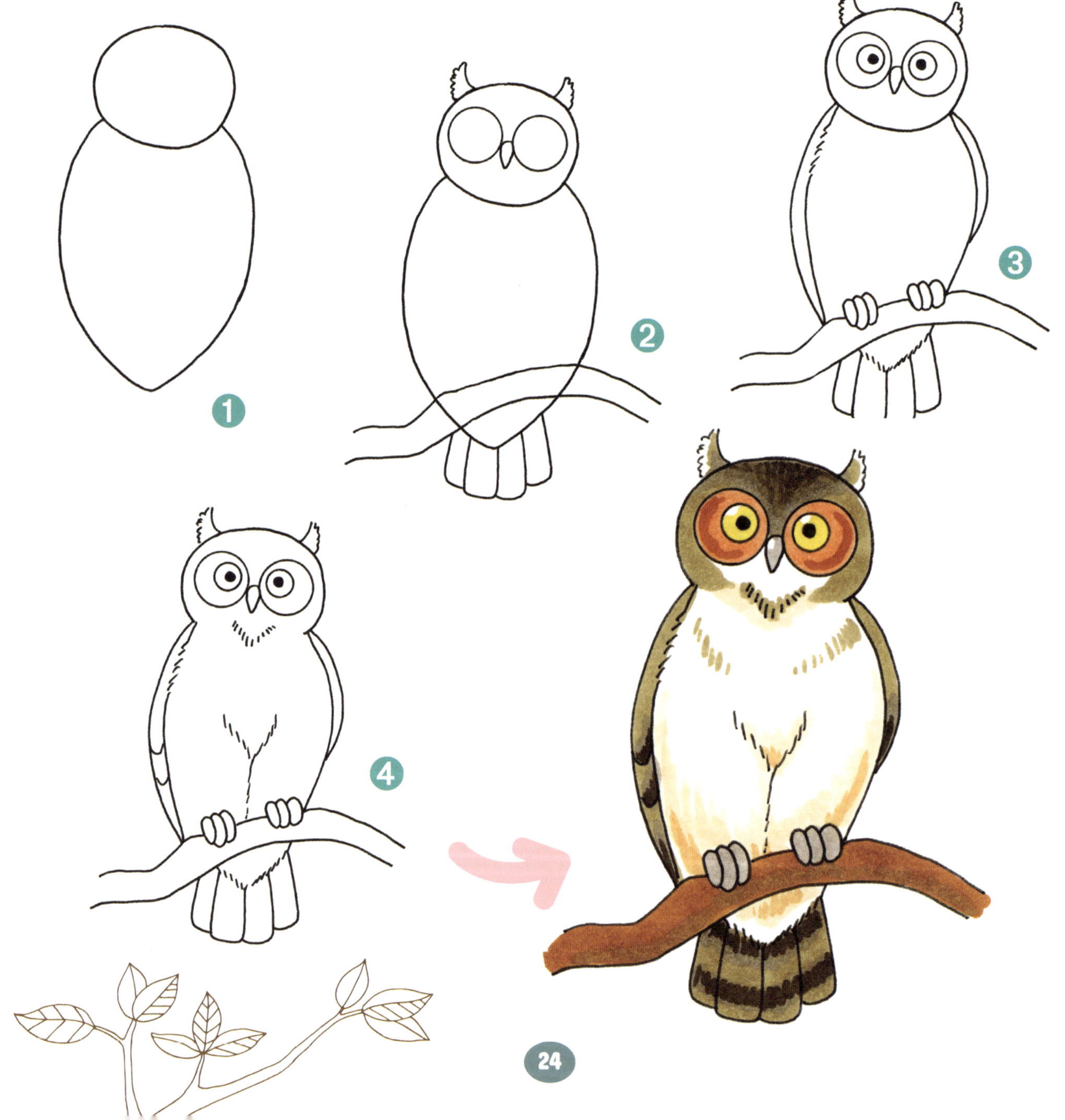

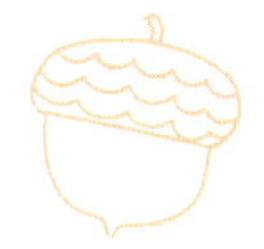

Squirrel

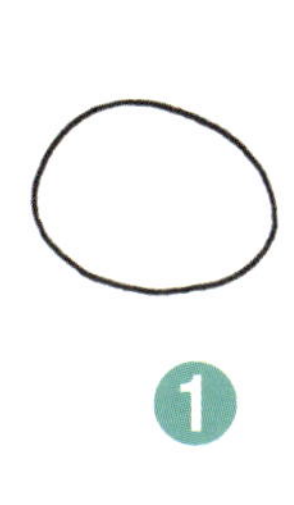

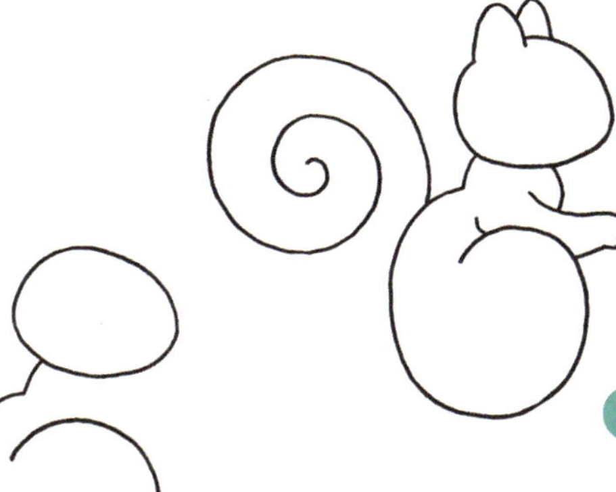

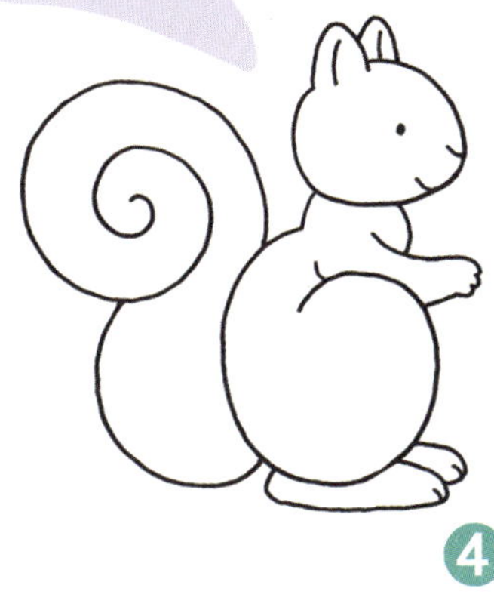

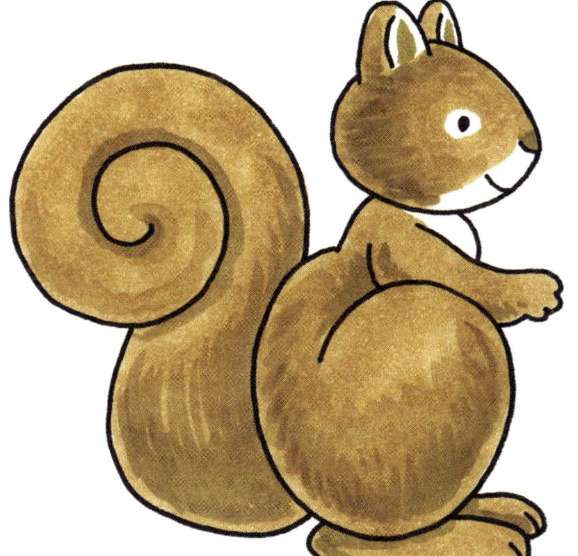

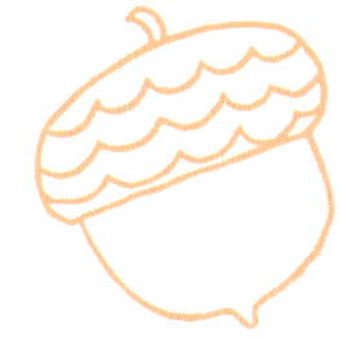

Make it a CHIPMUNK!

You just need to change the shape of the tail, add striping, and adjust the coloring.

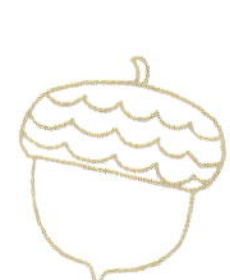

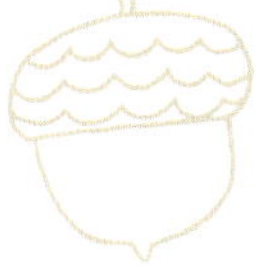

Badger

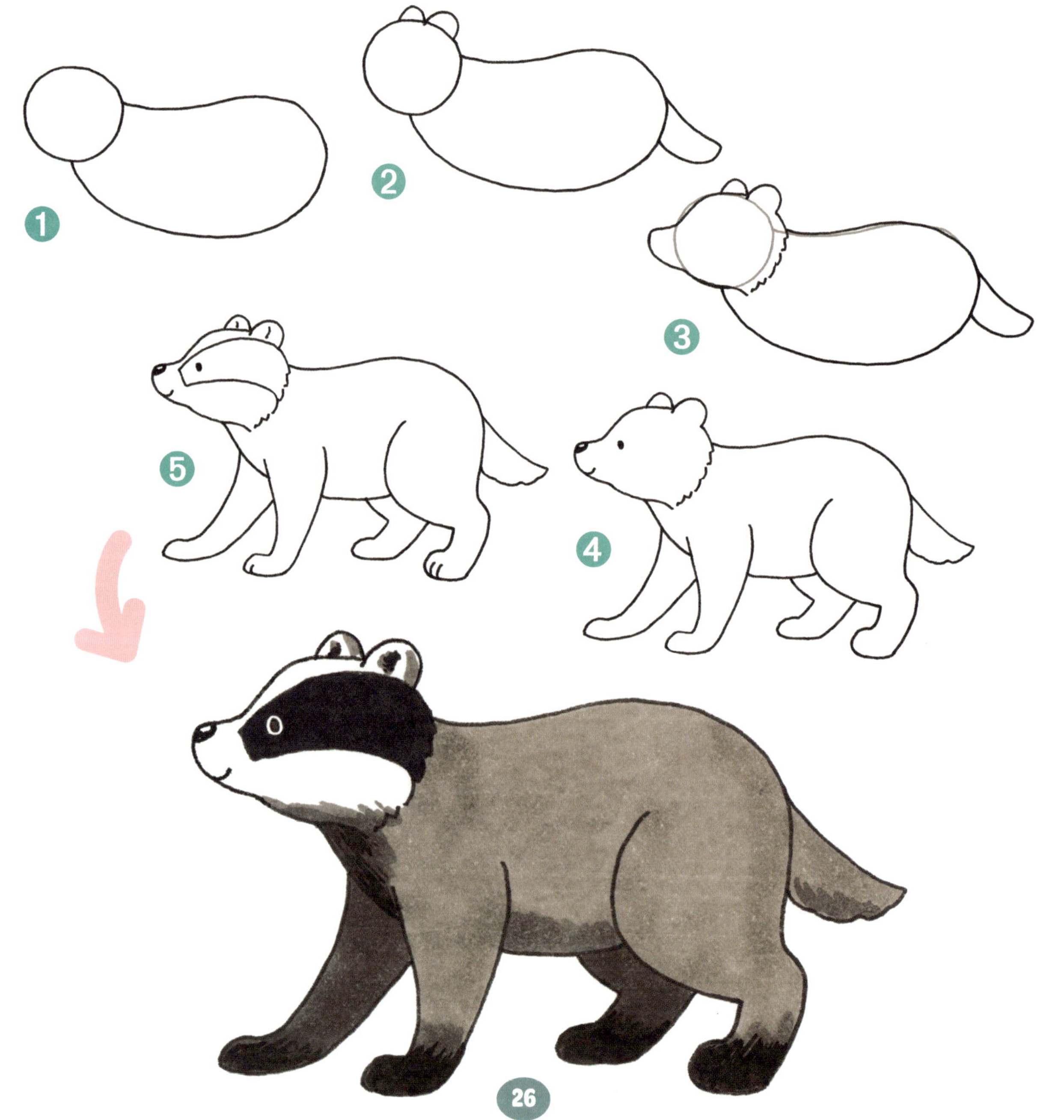

Rabbit

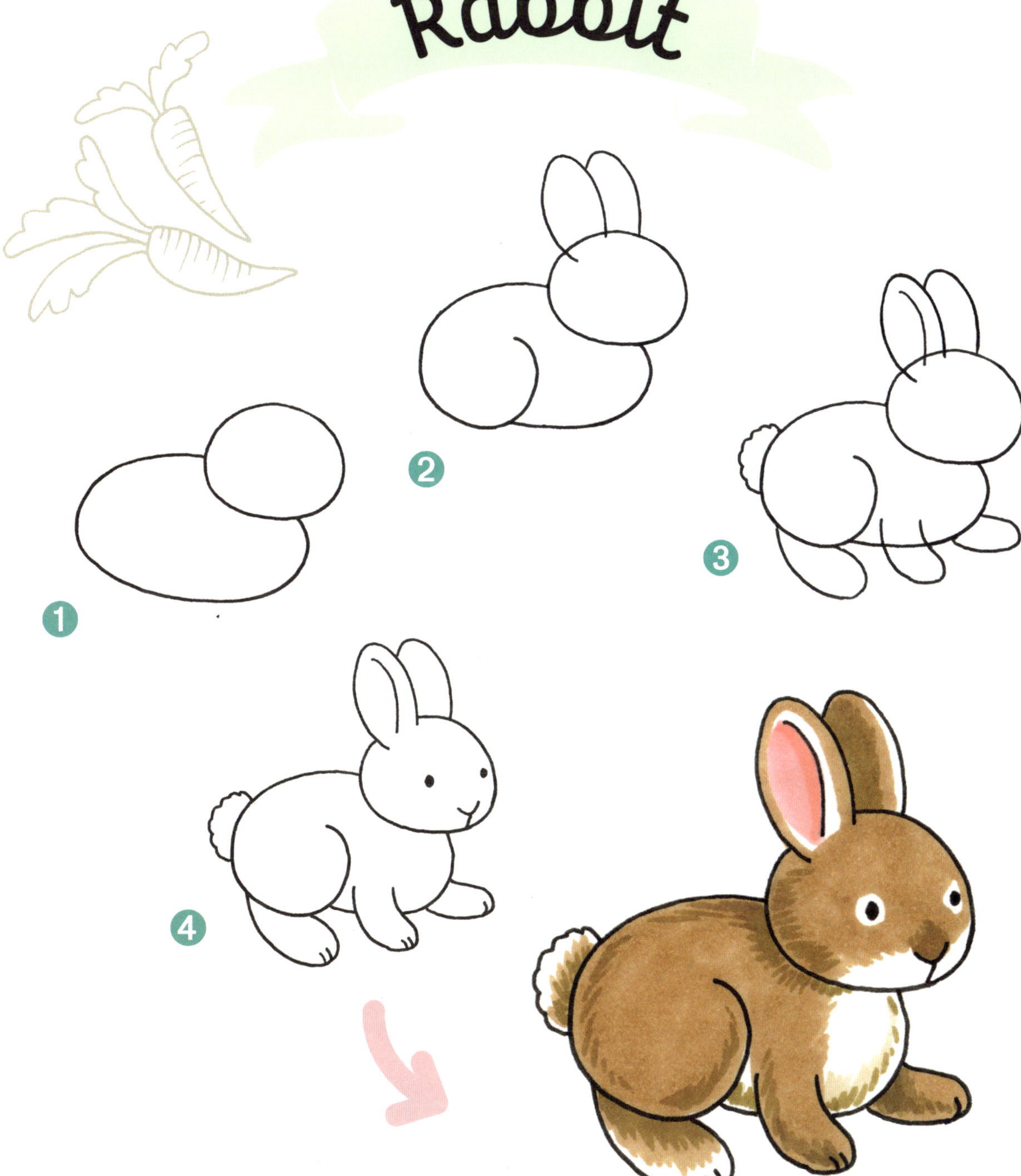

Beaver

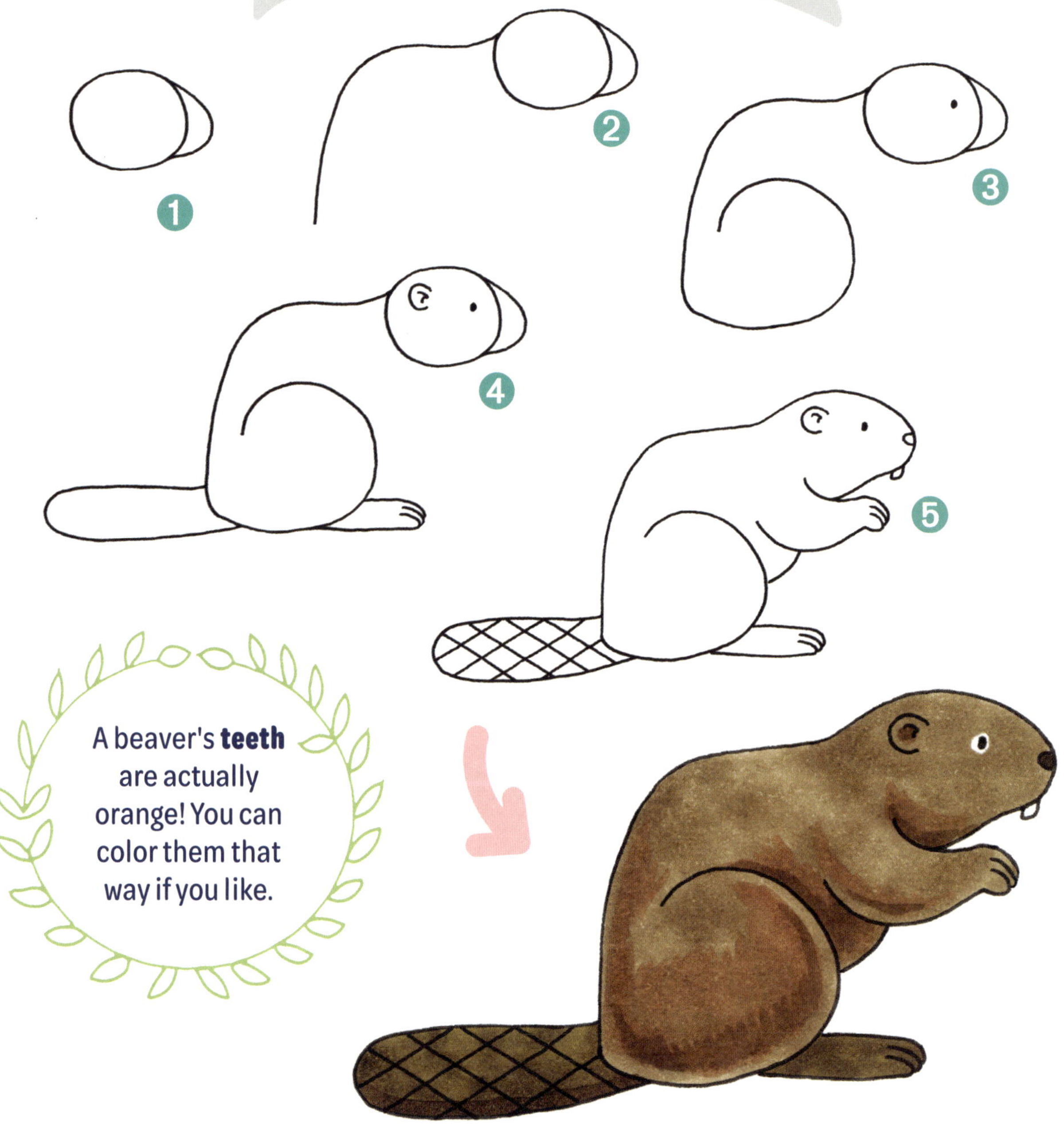

A beaver's **teeth** are actually orange! You can color them that way if you like.

Skunk

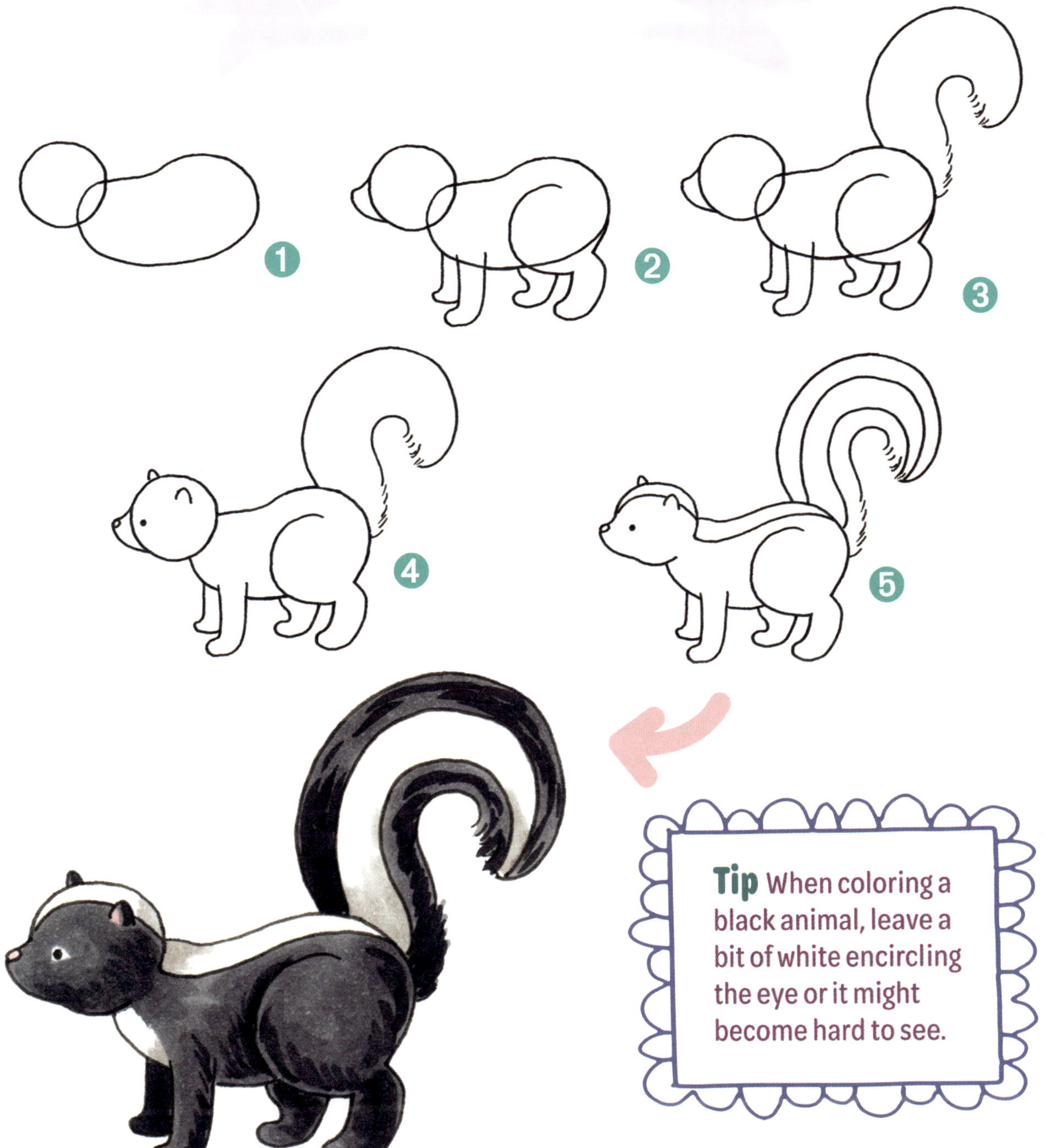

Tip When coloring a
black animal, leave a
bit of white encircling
the eye or it might
become hard to see.

Bear

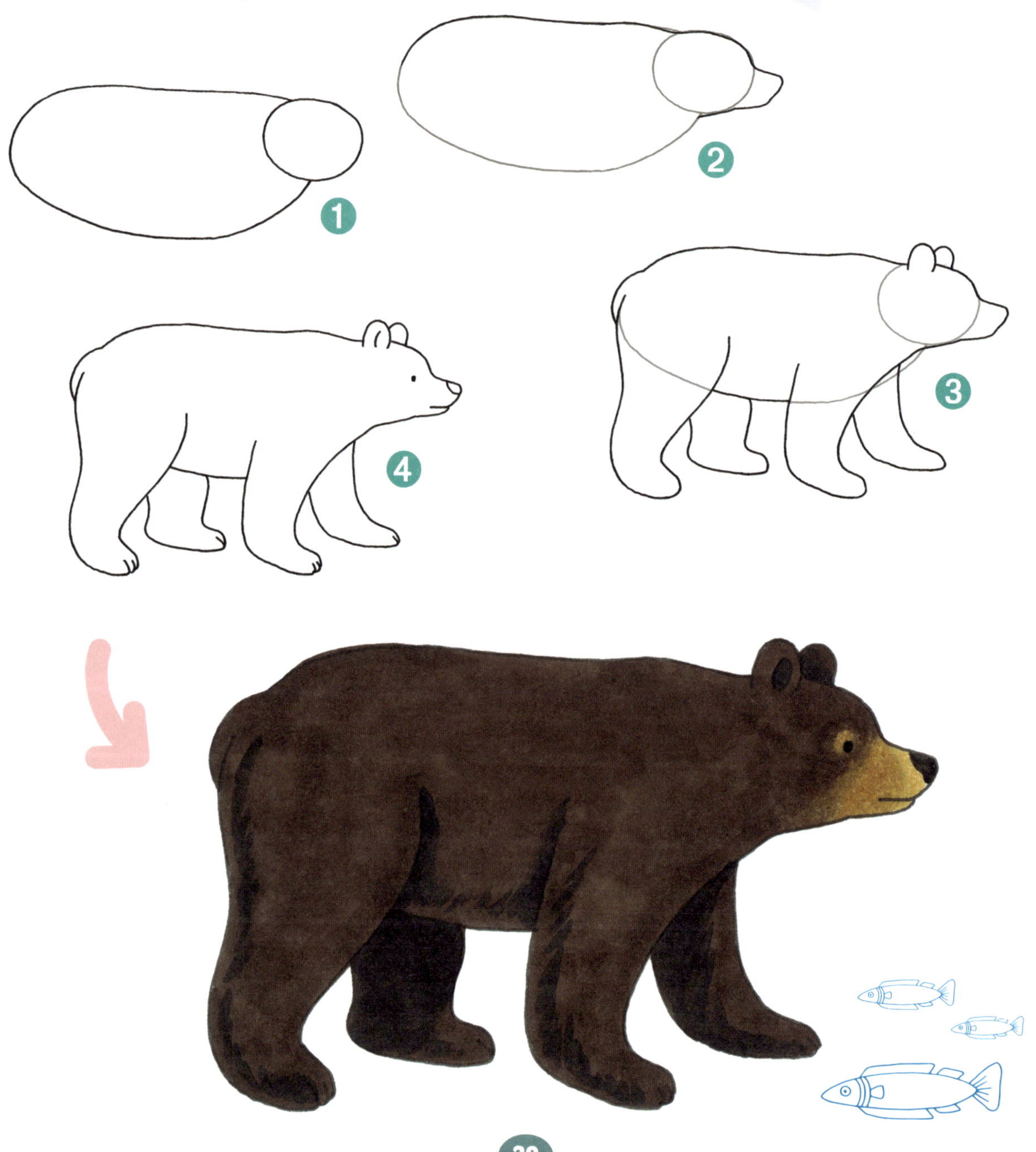

Fawn

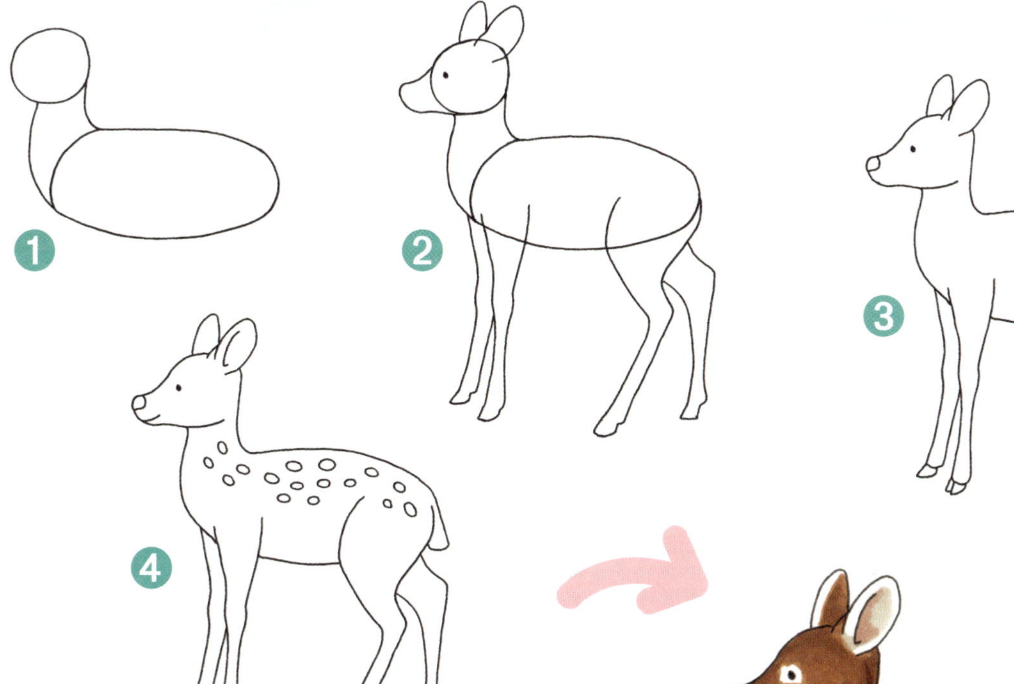

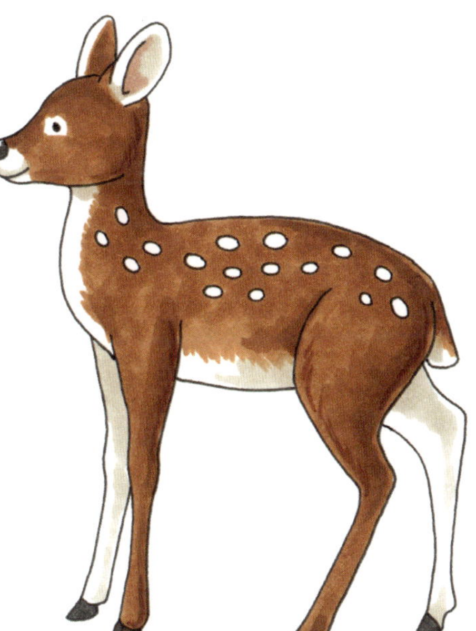

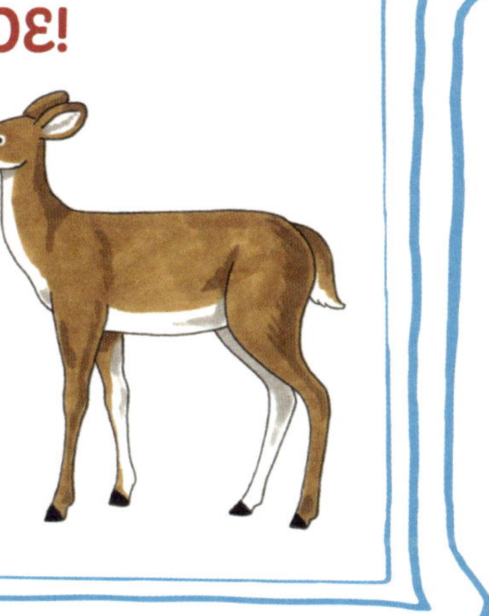

Make it a **DOE!**

Adjust the proportions for a mama deer. The fawn has a larger head and shorter neck in relation to its body.

Fox

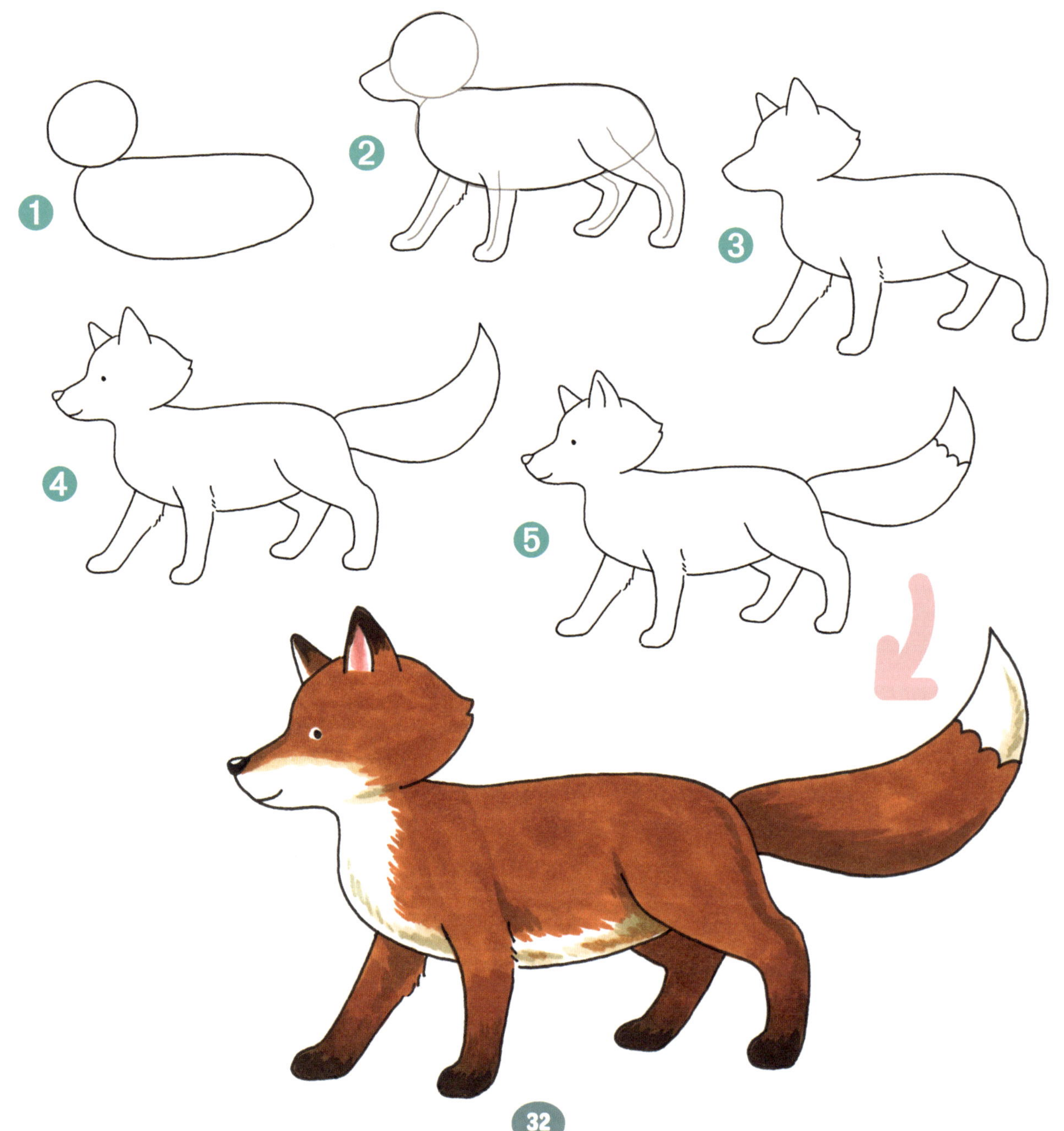

Berries

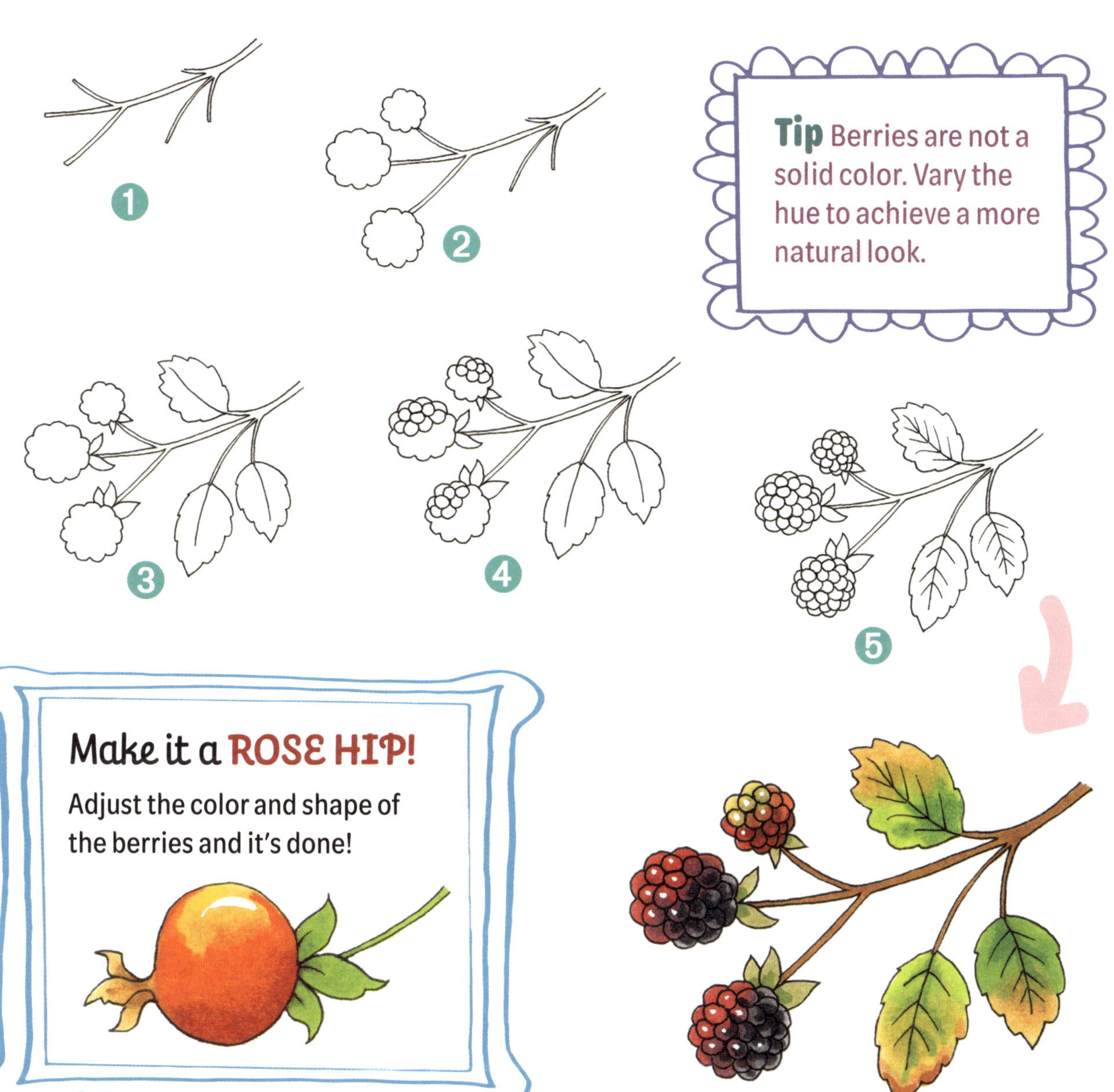

1
2
3
4
5
Tip Berries are not a solid color. Vary the hue to achieve a more natural look.

Make it a ROSE HIP!

Adjust the color and shape of the berries and it's done!

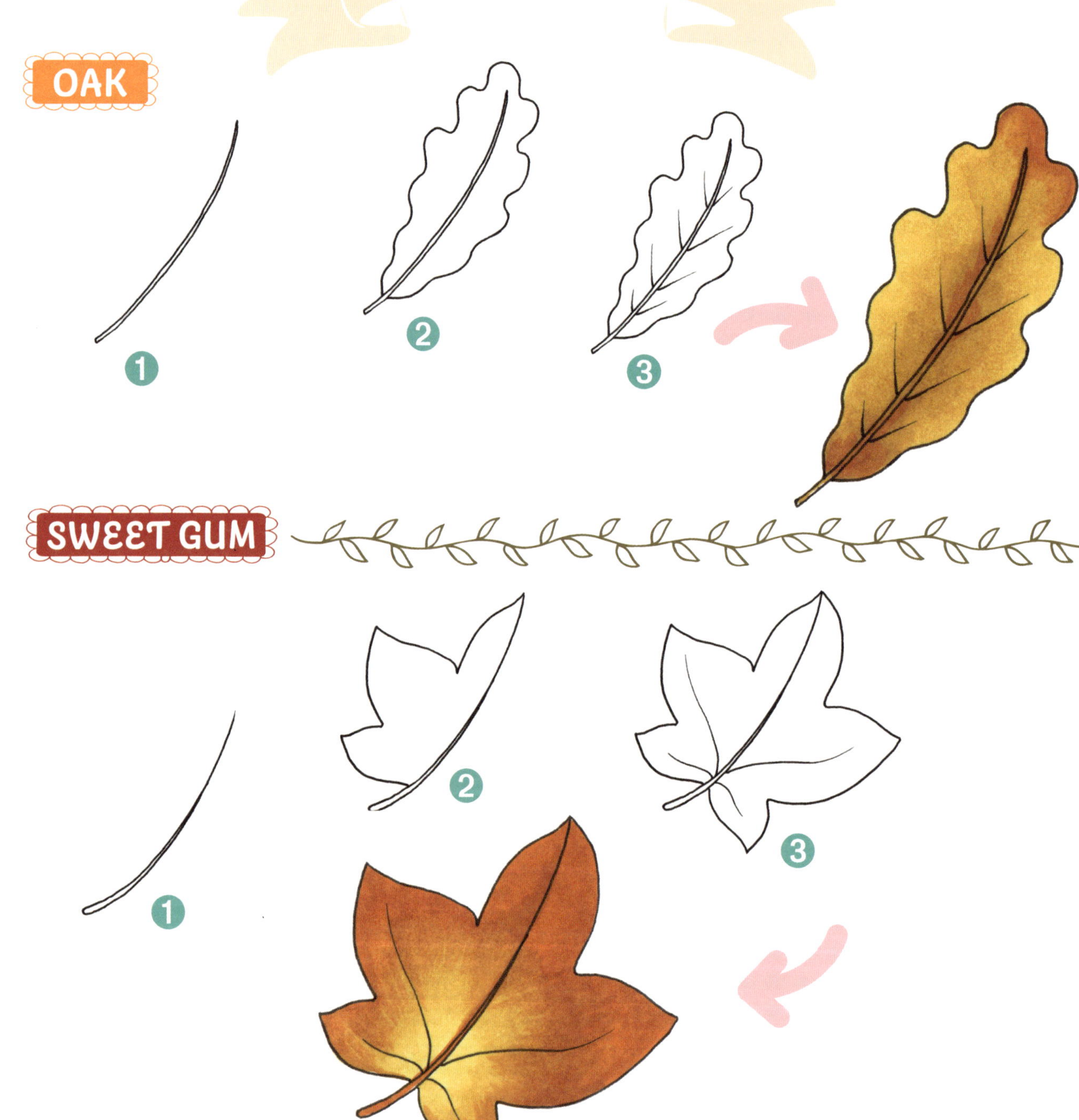

Leaves
OAK
1
2
3
SWEET GUM
1
2
3
34

ASH

MAPLE

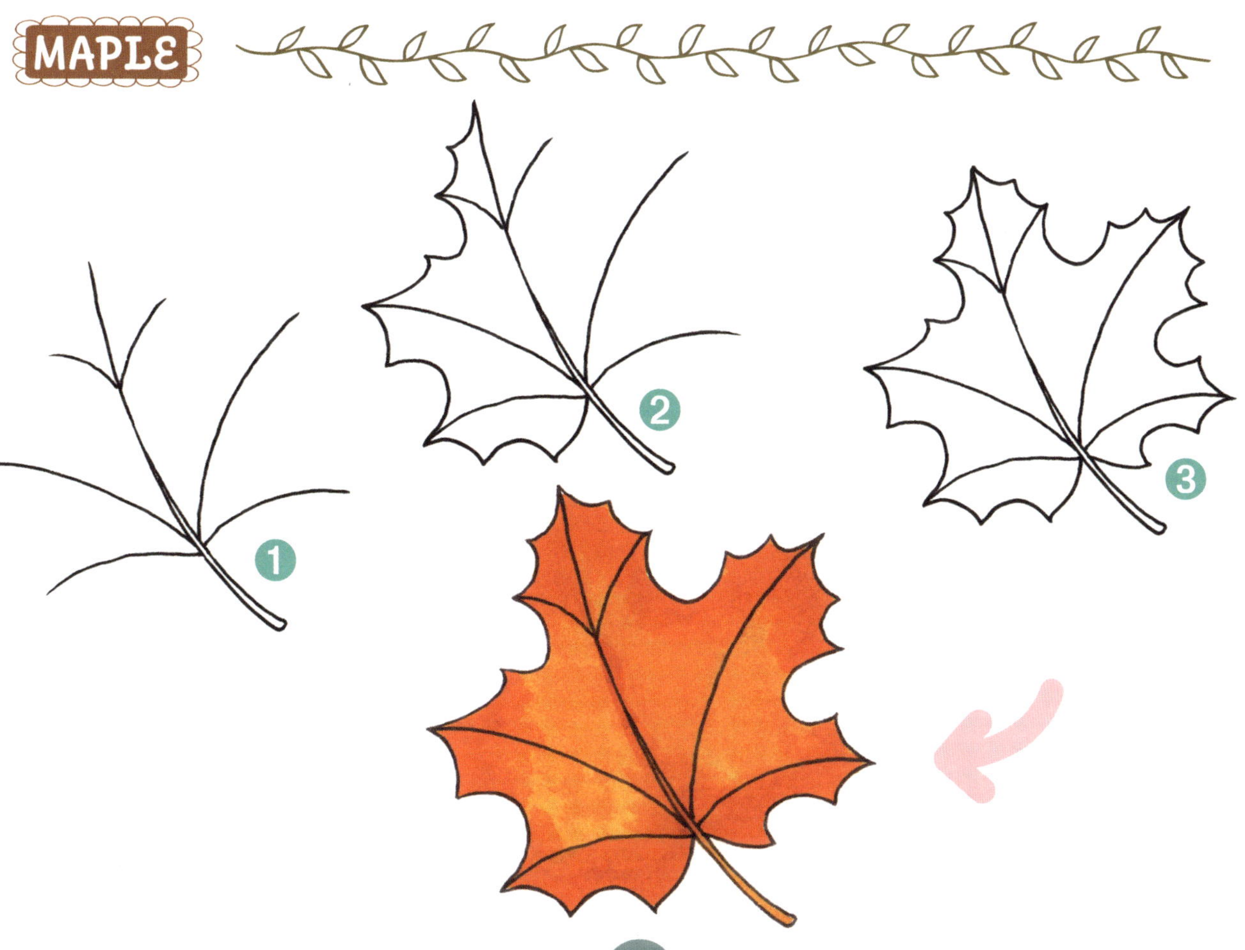

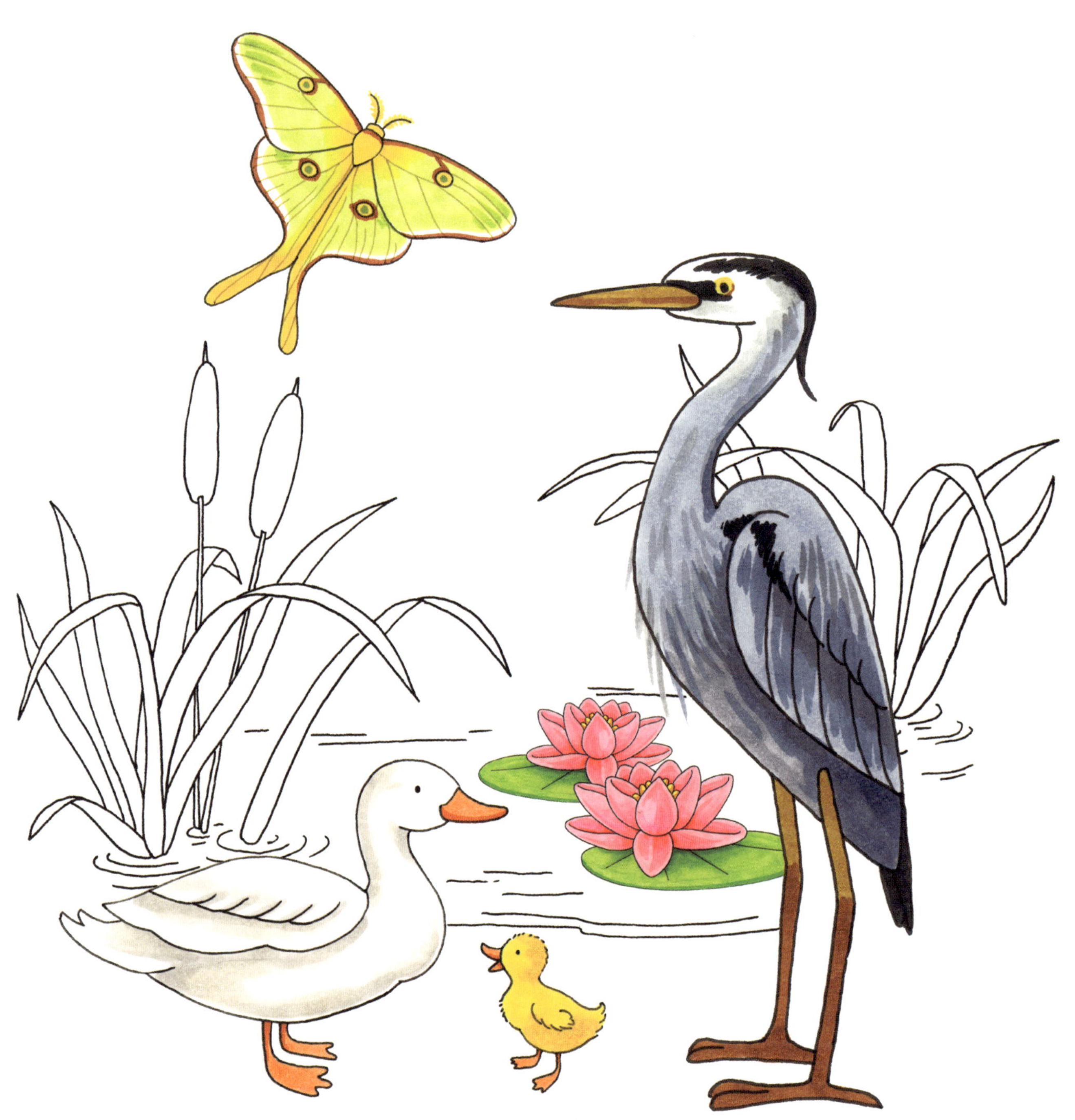

CHAPTER

3

Taking Wing

Birds are always a popular subject to draw. In this chapter, you will find a variety of feathered friends, from the tiny hummingbird to the majestic eagle. Other winged subjects you'll find here include the butterfly, bat, and a pretty moth.

Butterfly

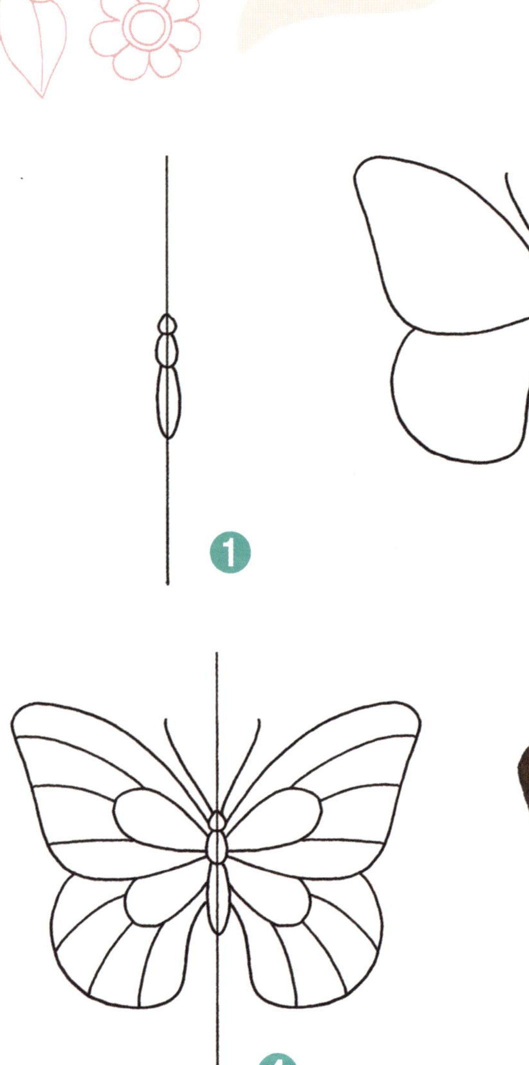

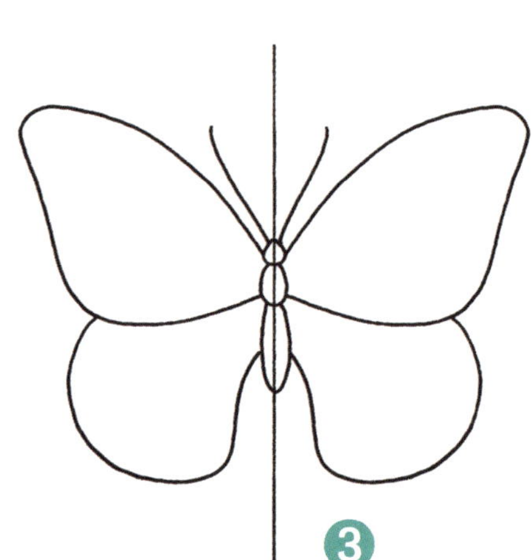

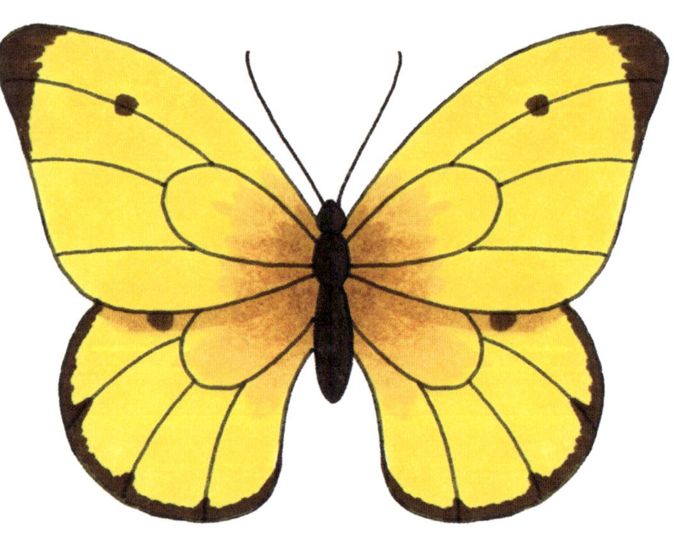

Luna Moth

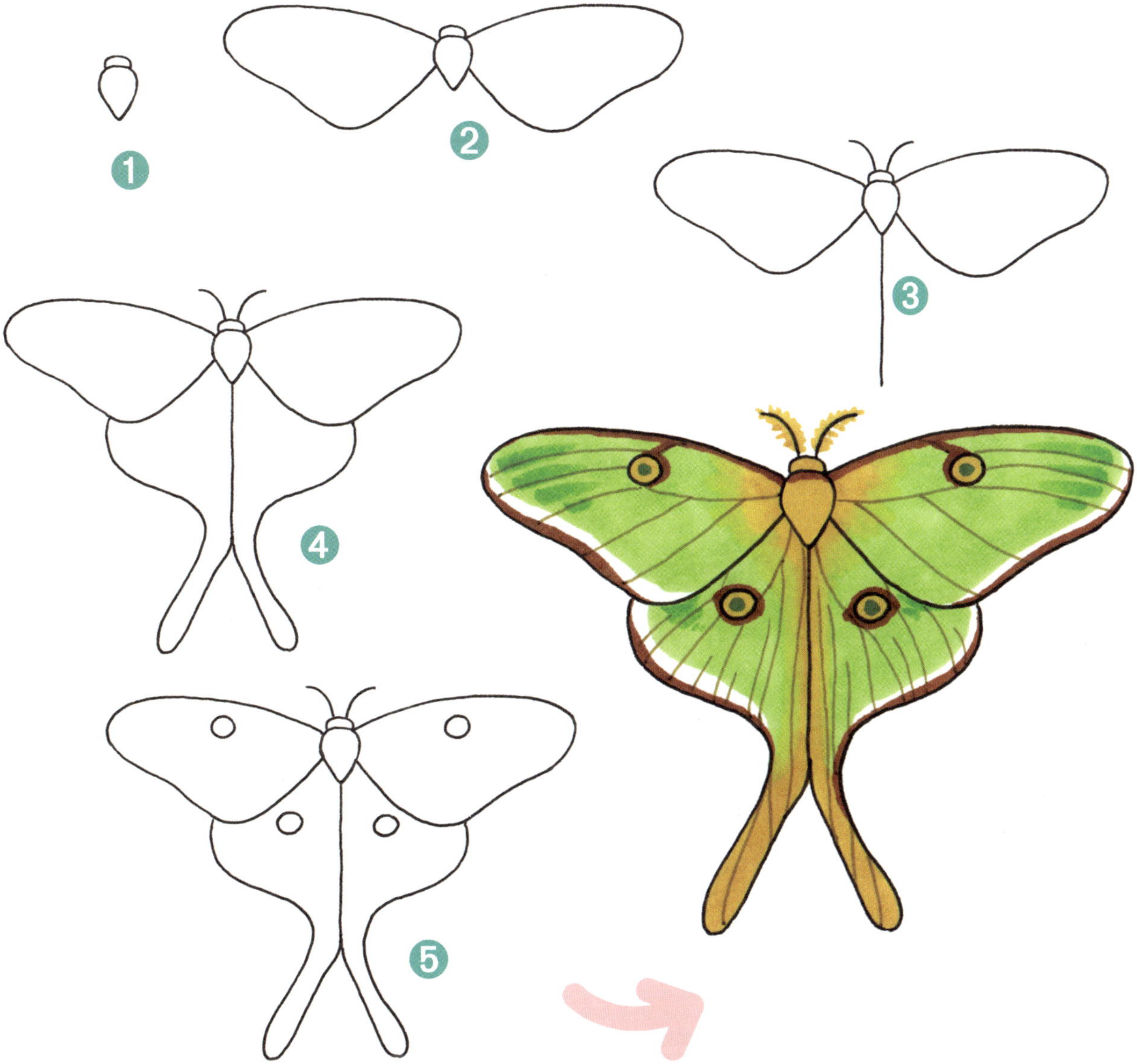

1

2

3

4

5

Flamingo

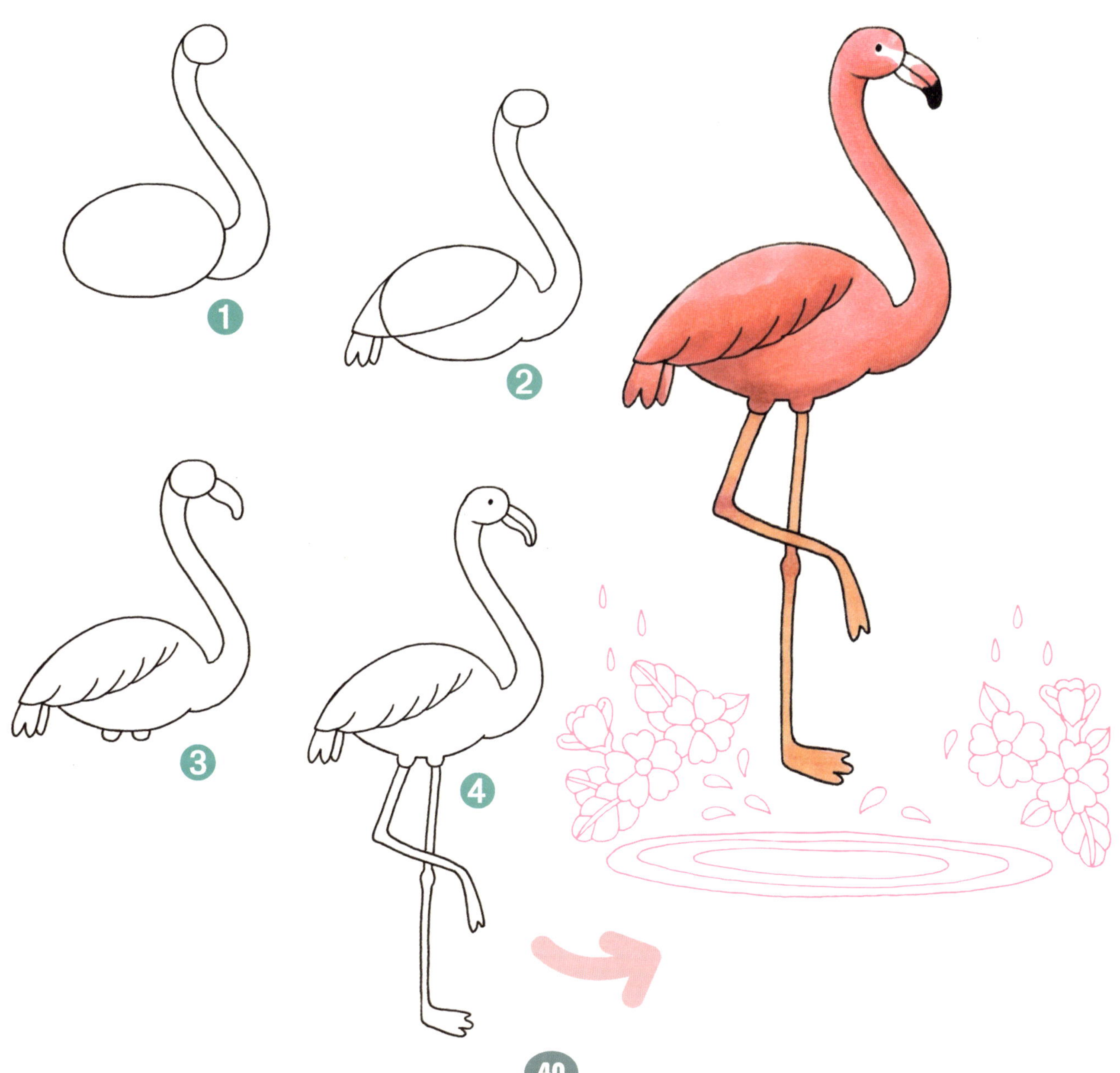

Puffin

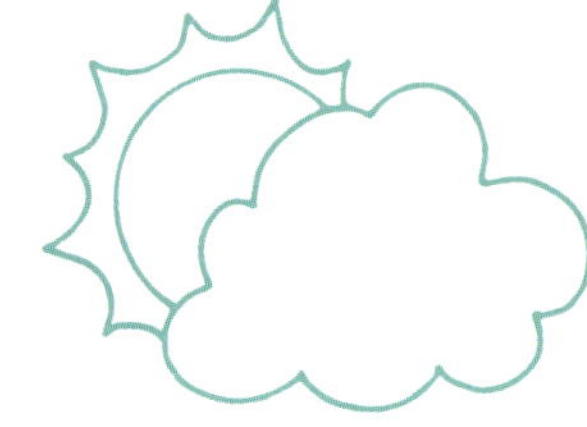

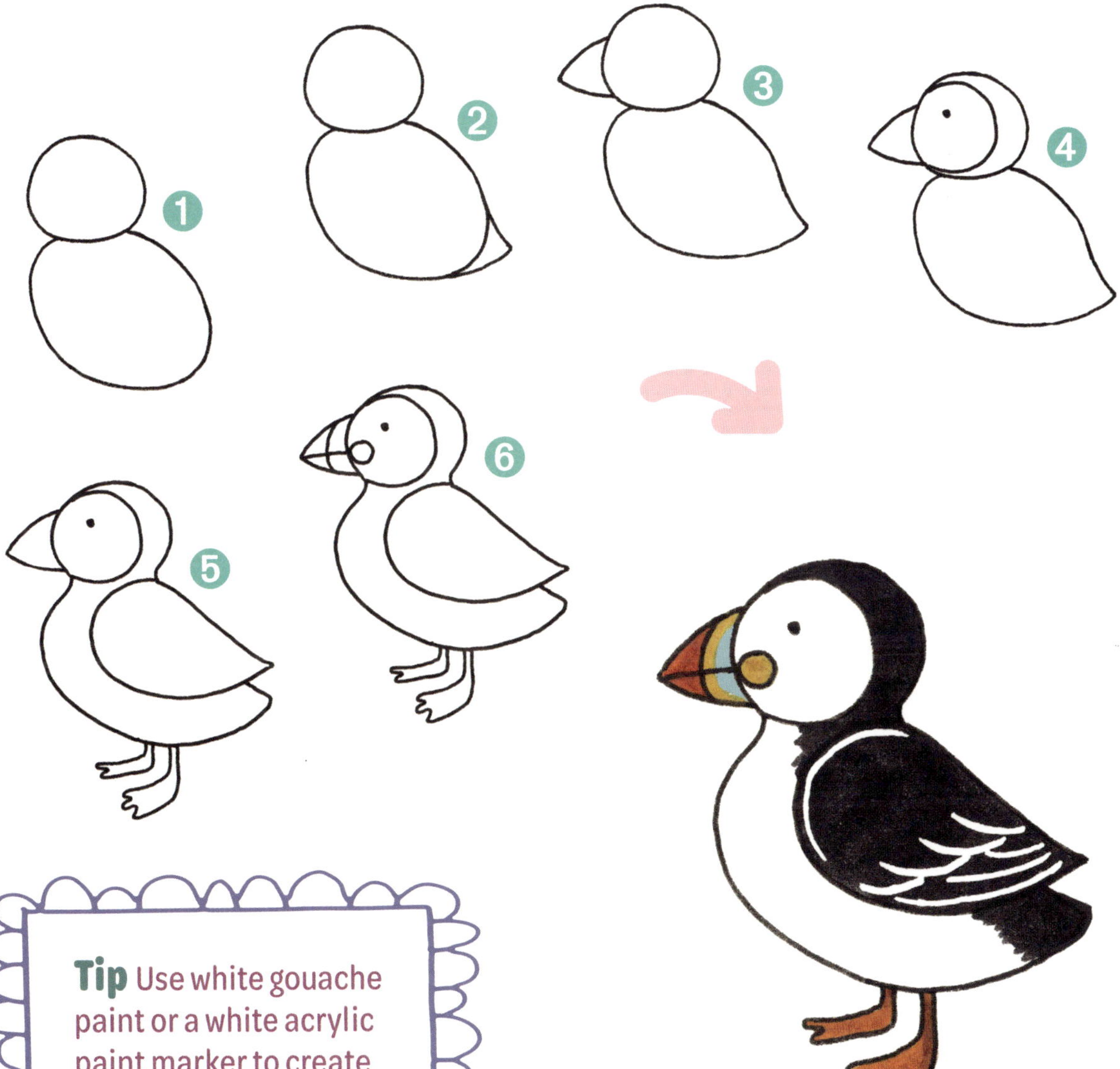

Tip Use white gouache paint or a white acrylic paint marker to create details on black areas.

Hummingbird

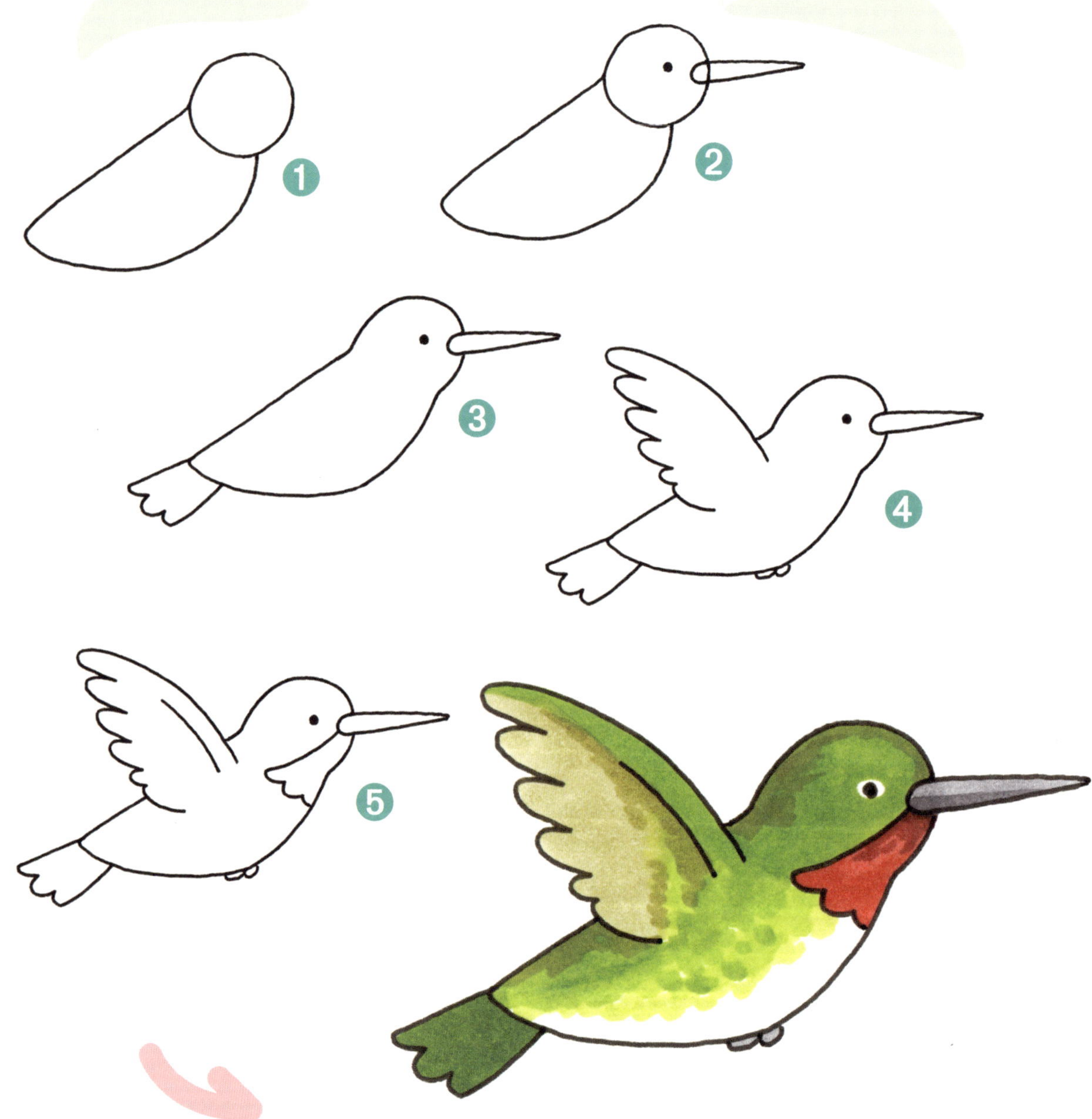

Heron

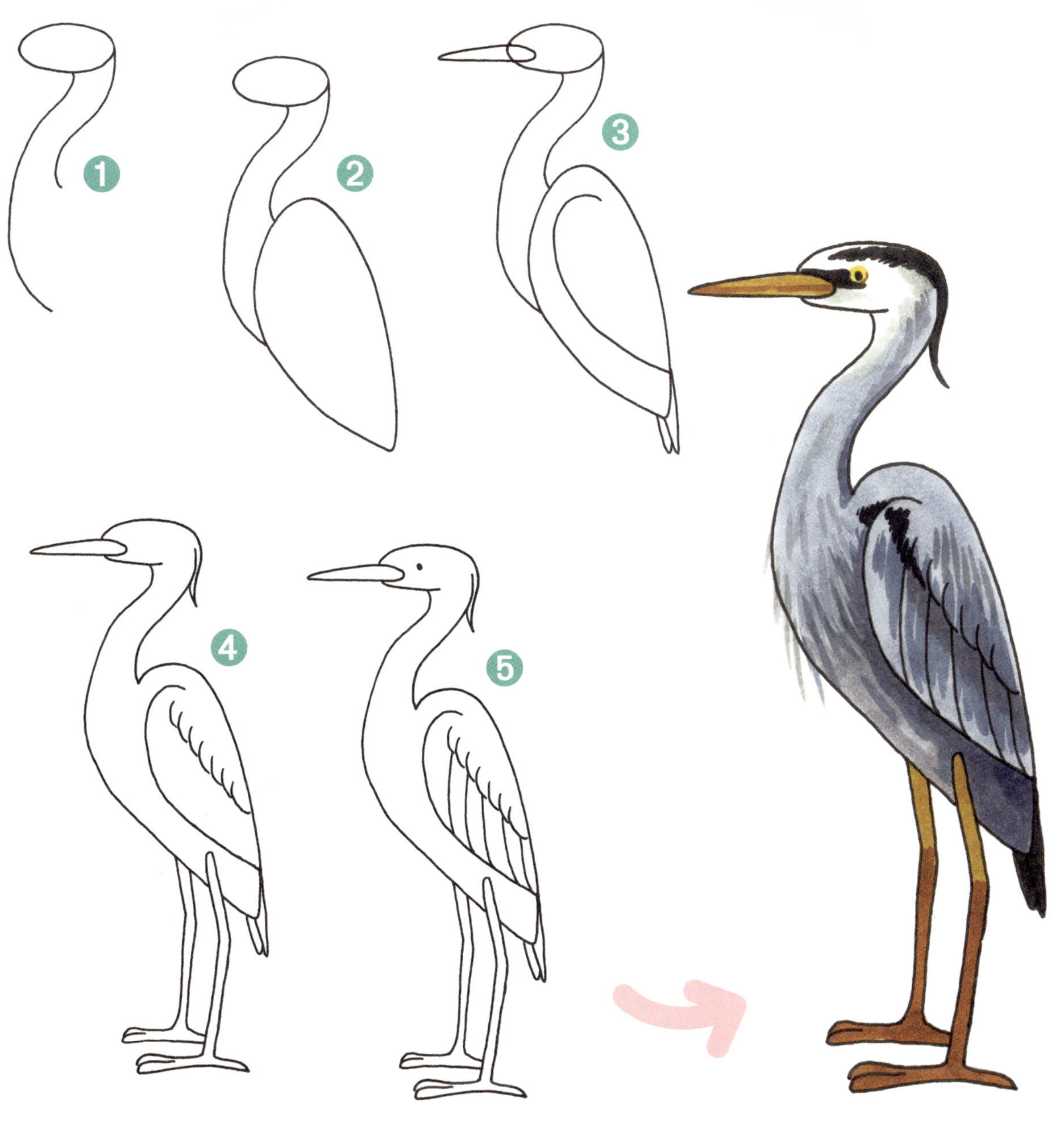

Toucan

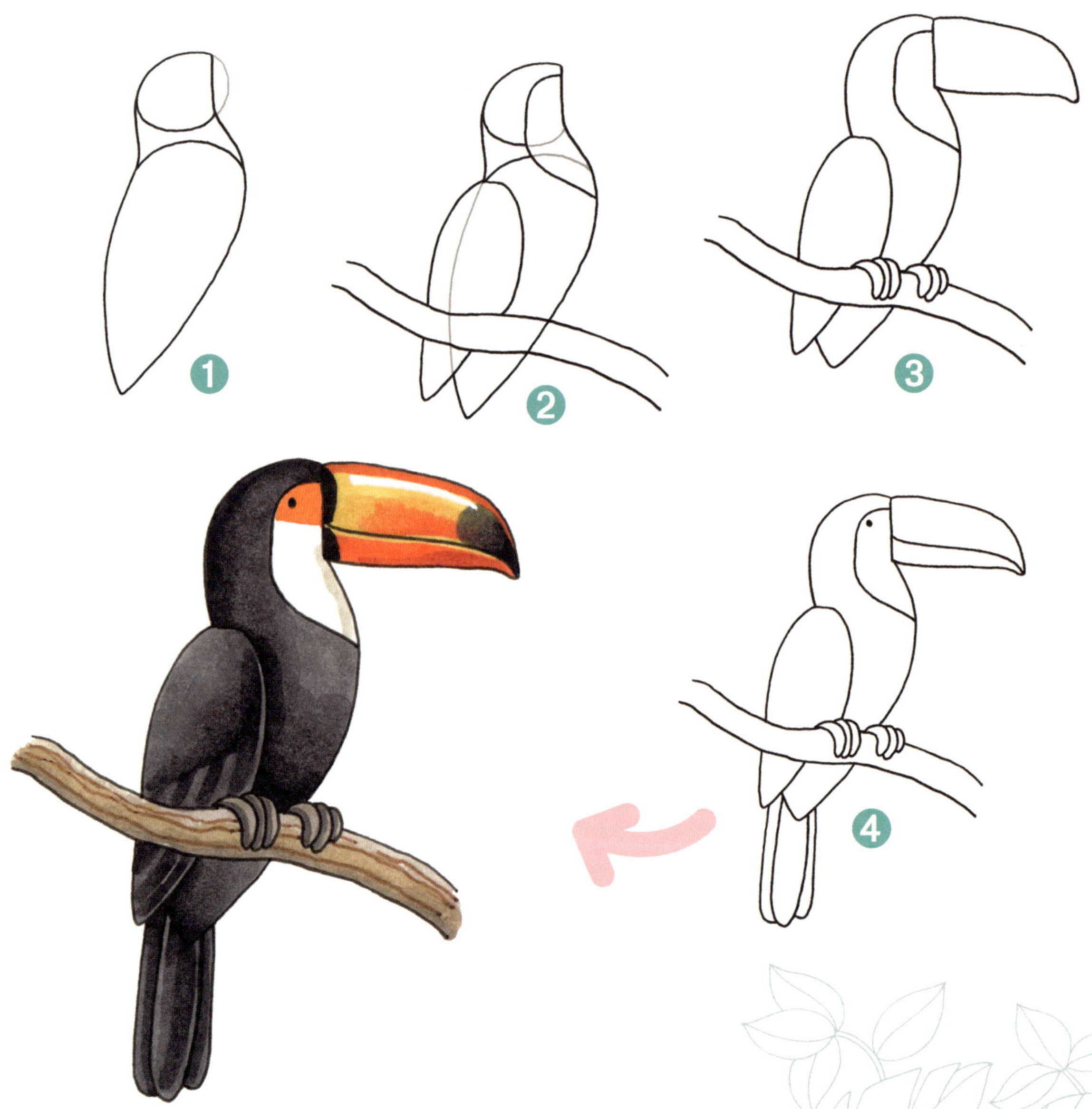

Swan

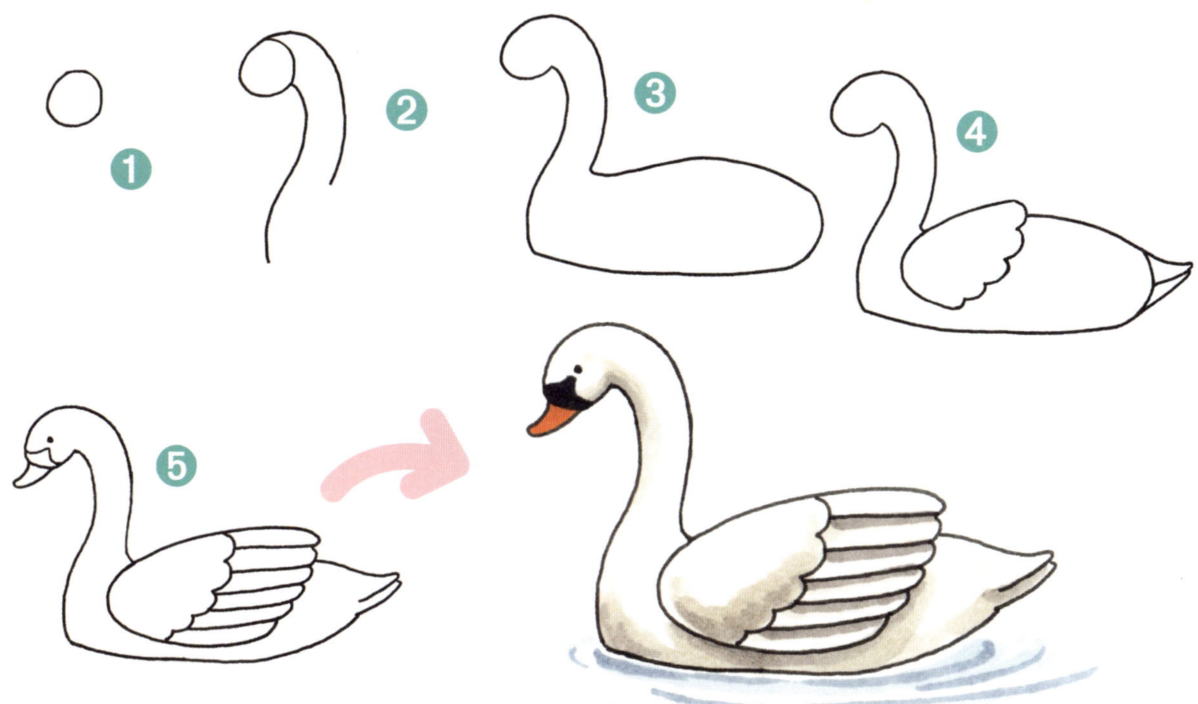

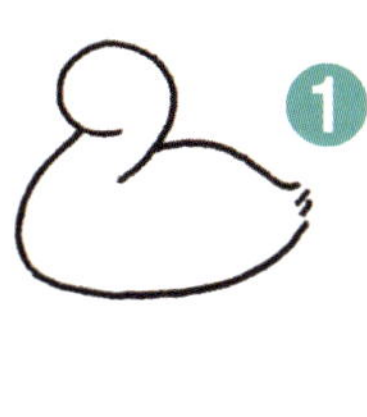

CYGNET

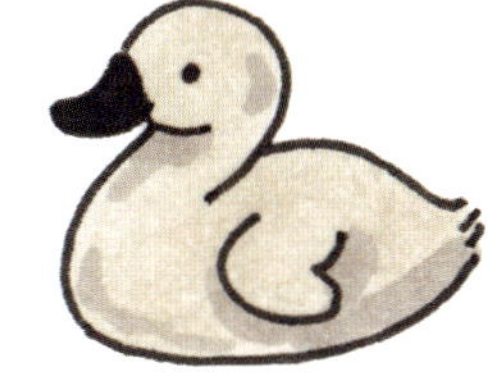

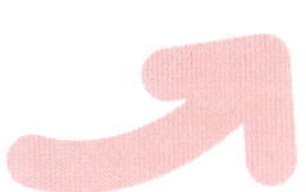

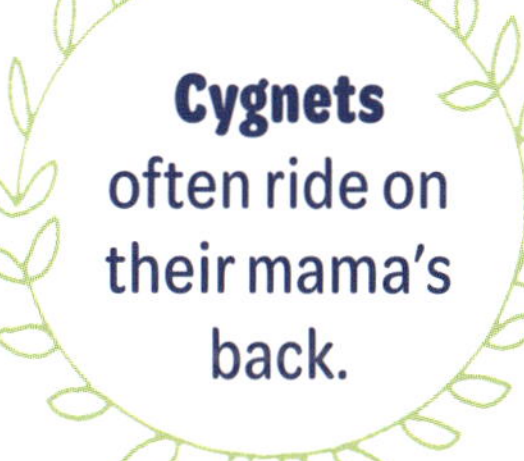

penguin

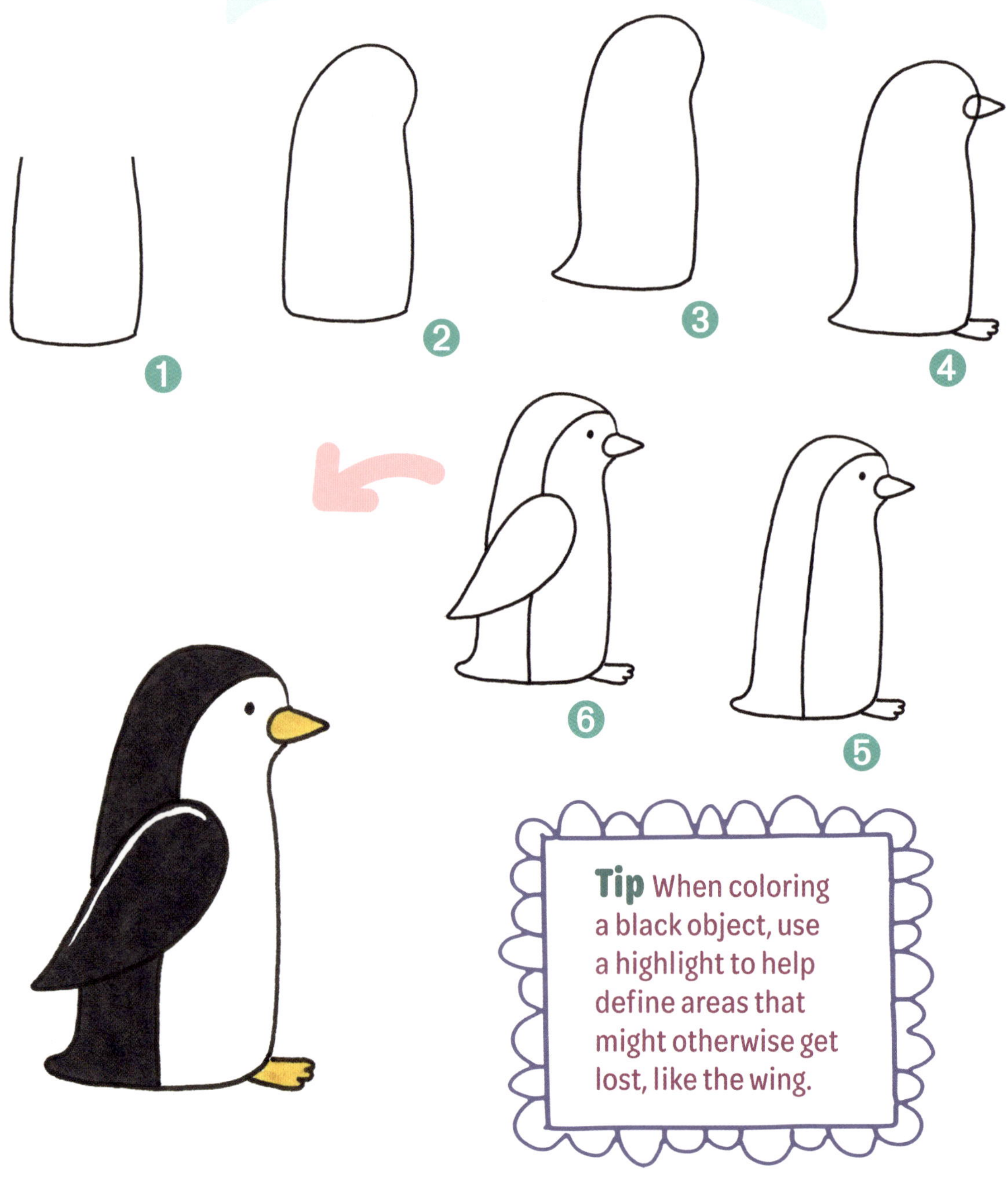

Tip When coloring
a black object, use
a highlight to help
define areas that
might otherwise get
lost, like the wing.

Eagle

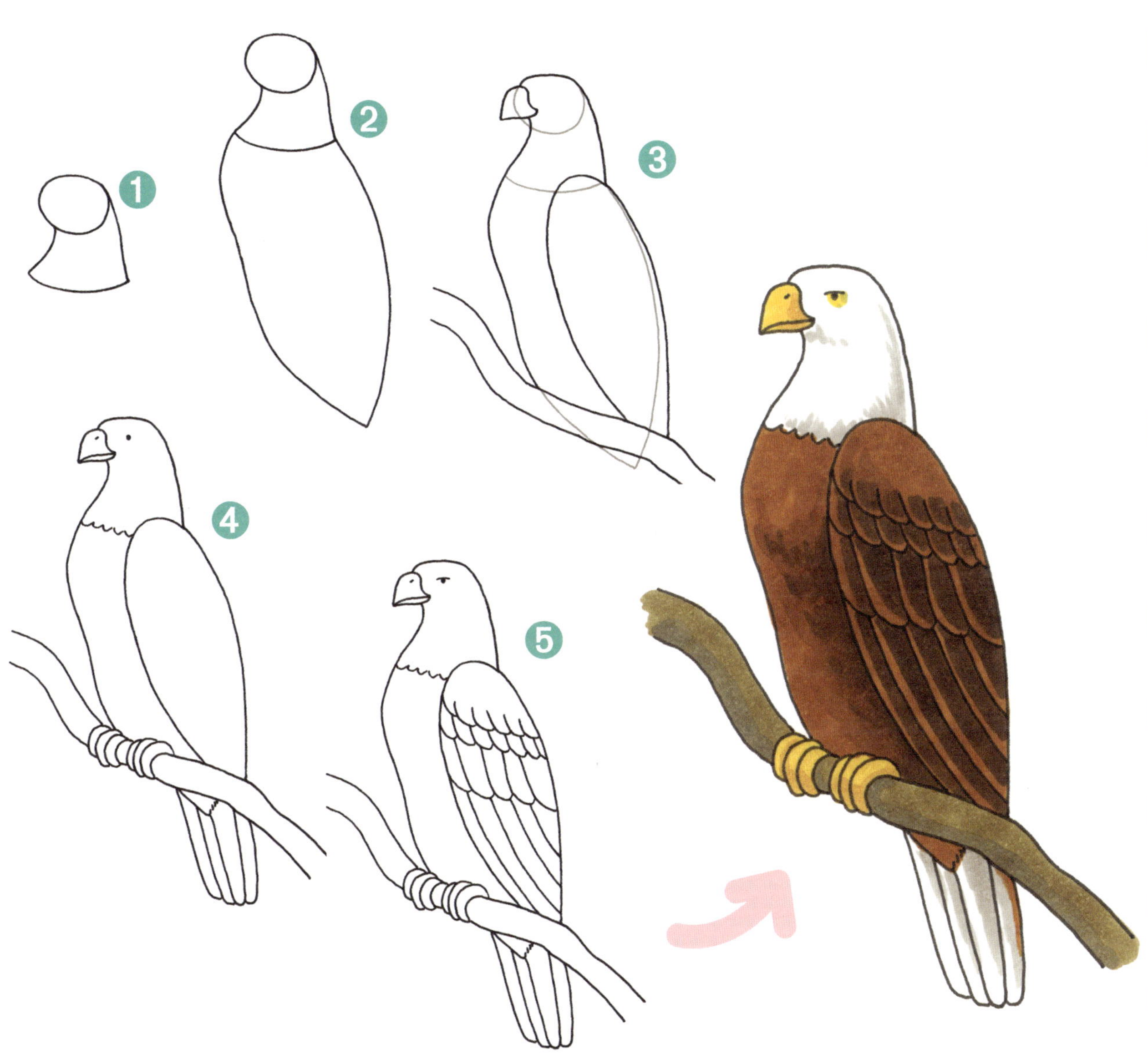

Ostrich

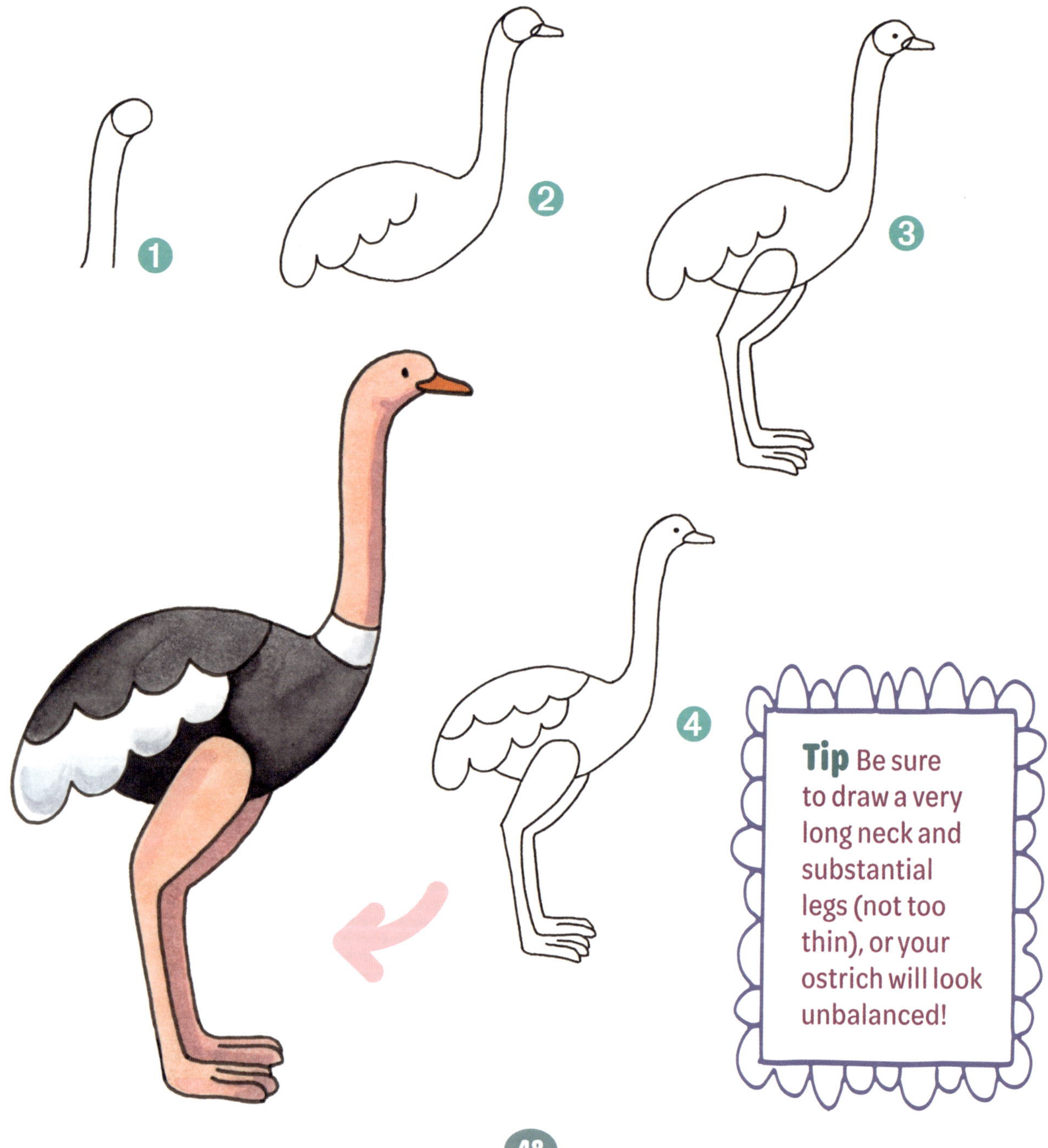

Tip Be sure to draw a very long neck and substantial legs (not too thin), or your ostrich will look unbalanced!

Macaw

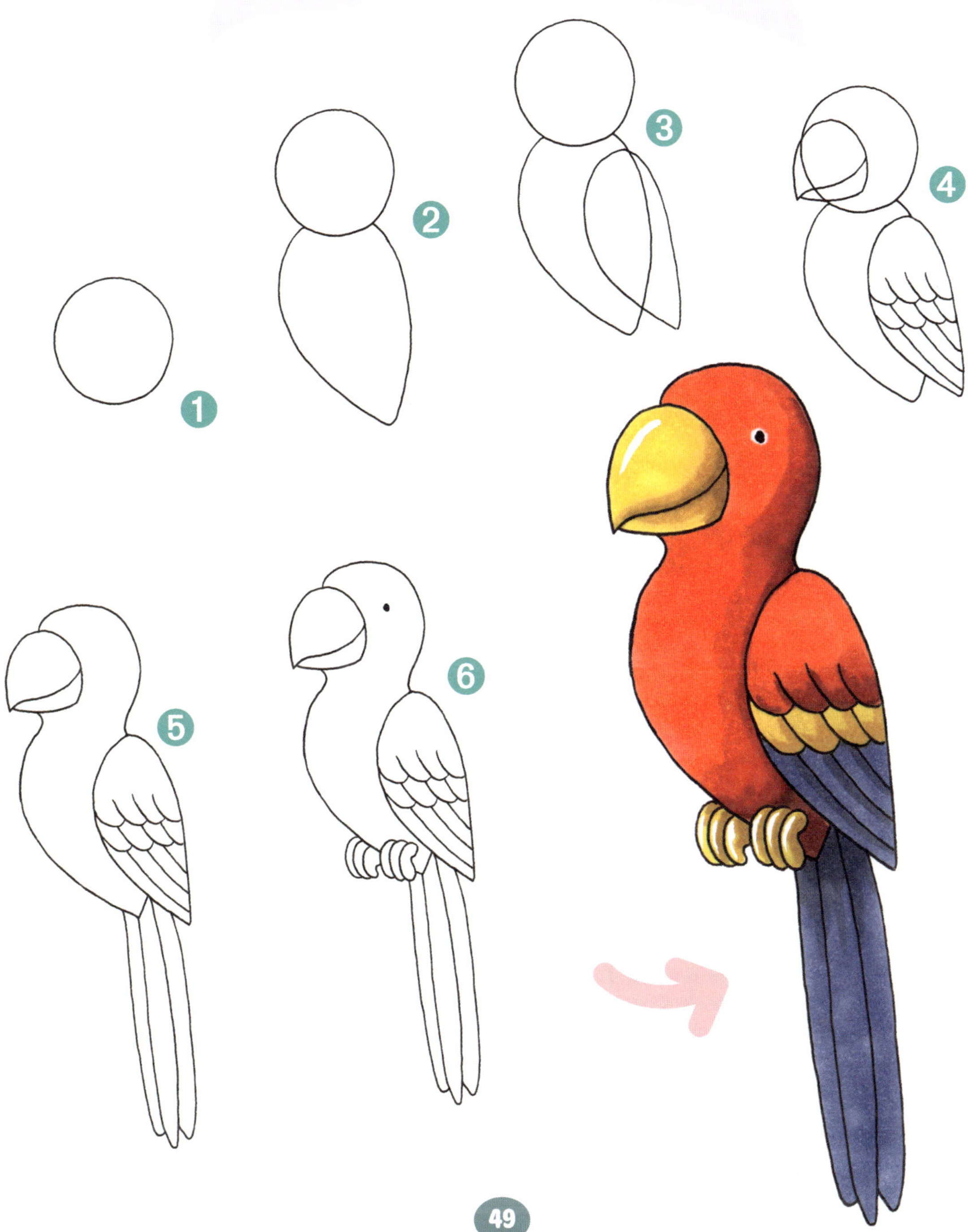

Duck

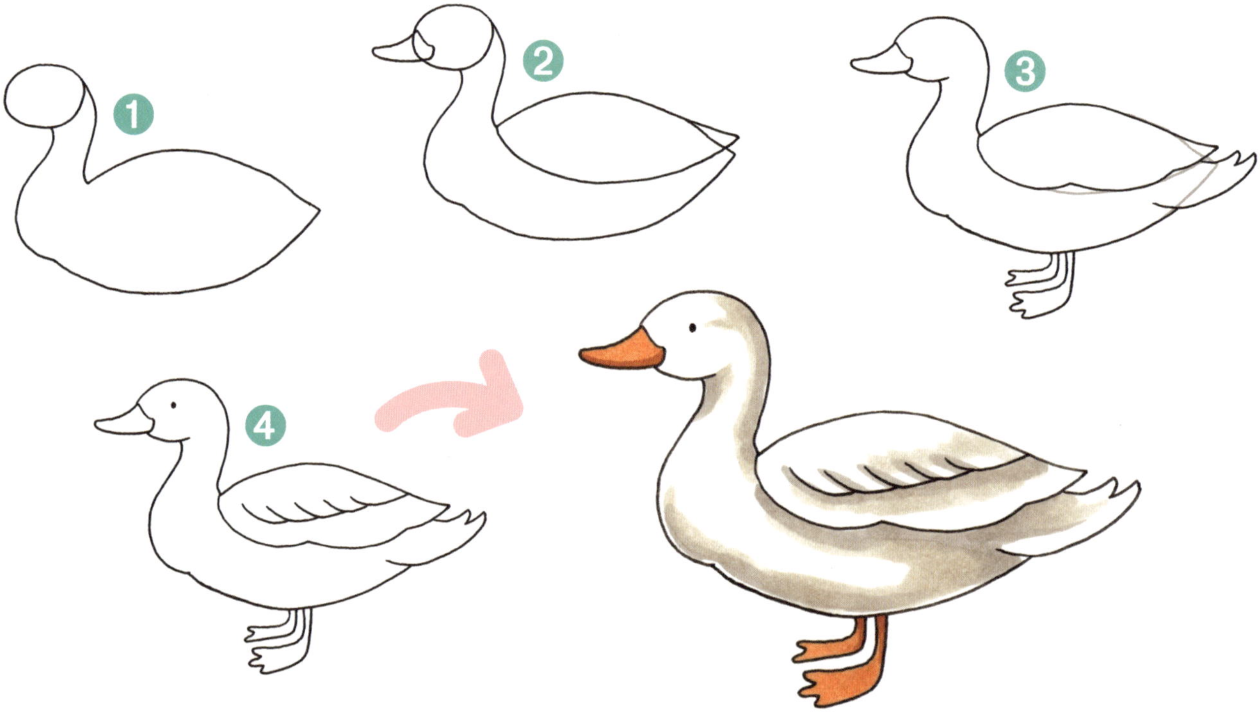

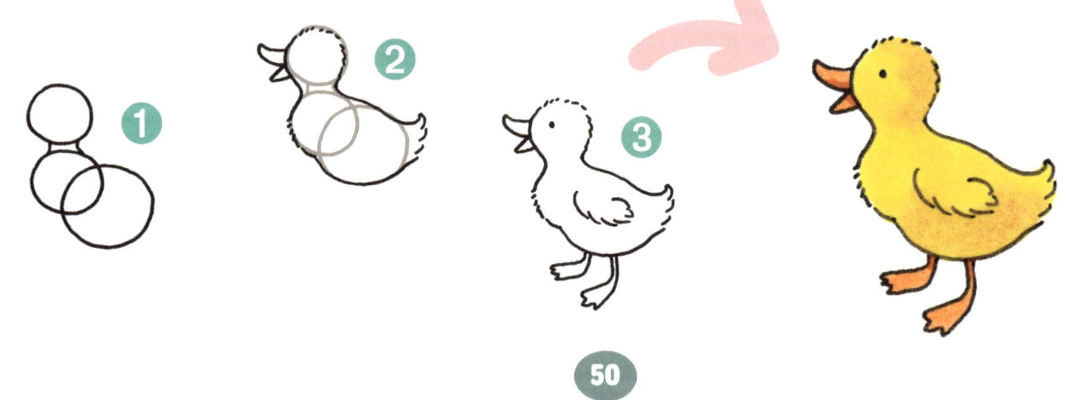

DUCKLING

Bat

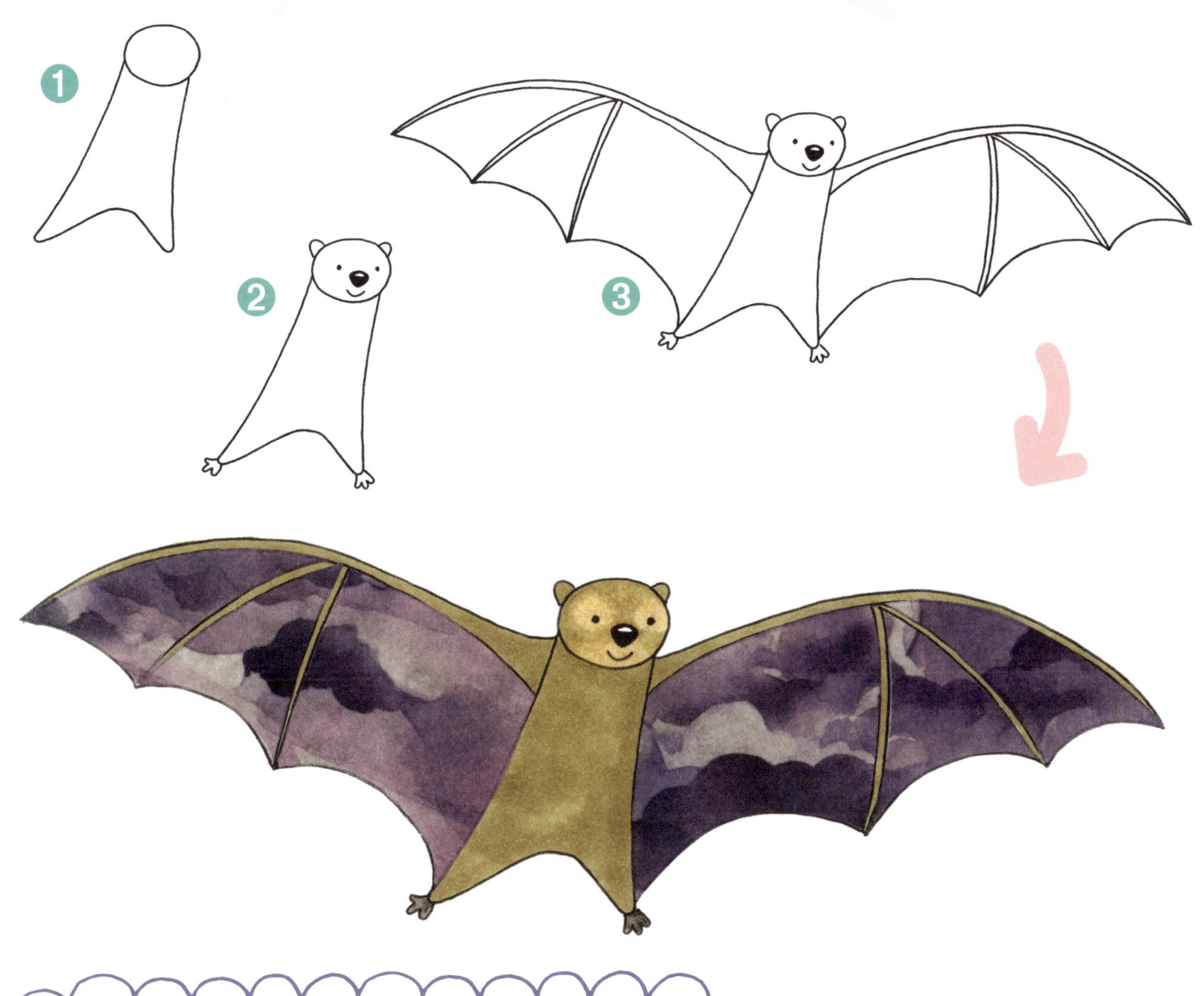

Tip For fun, collage the bat's wings with washi tape trimmed to fit. Choose a tape that is somewhat transparent to make this easier.

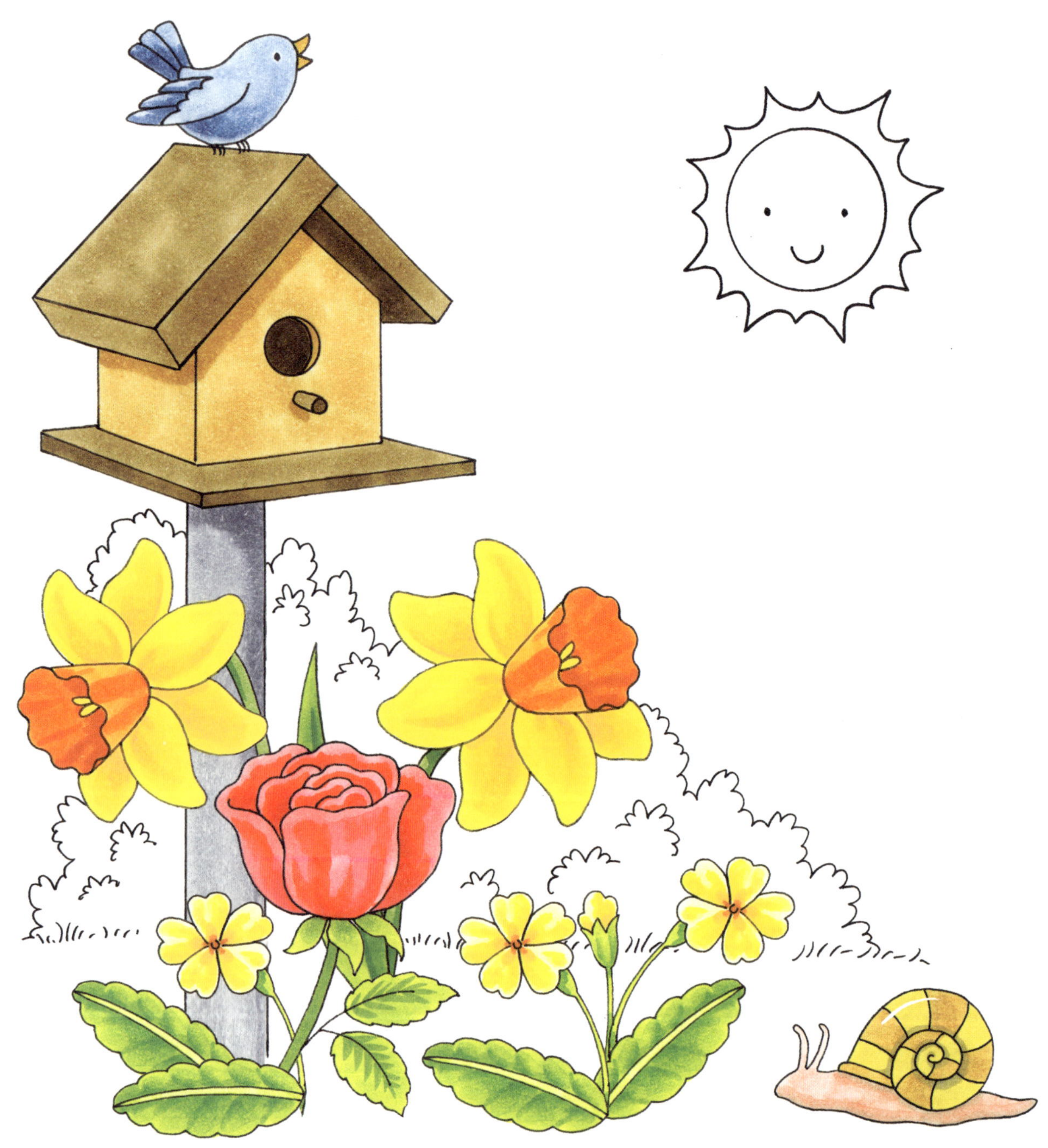

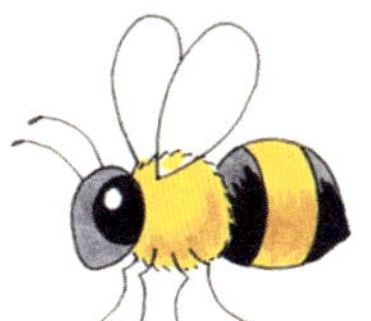

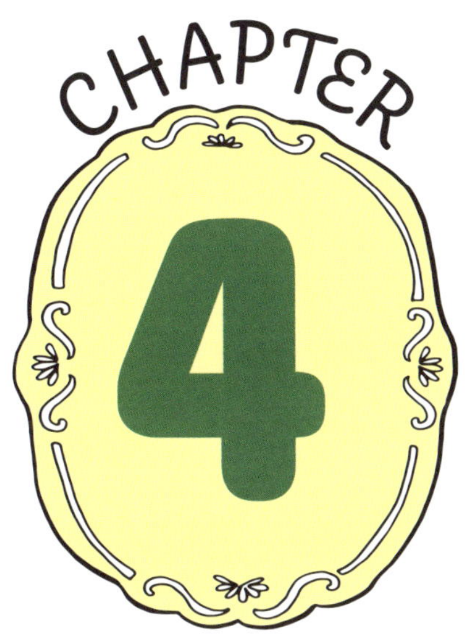

4

In the Garden

Your very own garden can provide lots of drawing inspiration—from plants to insects to objects. In this chapter, we will explore how to draw a selection of flowers as well as the creatures who visit there, like hummingbirds, bees, and butterflies, and garden tools.

Lizard

This is an **anole** lizard, native to the southern US.

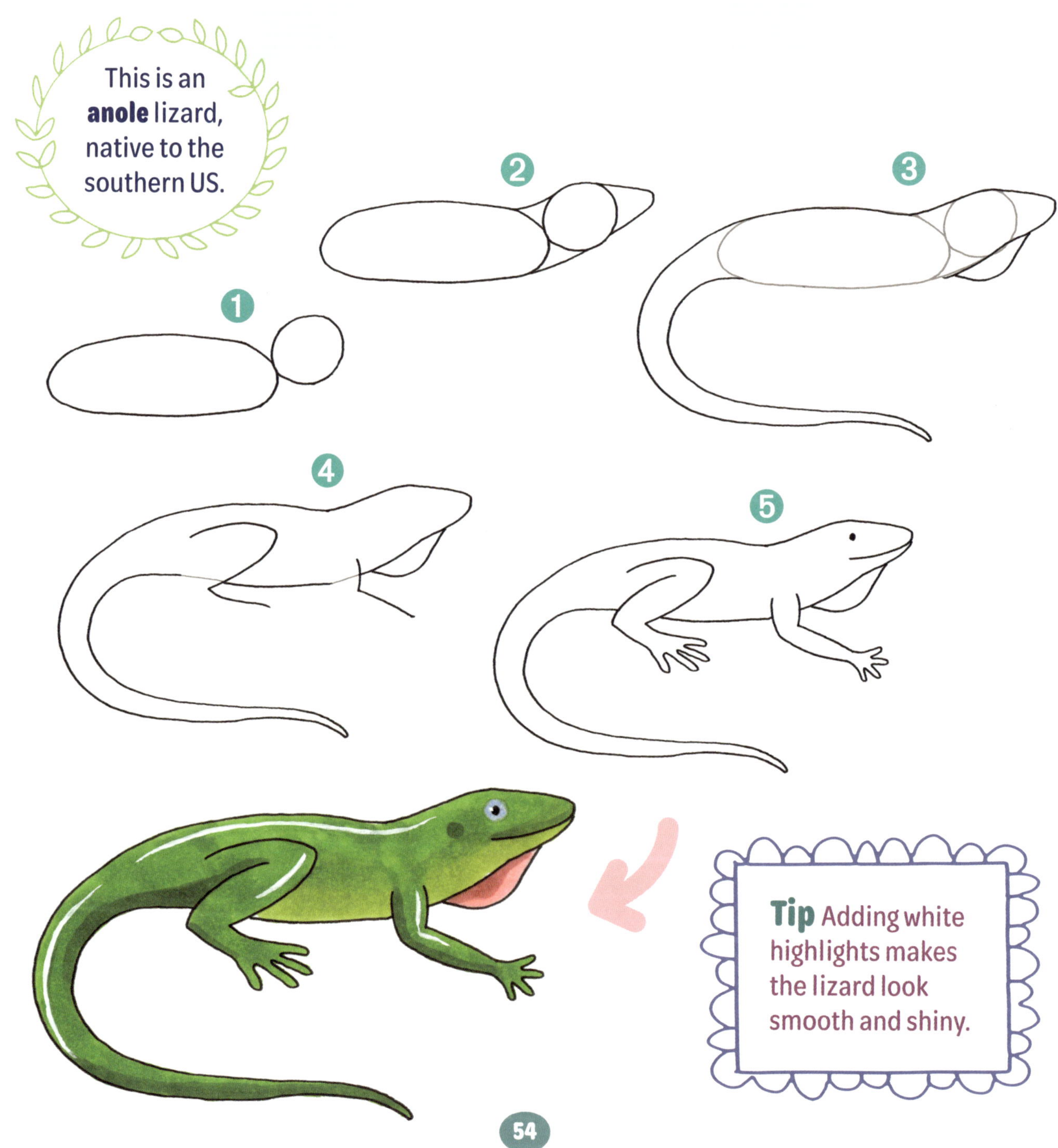

Tip Adding white highlights makes the lizard look smooth and shiny.

Garden Friends

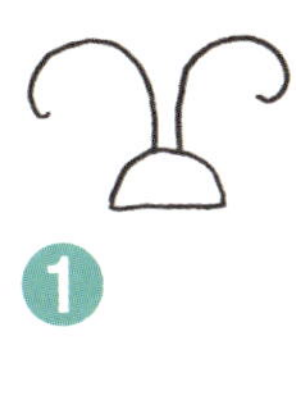 1

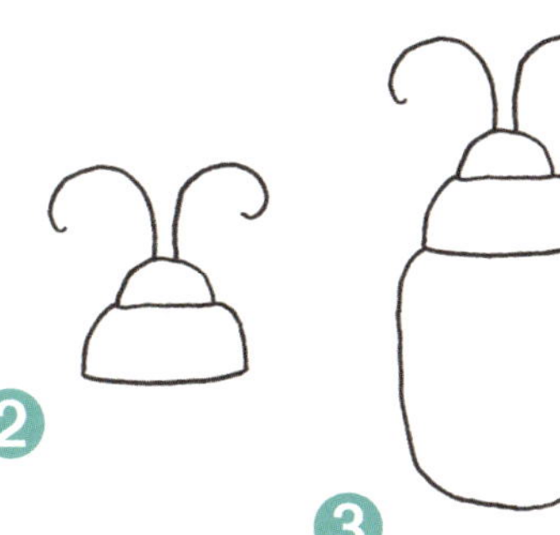 2

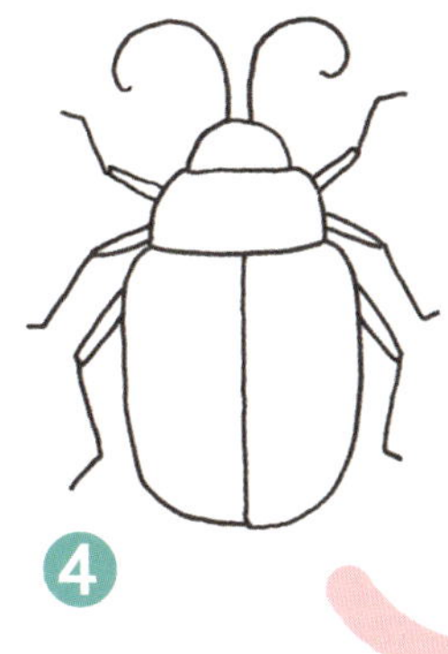 3

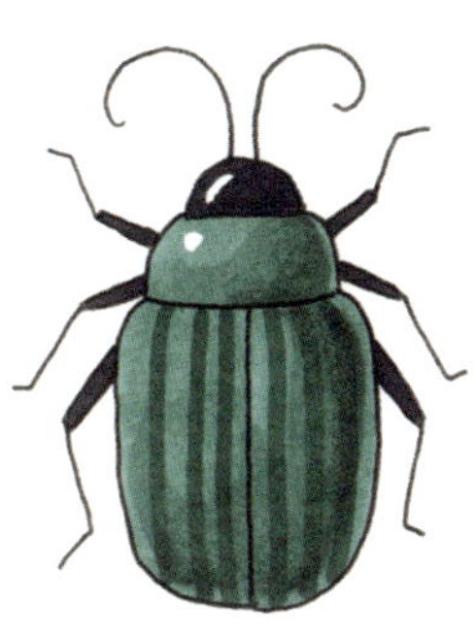 4

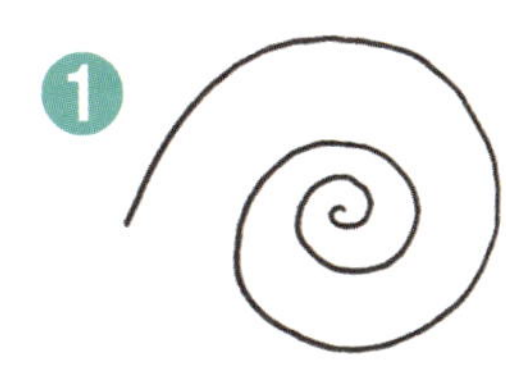 1

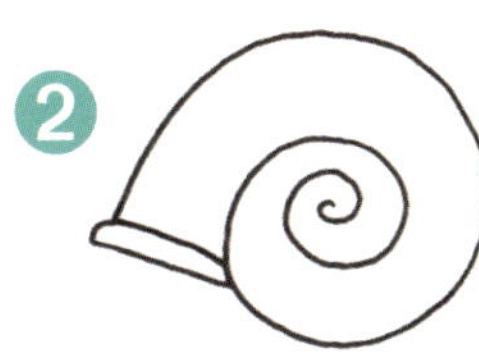 2

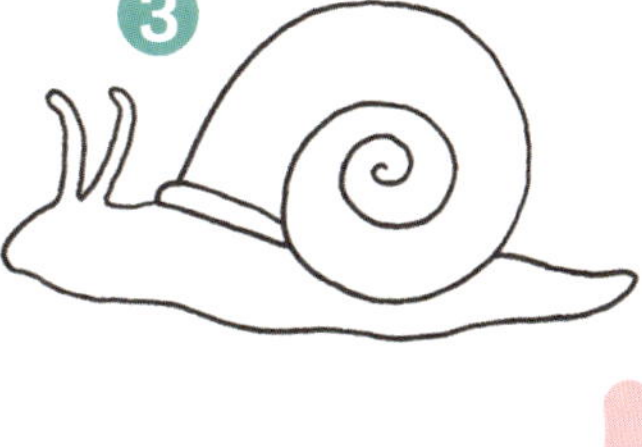 3

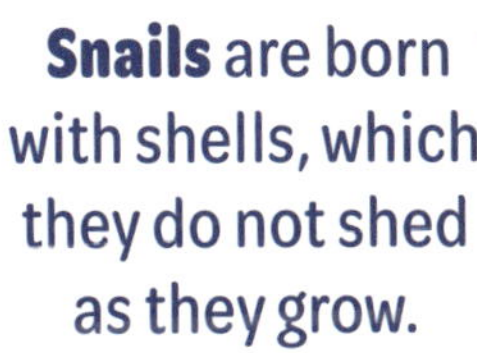

Snails are born with shells, which they do not shed as they grow.

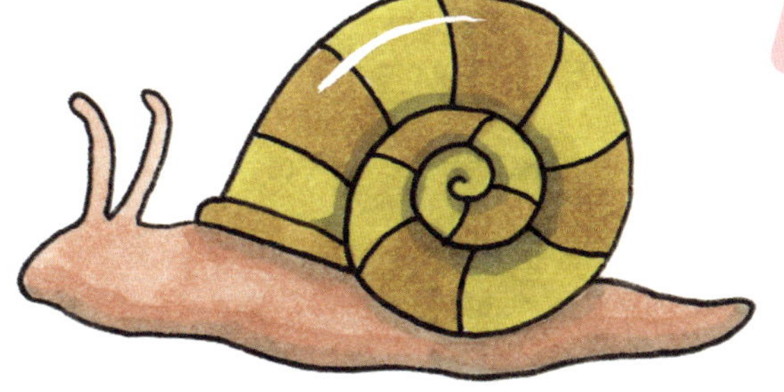

Watering Can

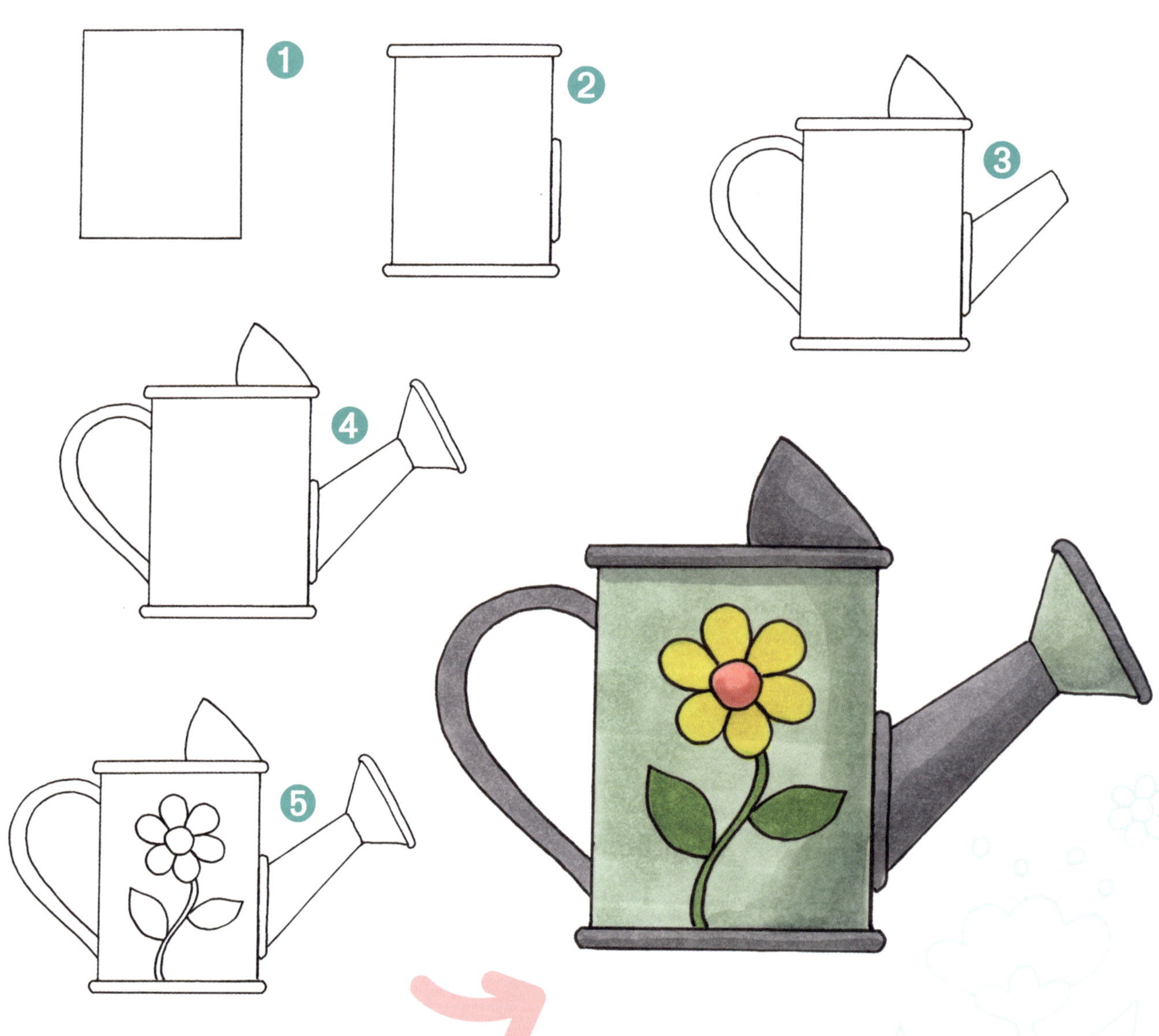

Buzzing About

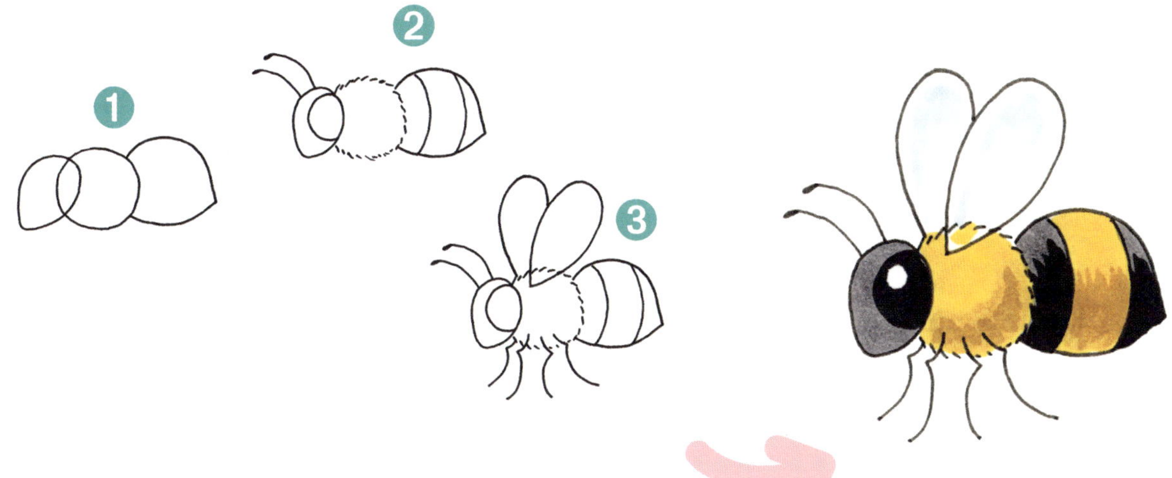

BEEHIVE

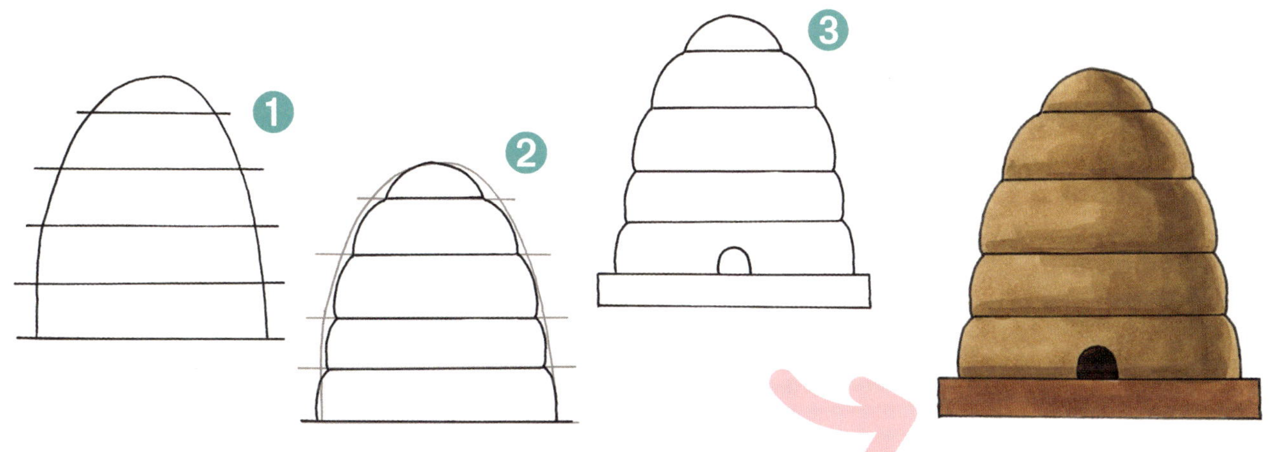

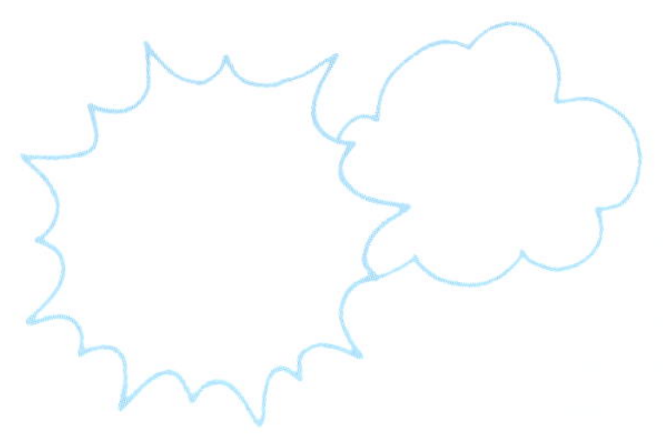

Birdhouse

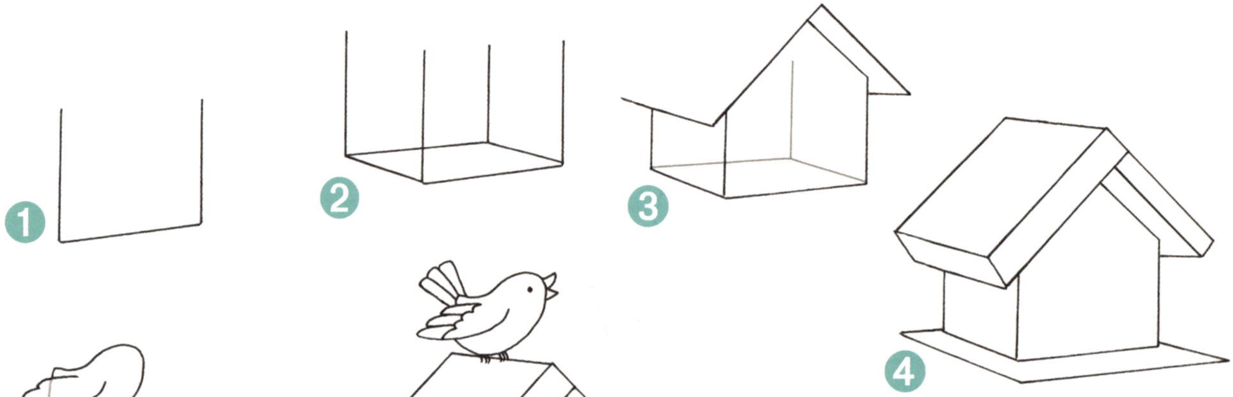

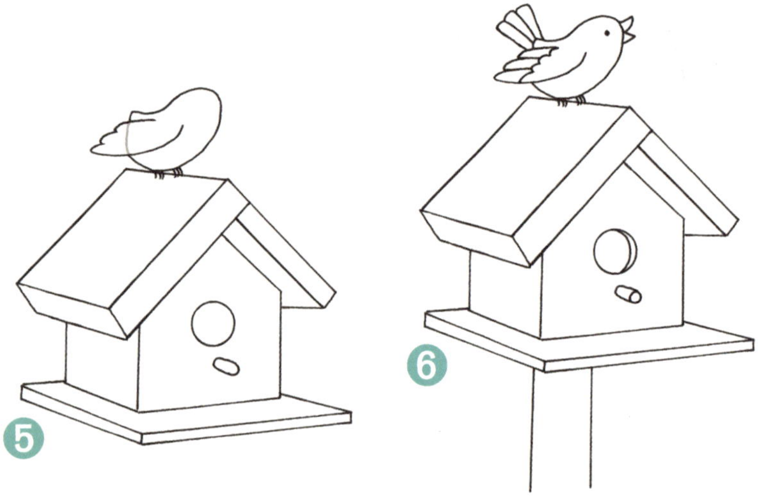

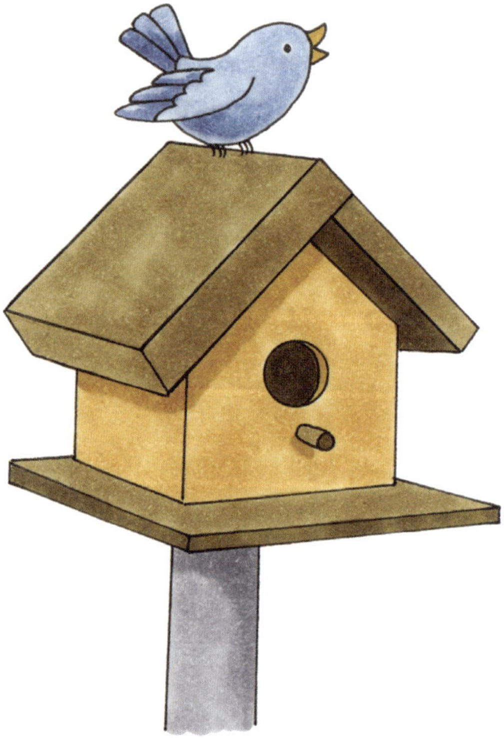

1

2

3

4

5

6

Goldfinch

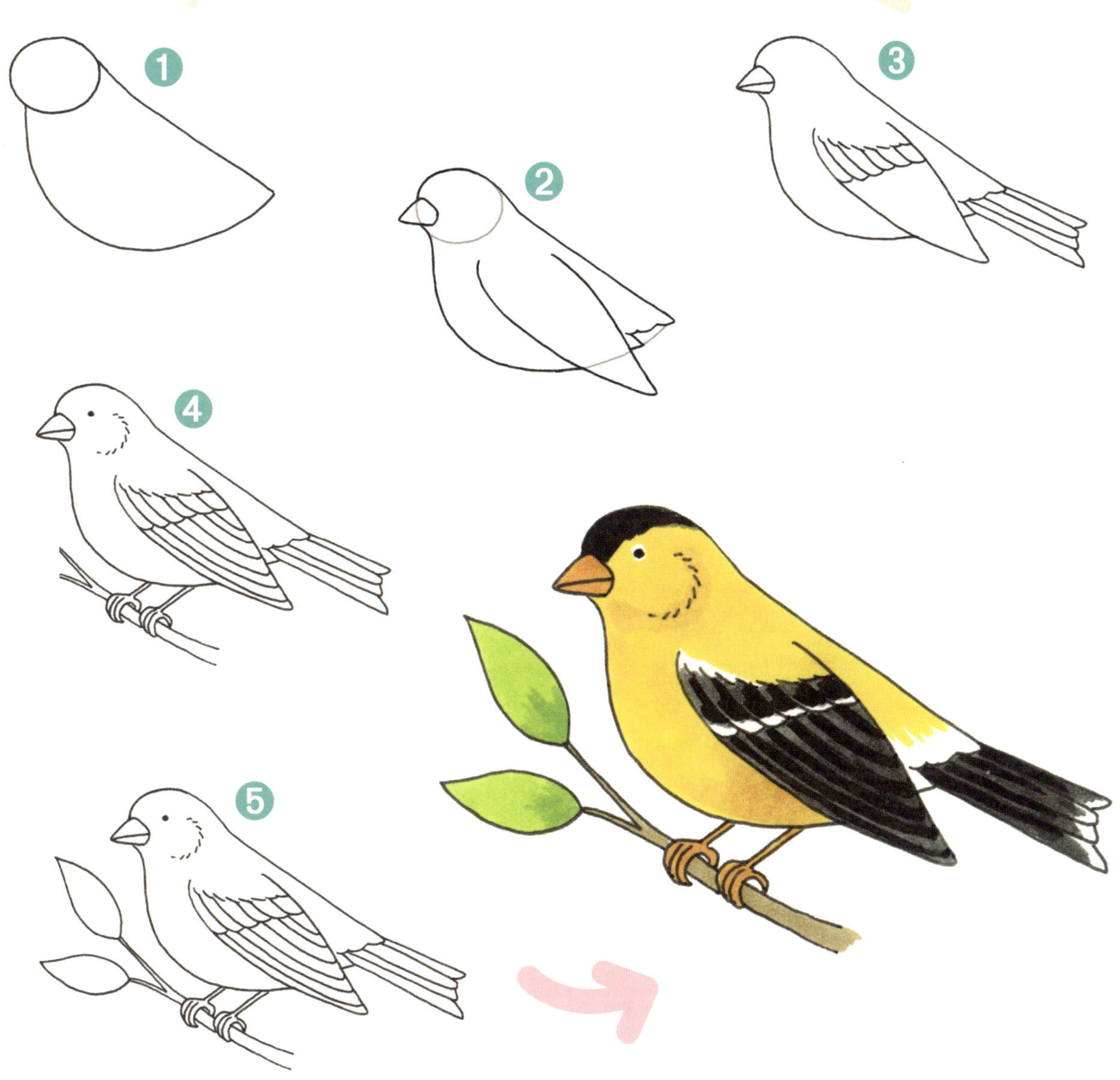

Rose

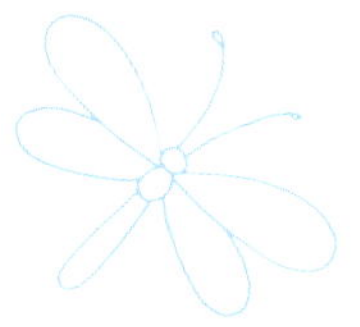

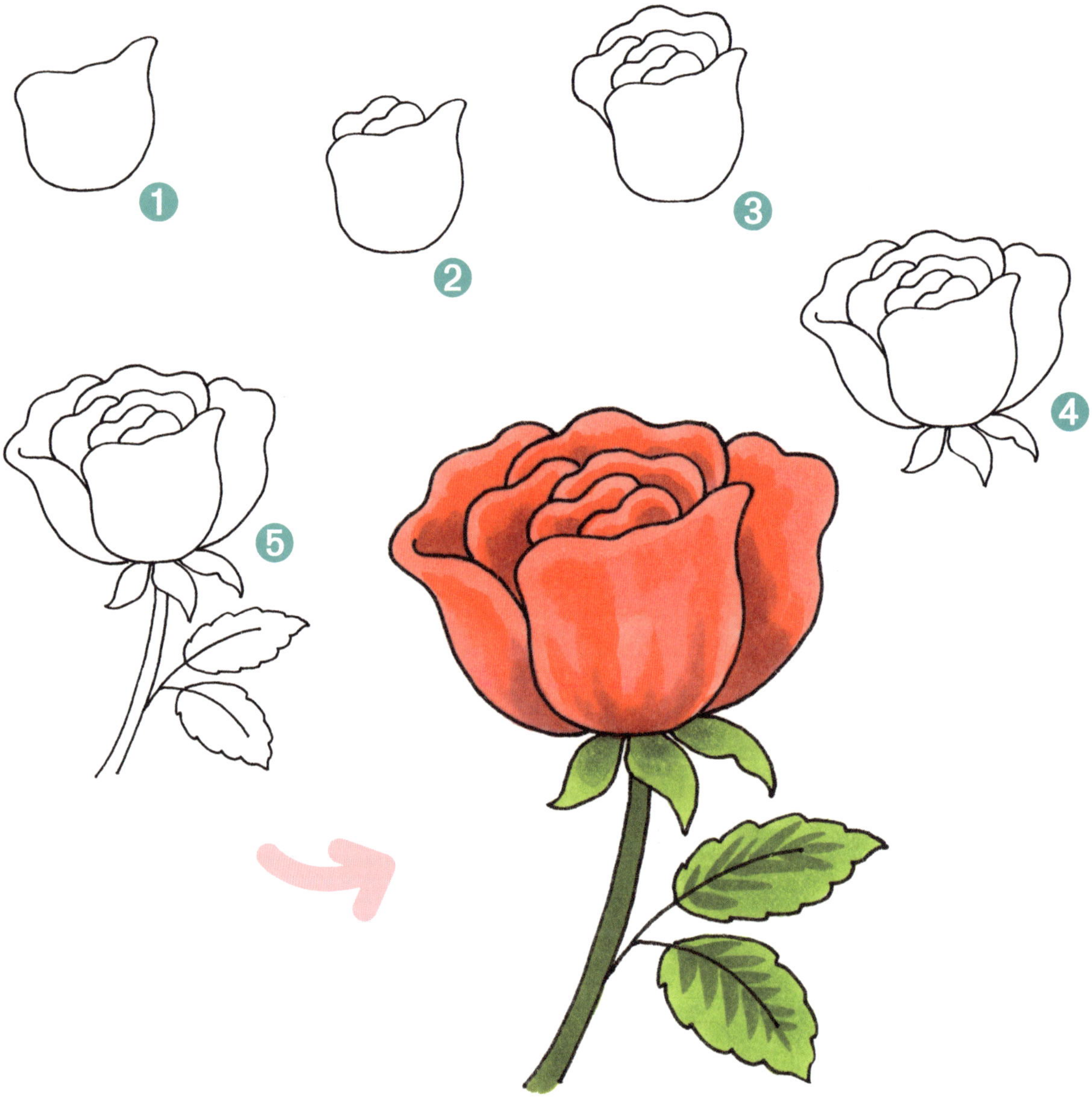

Tulip

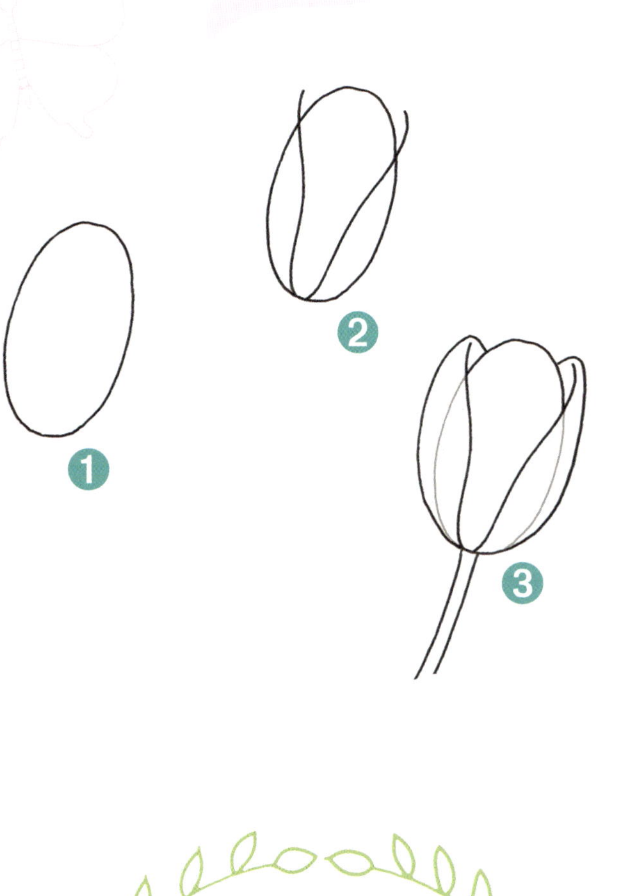

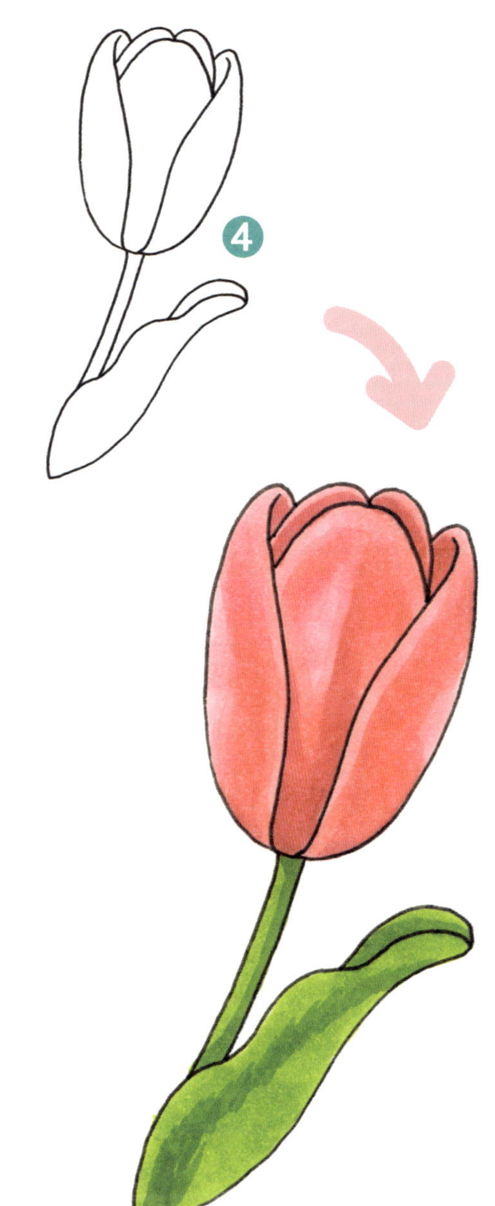

Tulips come in many different colors and patterns, so feel free to experiment with your coloring.

Daffodil

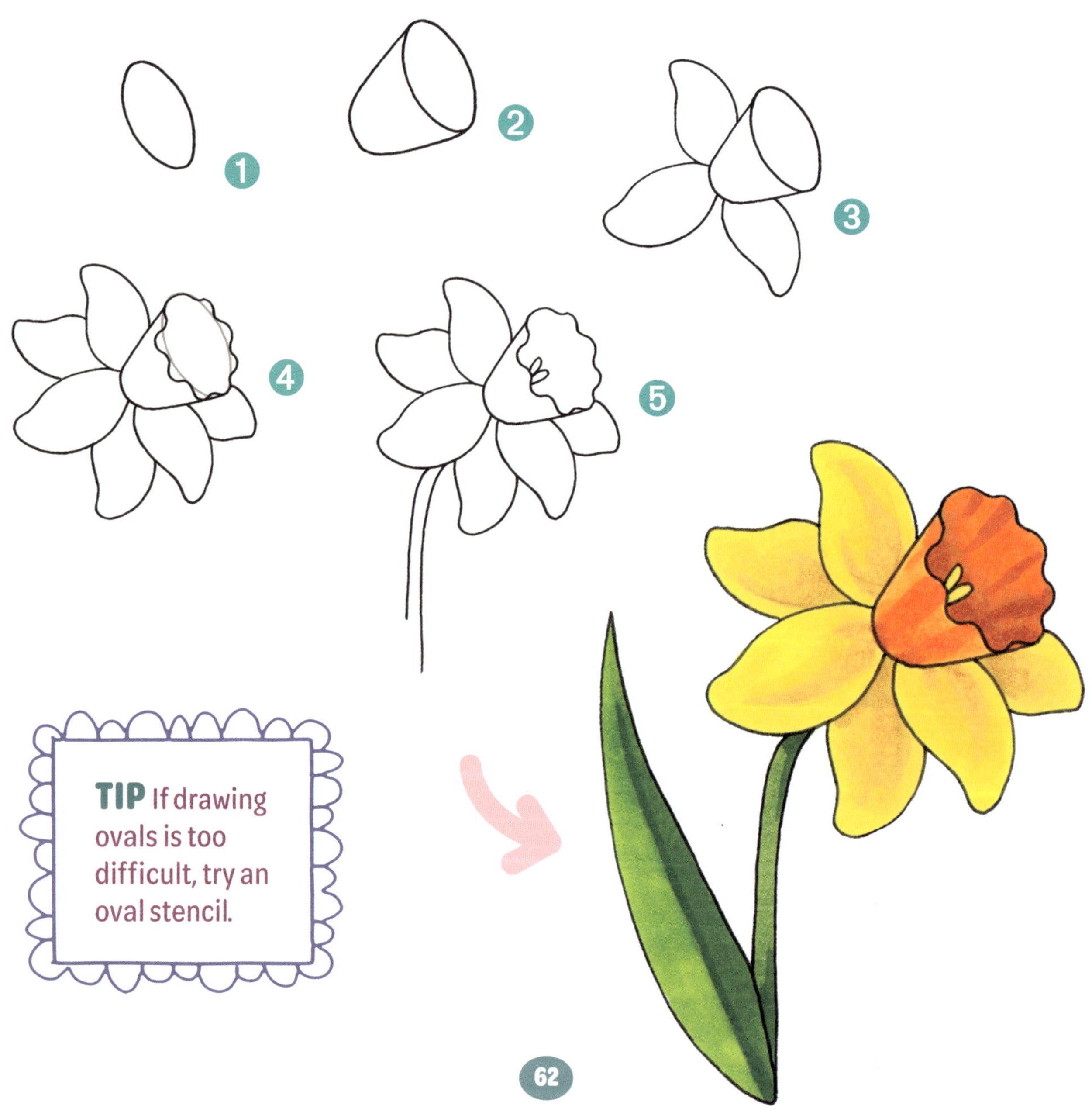

TIP If drawing ovals is too difficult, try an oval stencil.

Primrose

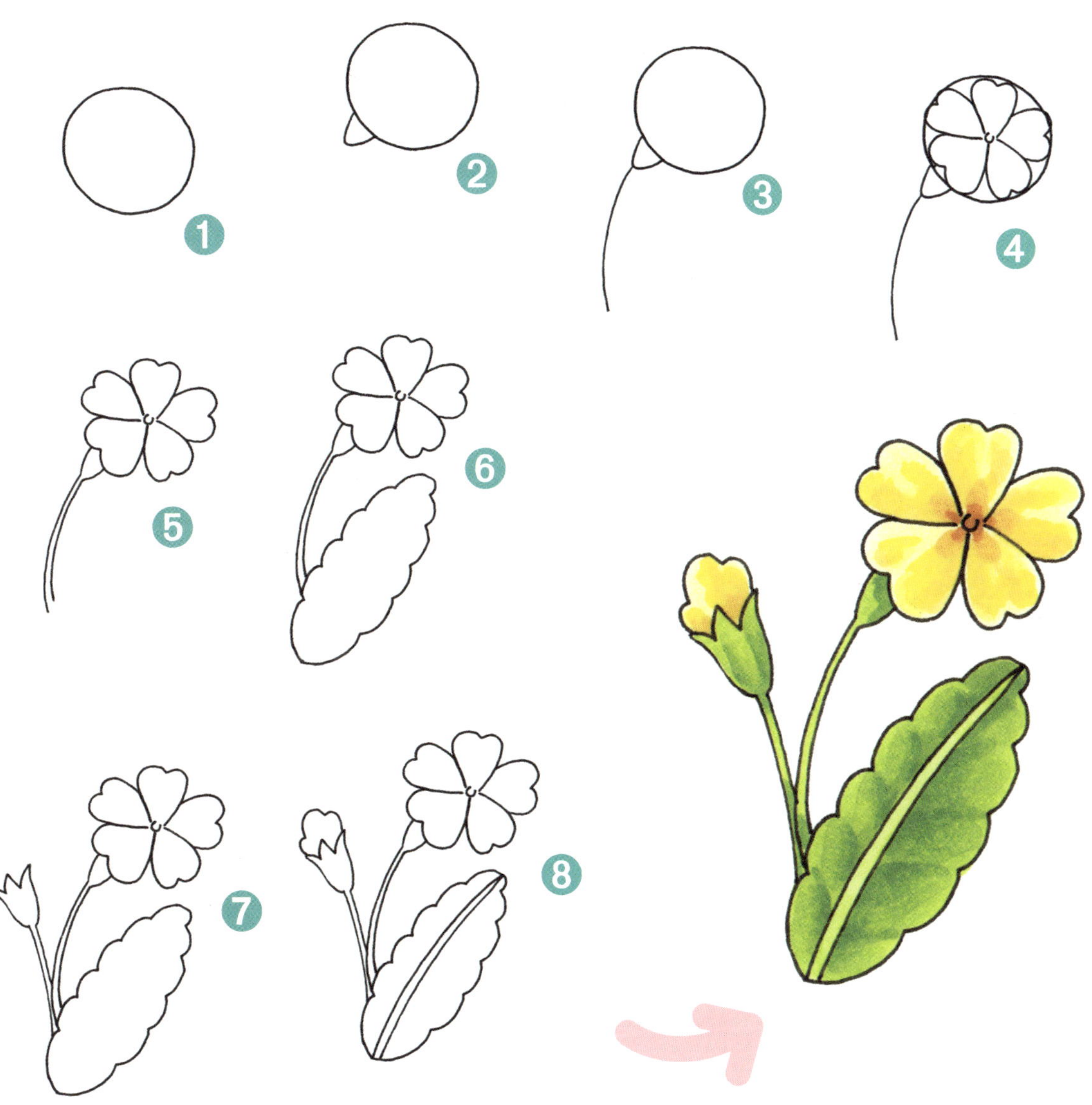

Radish

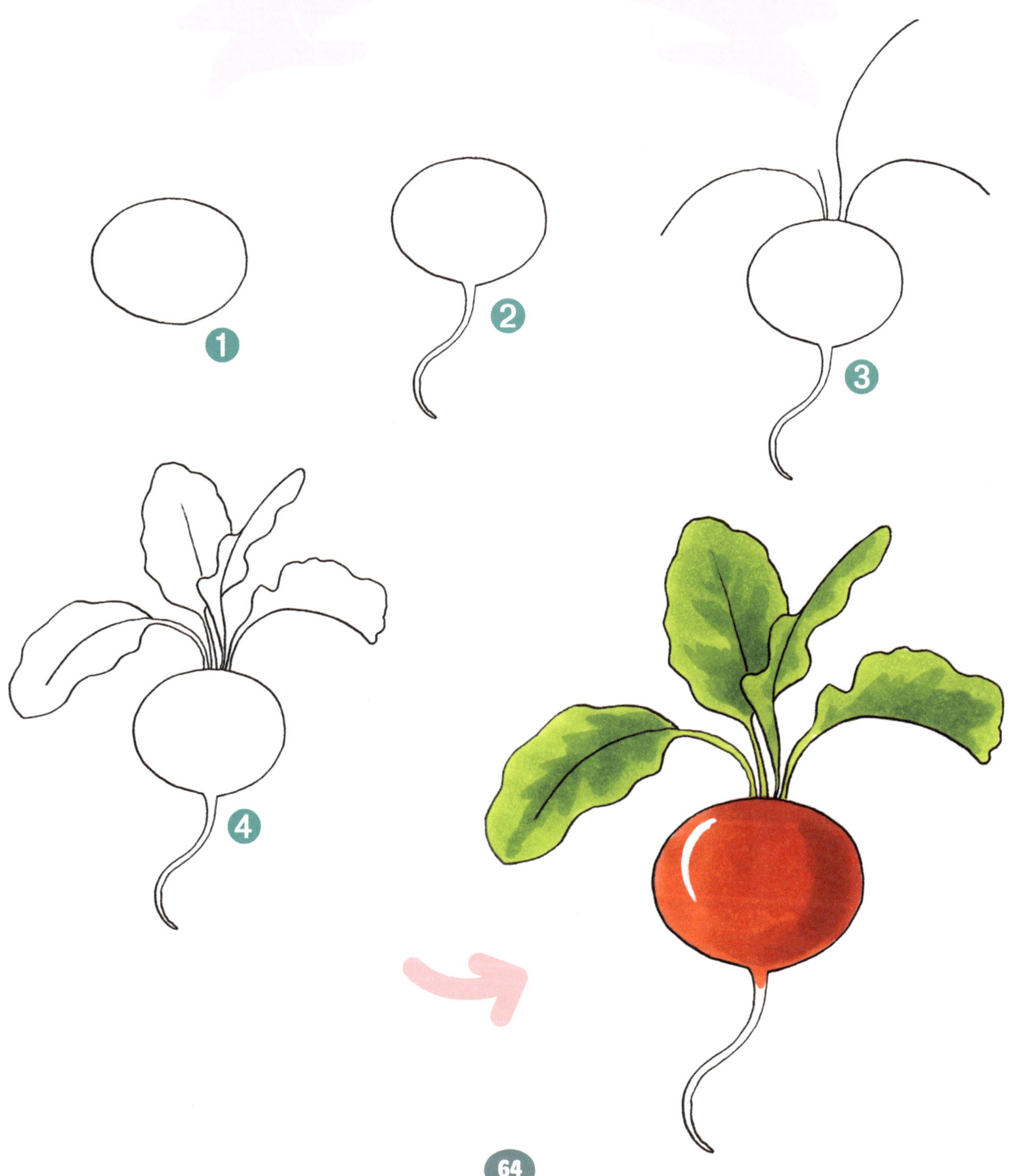

peppers

1 2 3

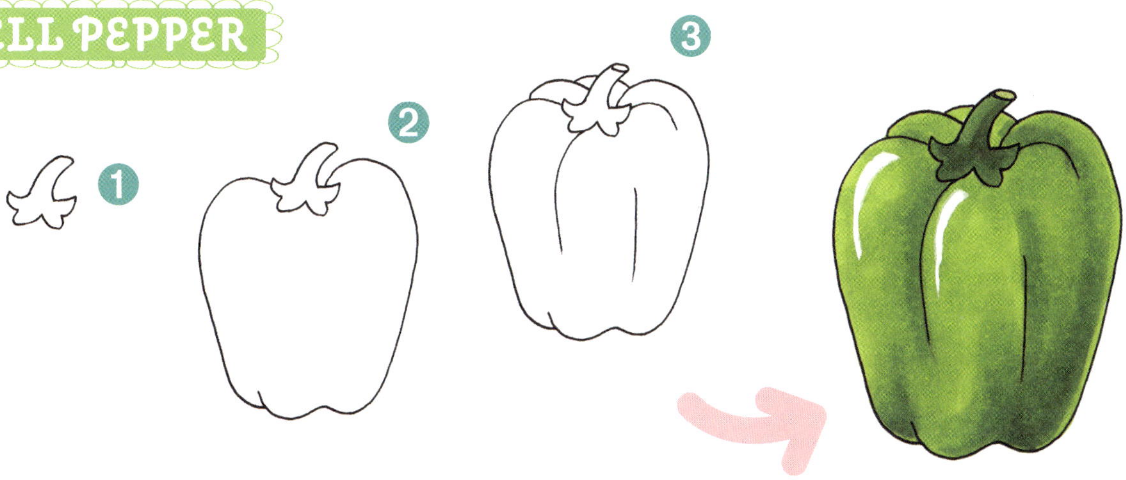

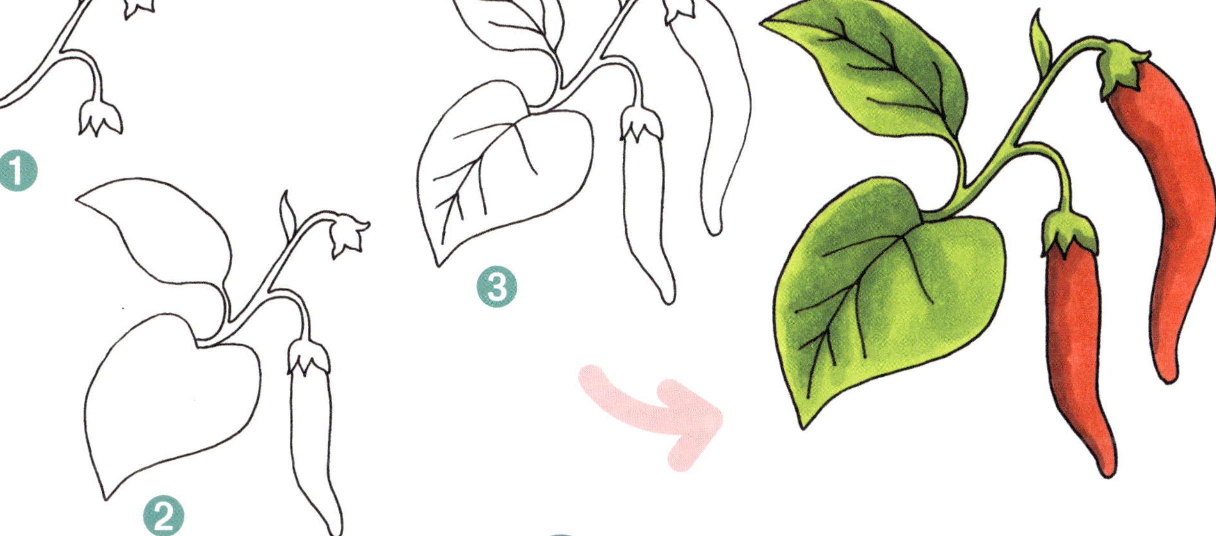

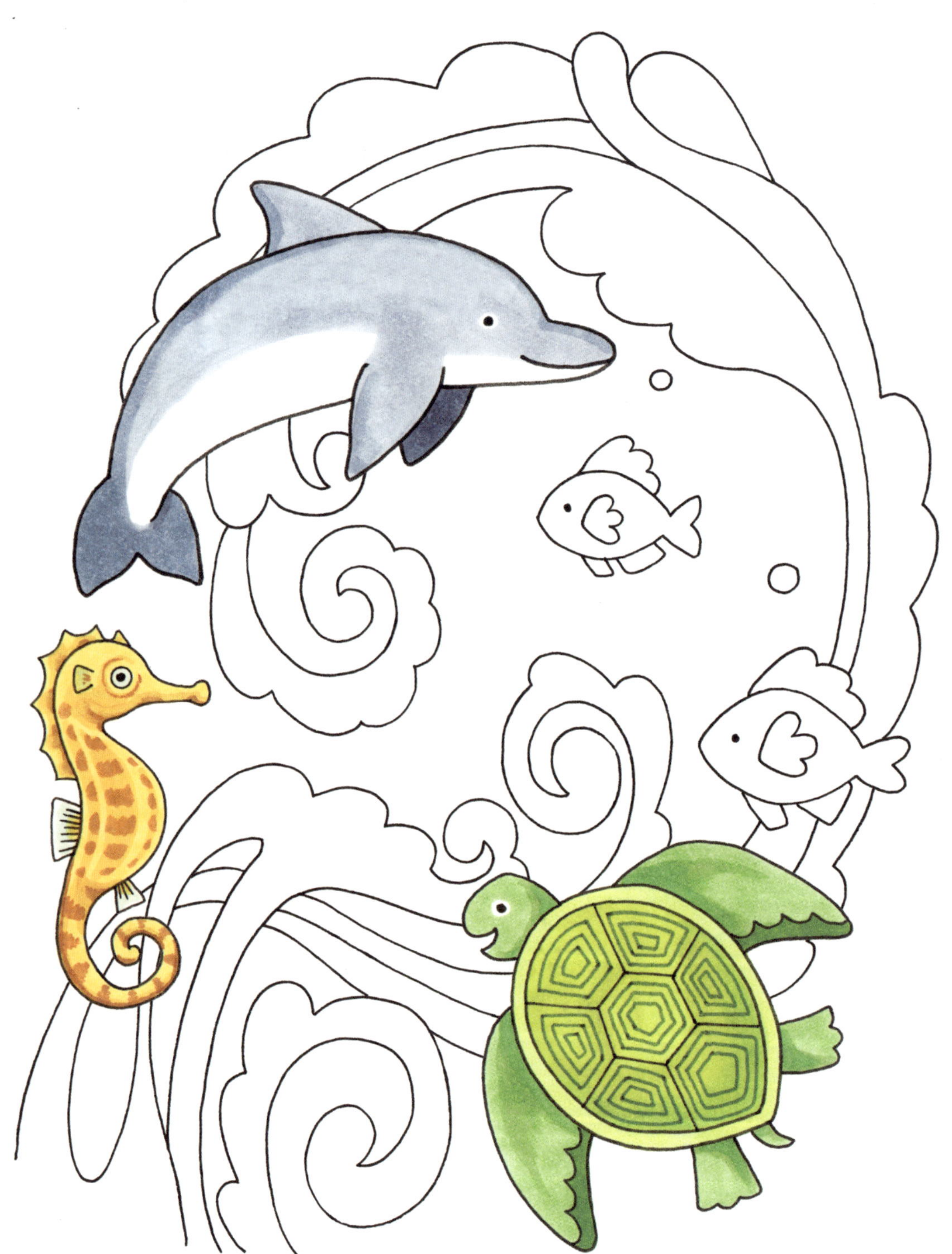

CHAPTER

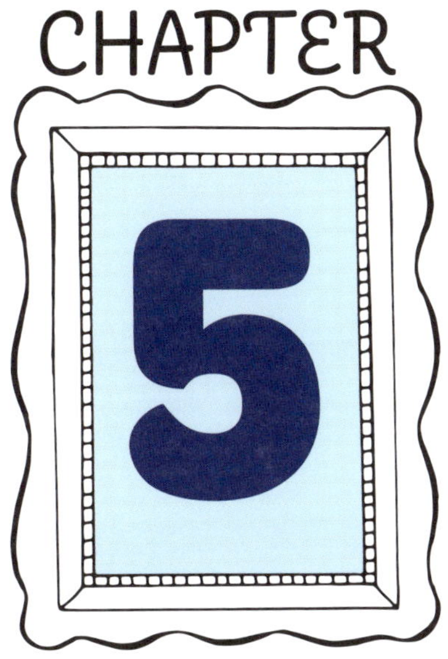

Water World

There is nothing more relaxing than being
by the water, whether it's the ocean,
a lake, a stream, or a pond. In this chapter,
we take a look at how to draw some
of the creatures you might find there,
both under and above the water.

Seagull

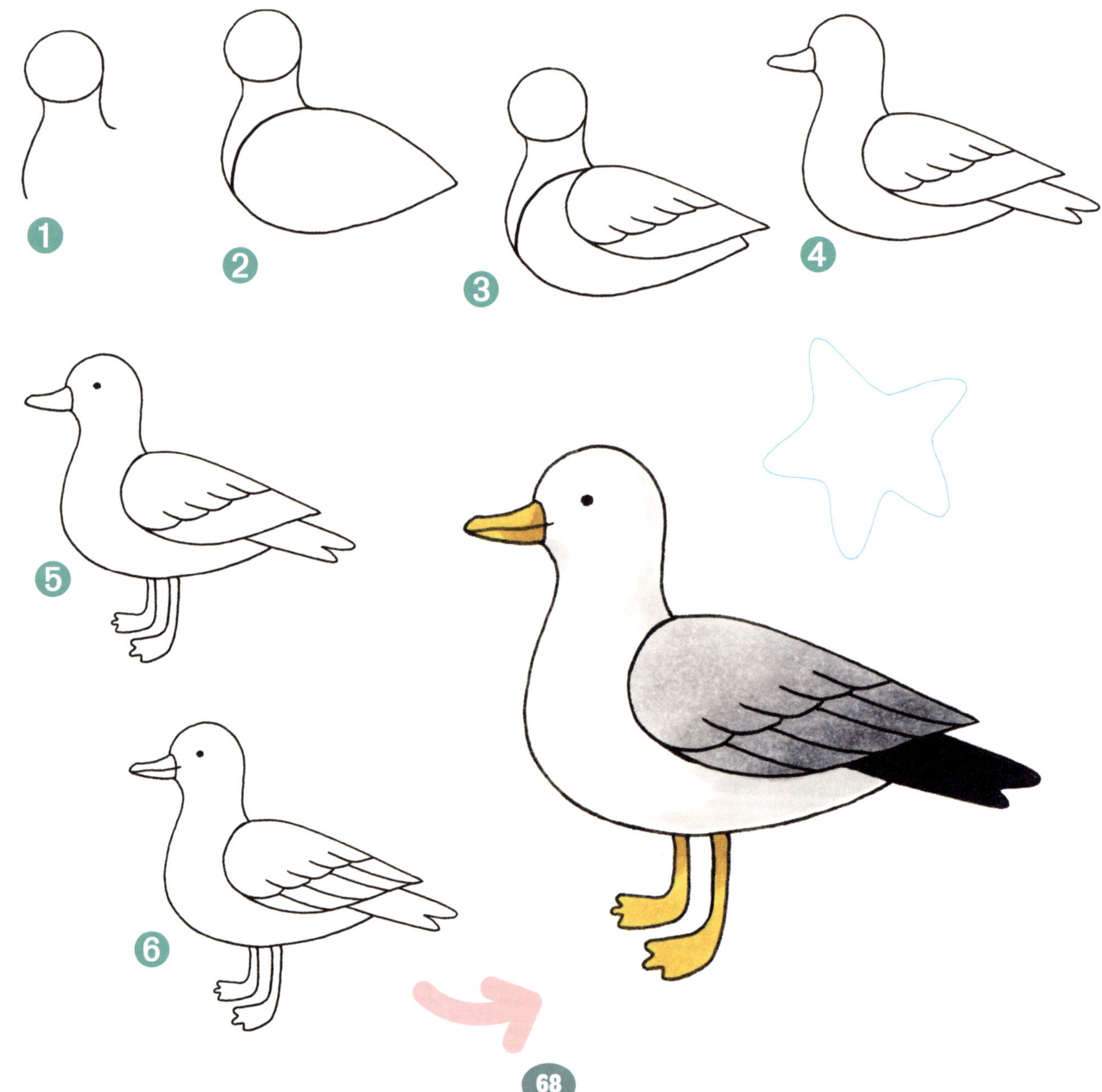

pelican

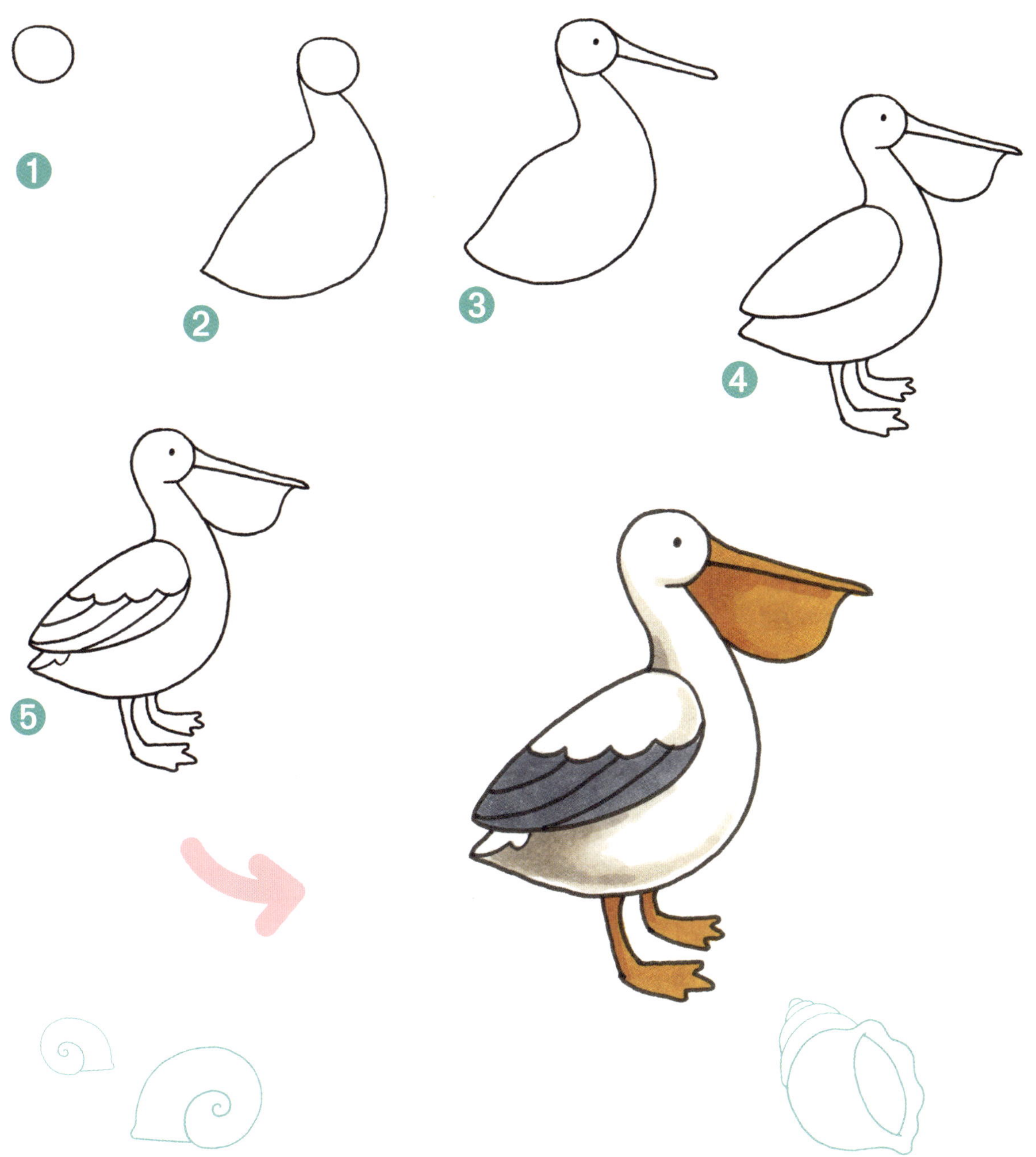

Sea Otter

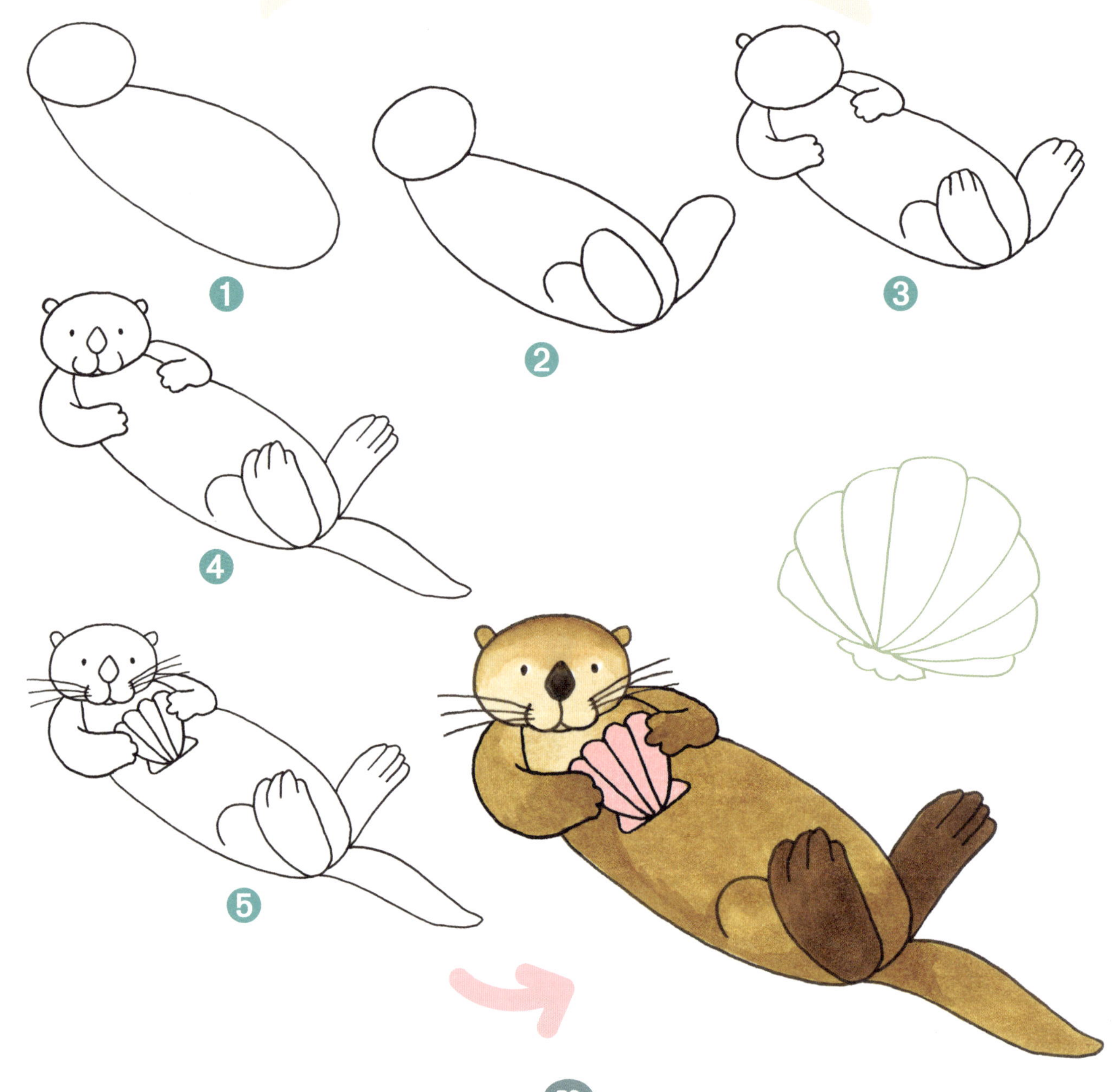

Sea Turtle

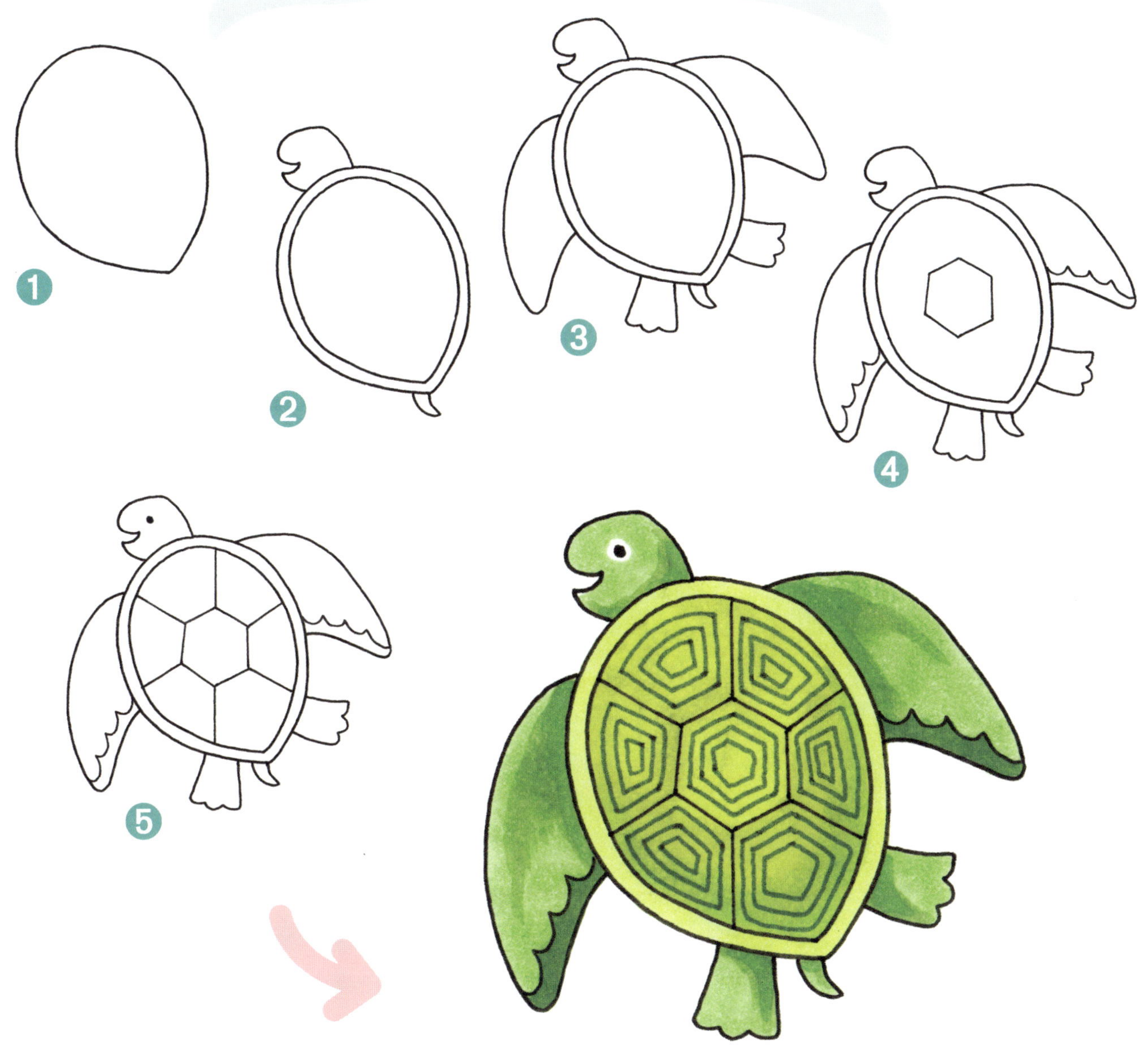

Walrus

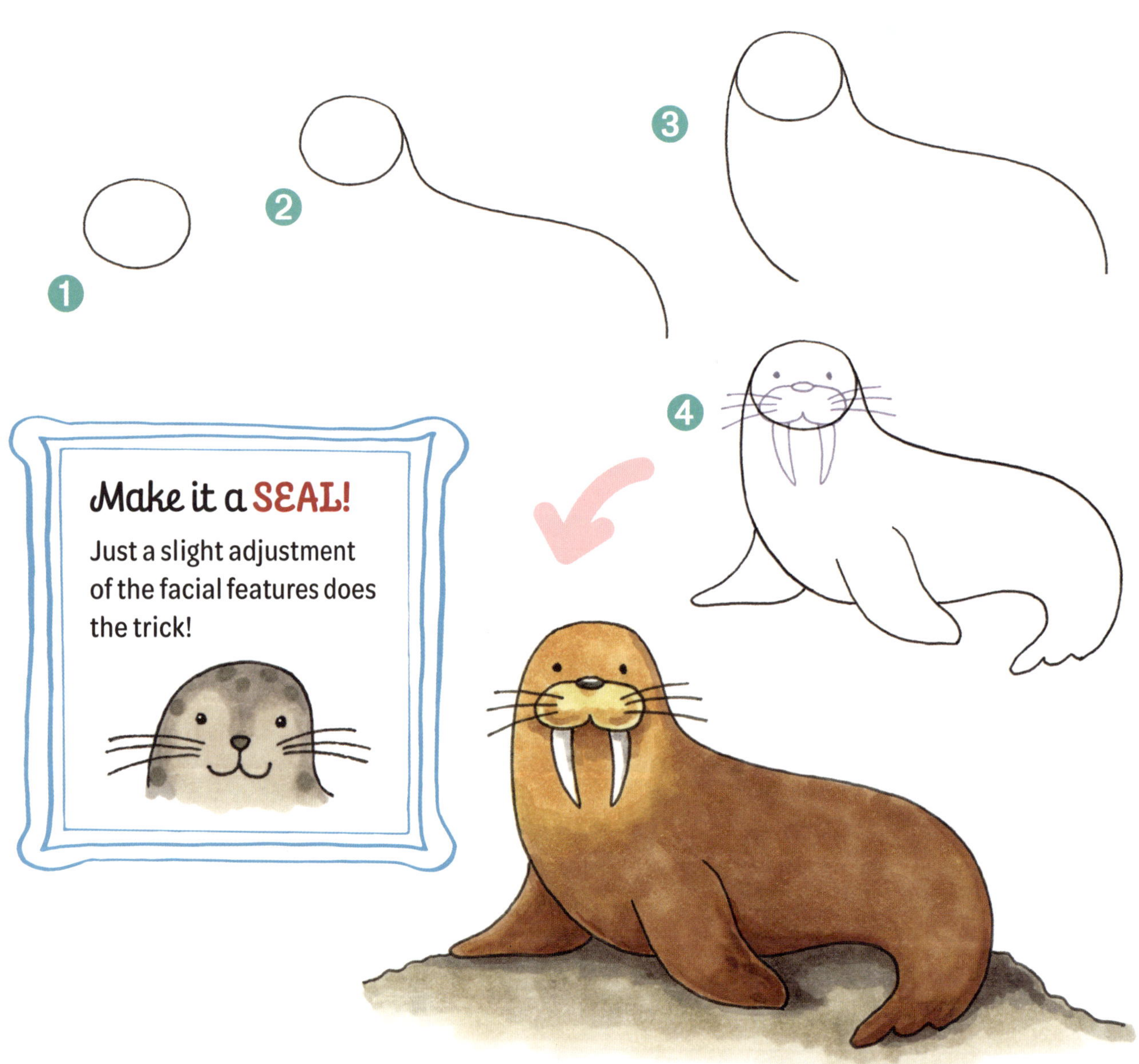

1
2
3
4
Make it a SEAL!
Just a slight adjustment of the facial features does the trick!

Orca Whale

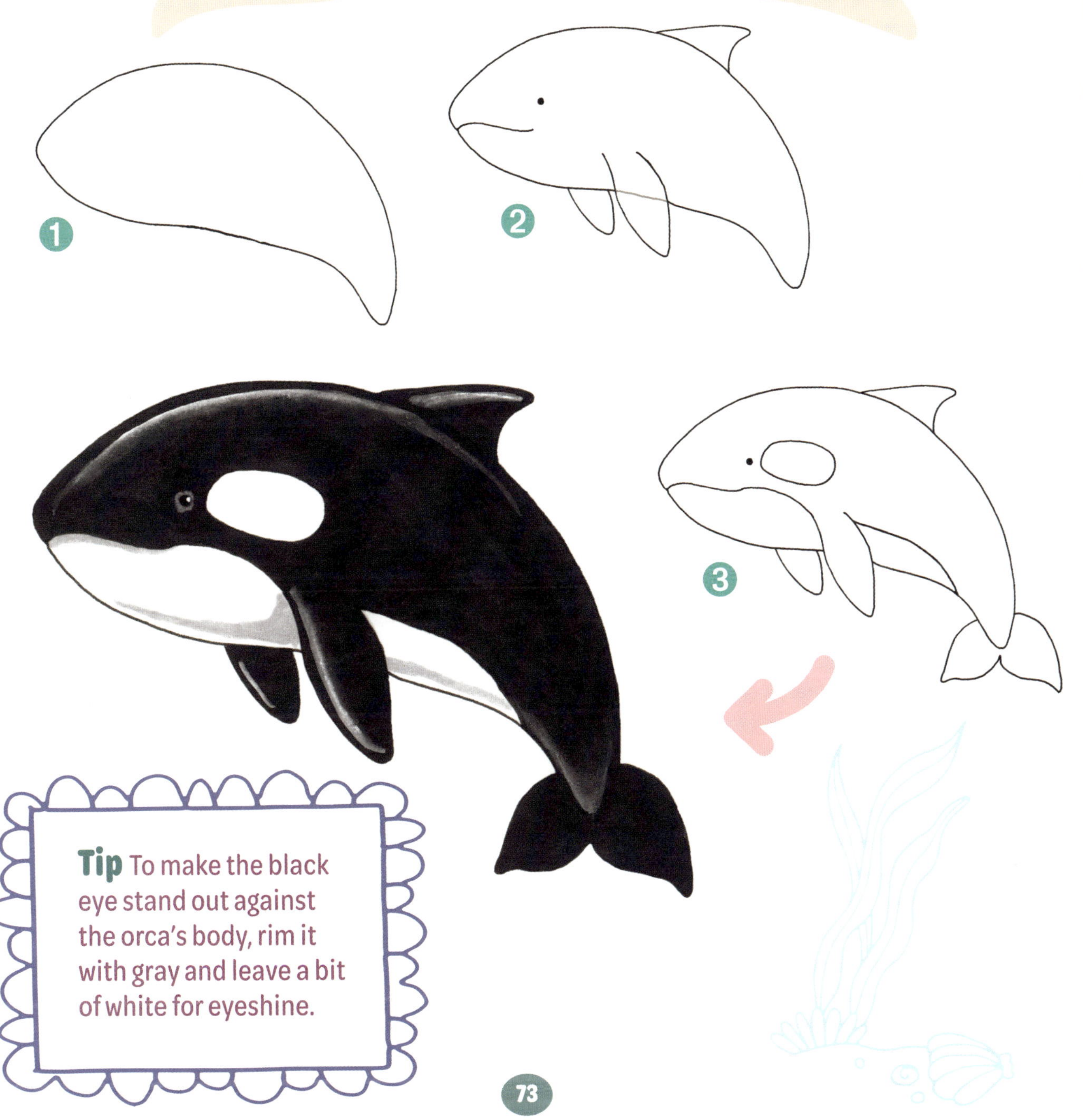

Tip To make the black eye stand out against the orca's body, rim it with gray and leave a bit of white for eyeshine.

Dolphin

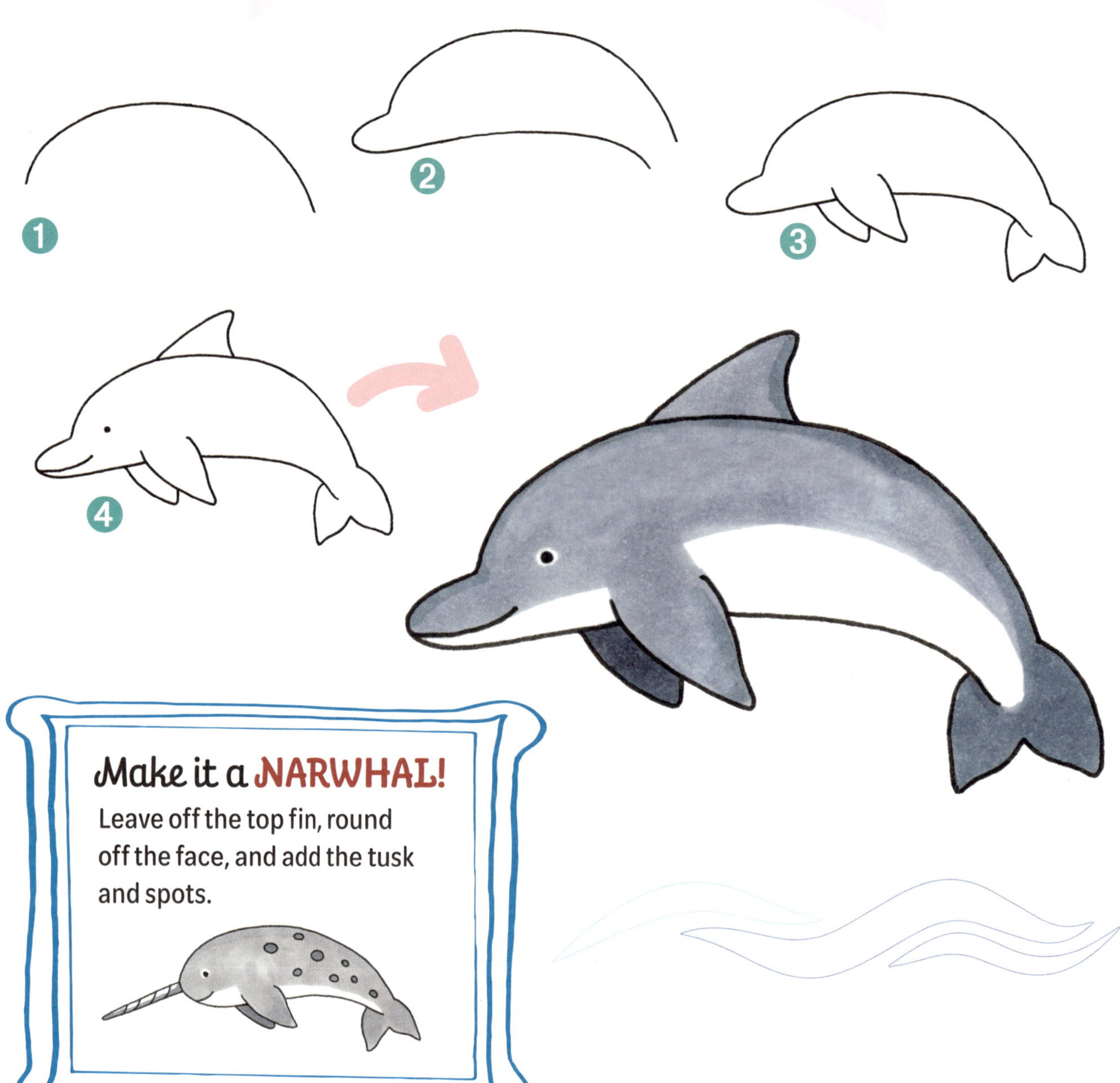

Make it a NARWHAL!

Leave off the top fin, round off the face, and add the tusk and spots.

seahorse

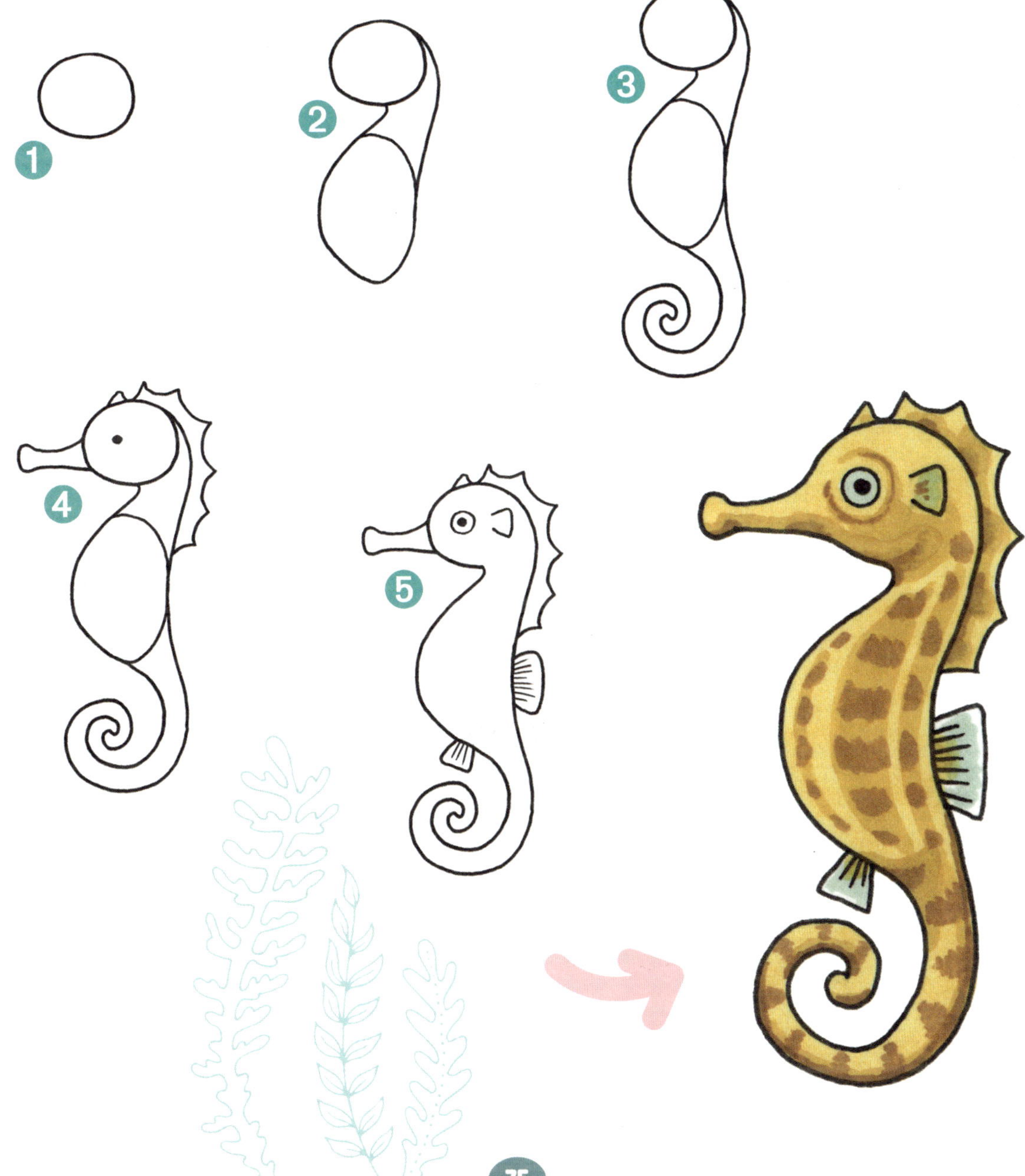

salmon

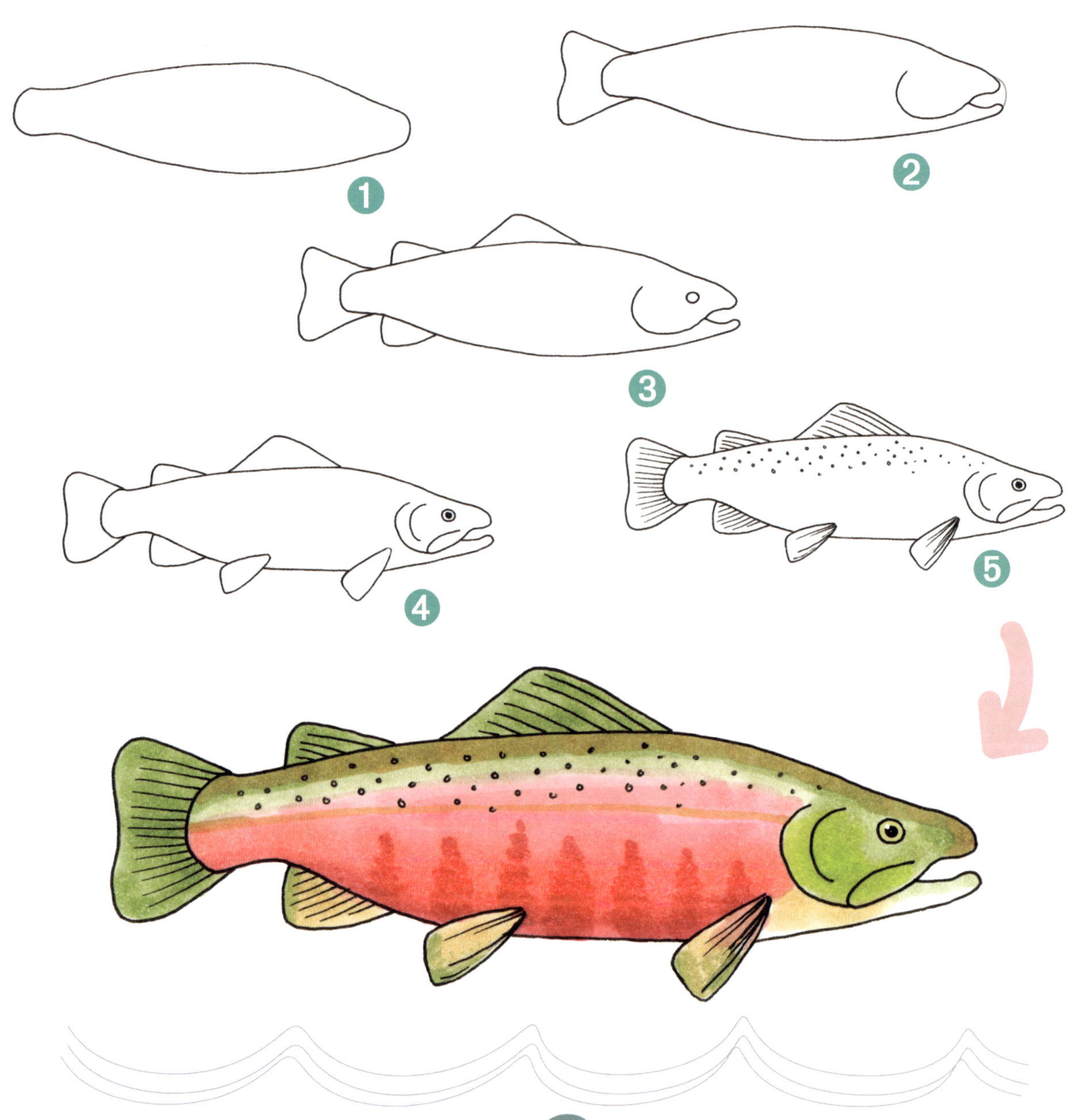

Frog

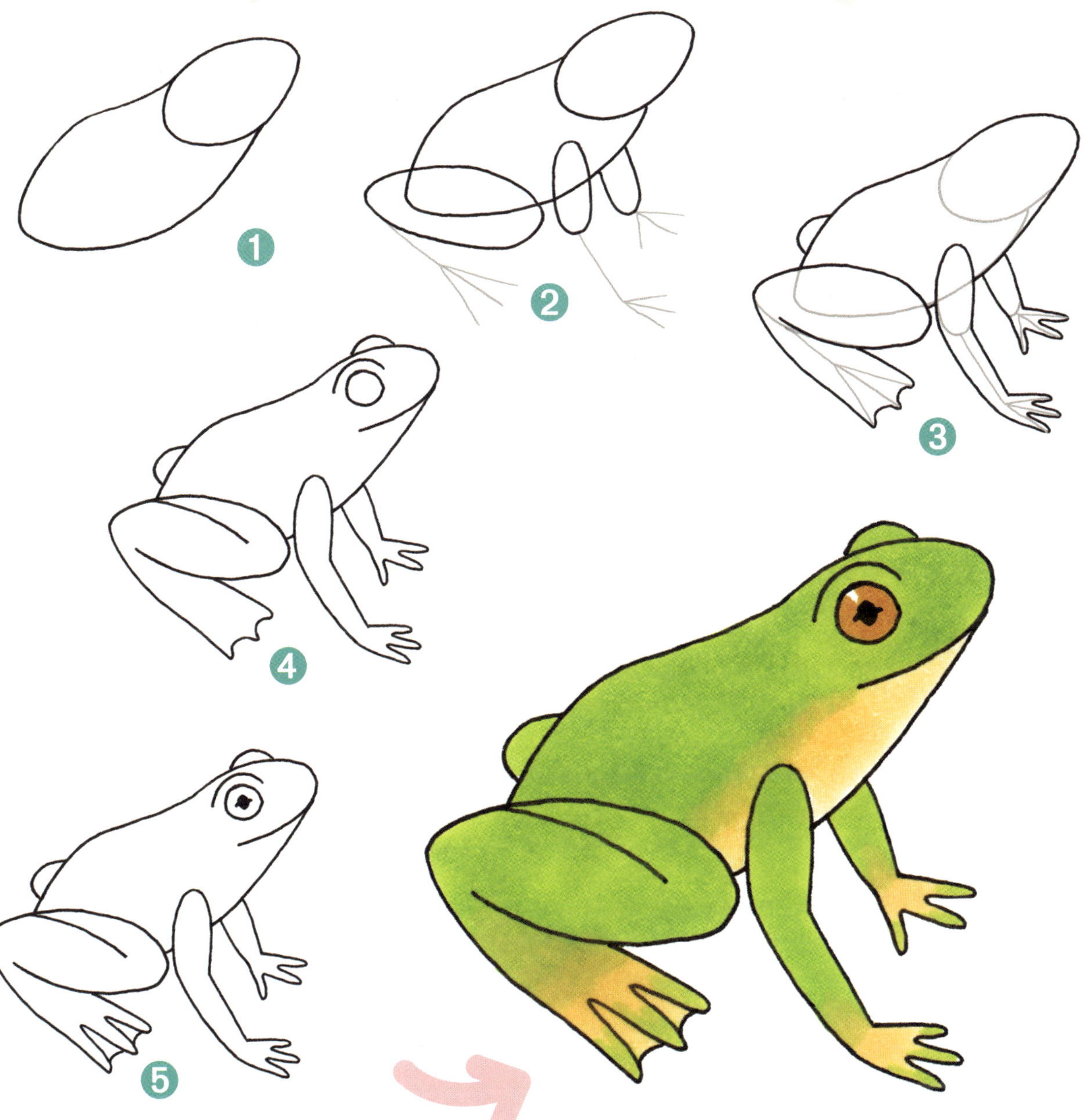

Water Lily

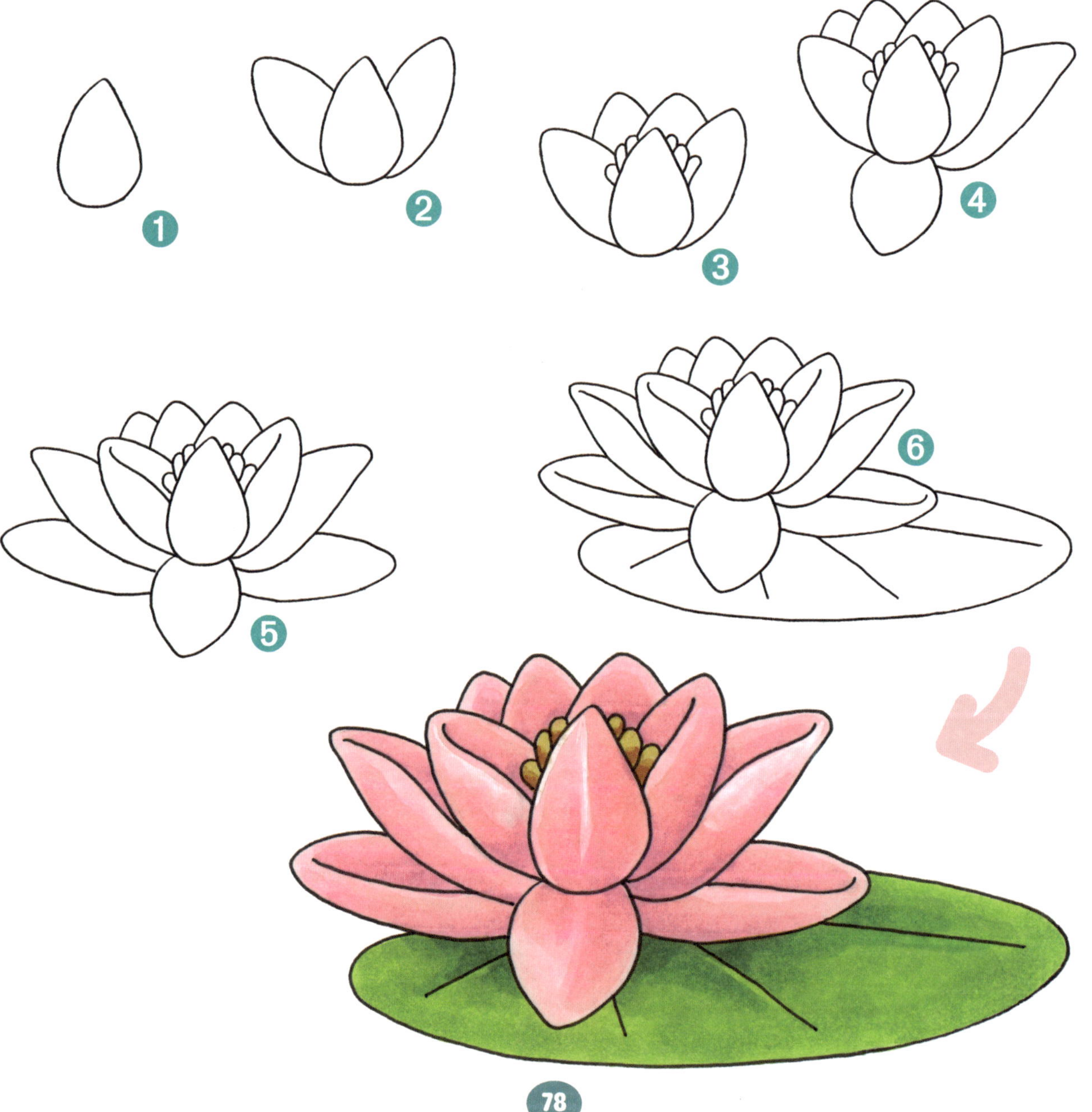

Dragonfly

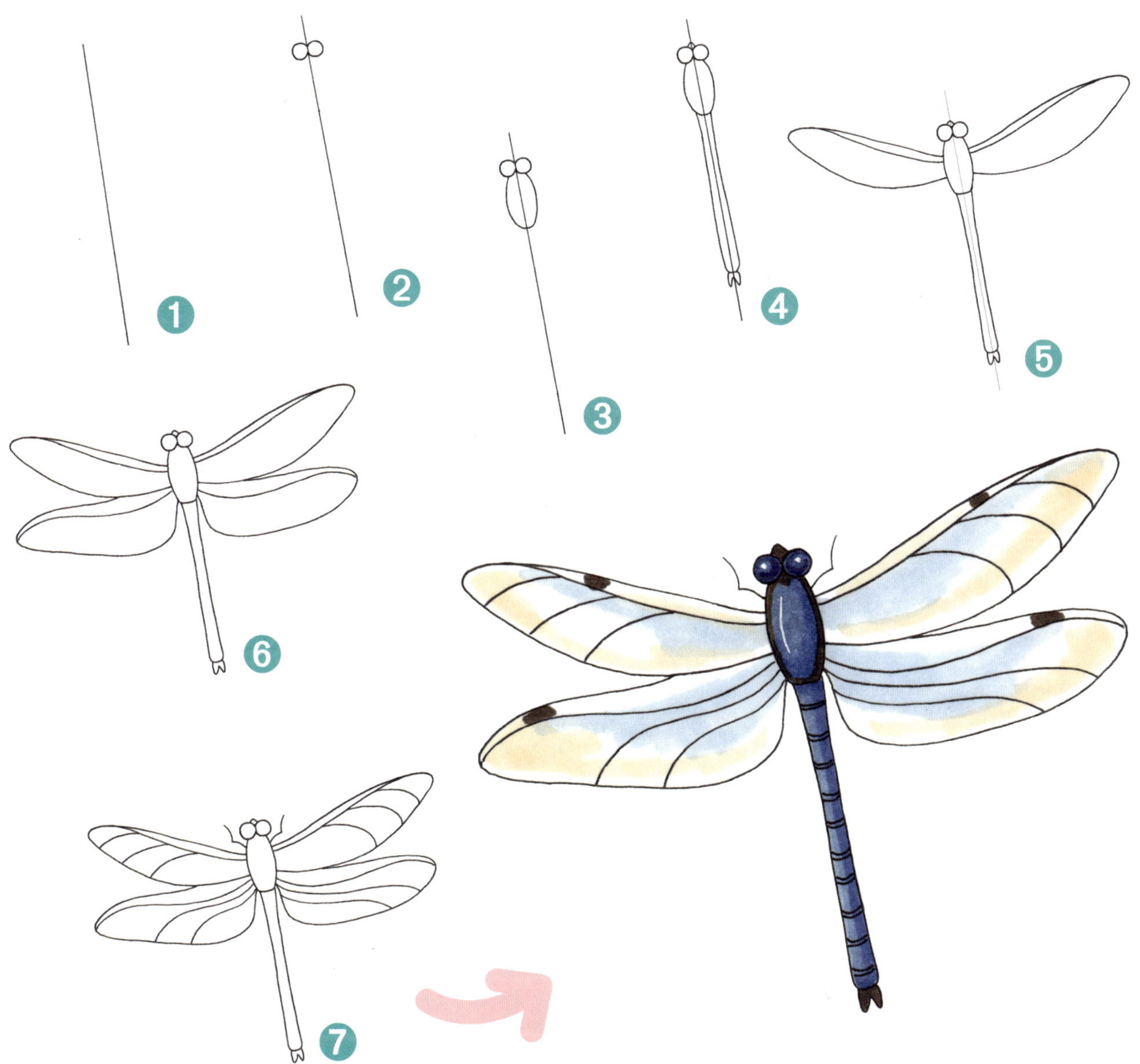

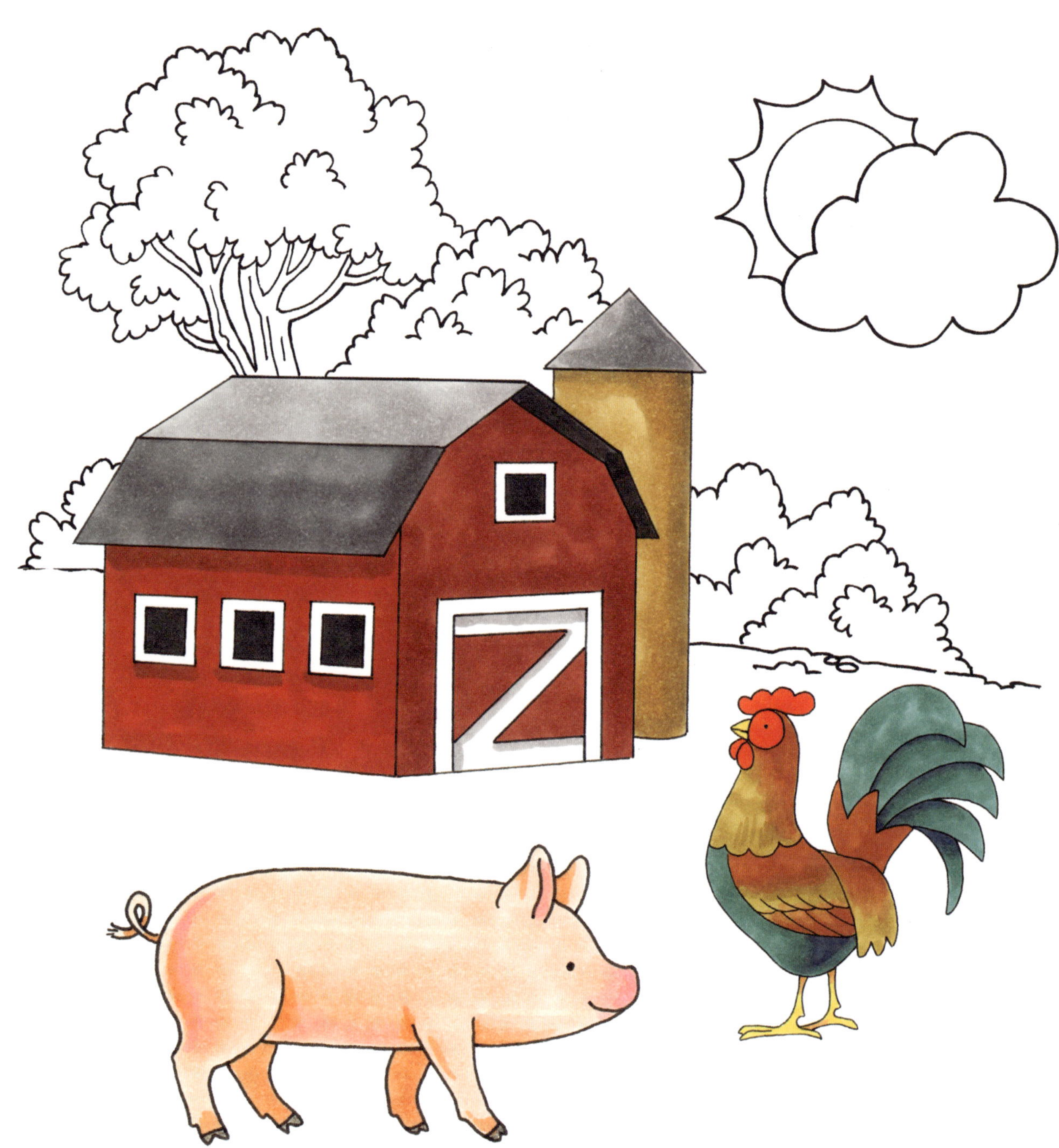

On the Farm & Cozy Comforts

It's fun to explore new places, but when you need comfort and relaxation, sometimes you want to stick close to home. In this chapter you will find farm animals and pets, as well as cozy items from home.

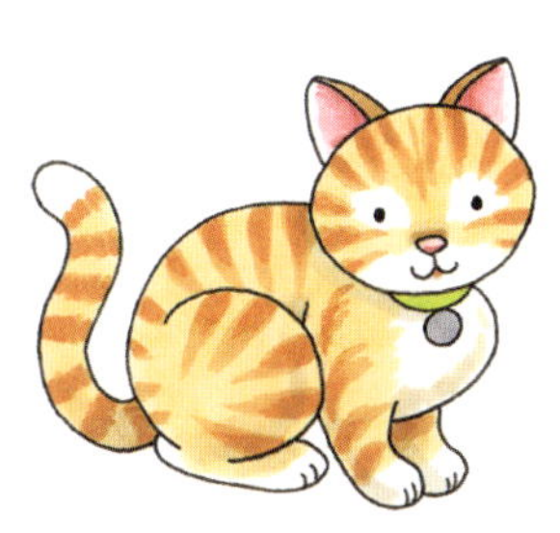

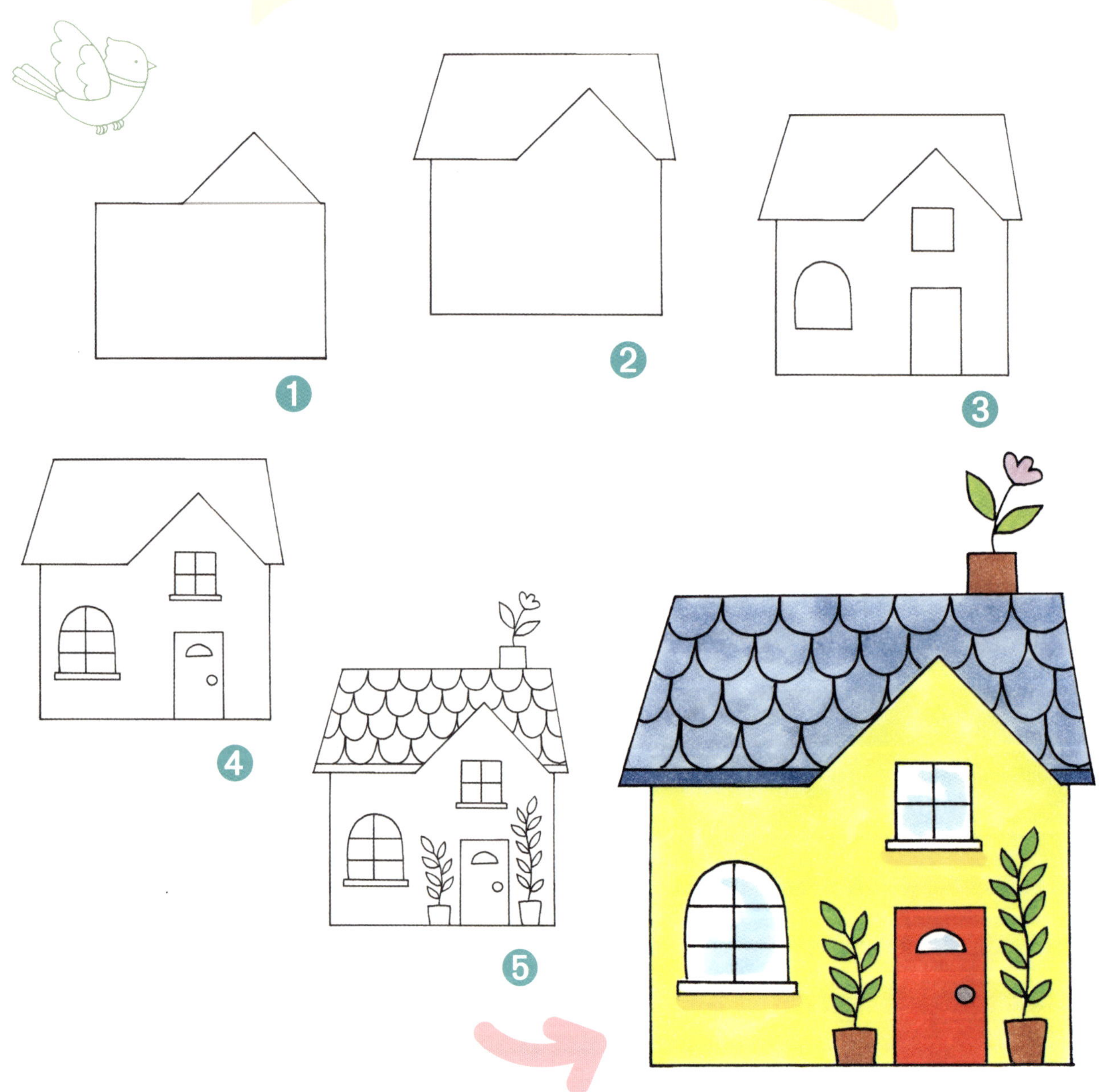

Cottage

Barn

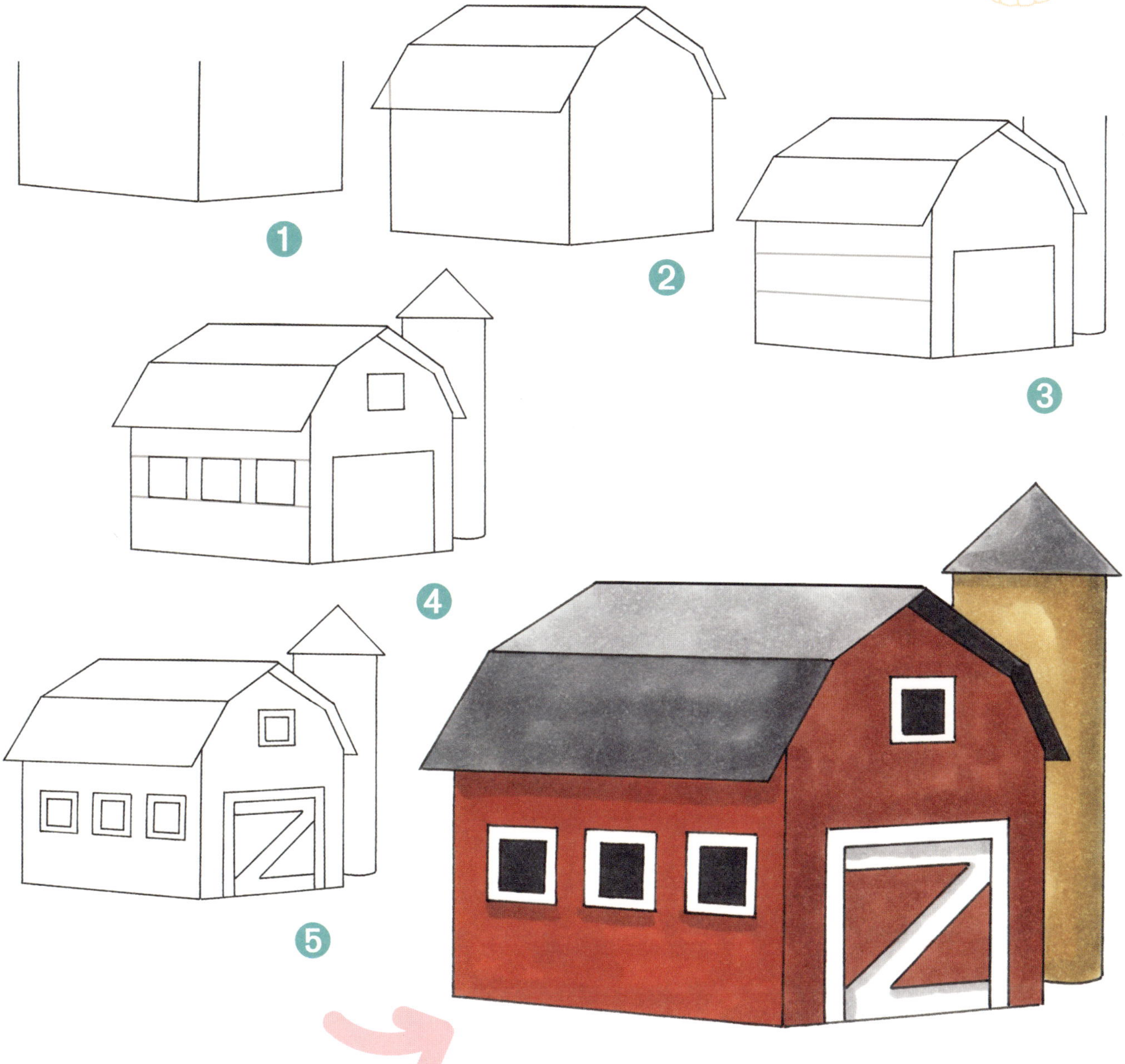

1

2

3

4

5

Cow

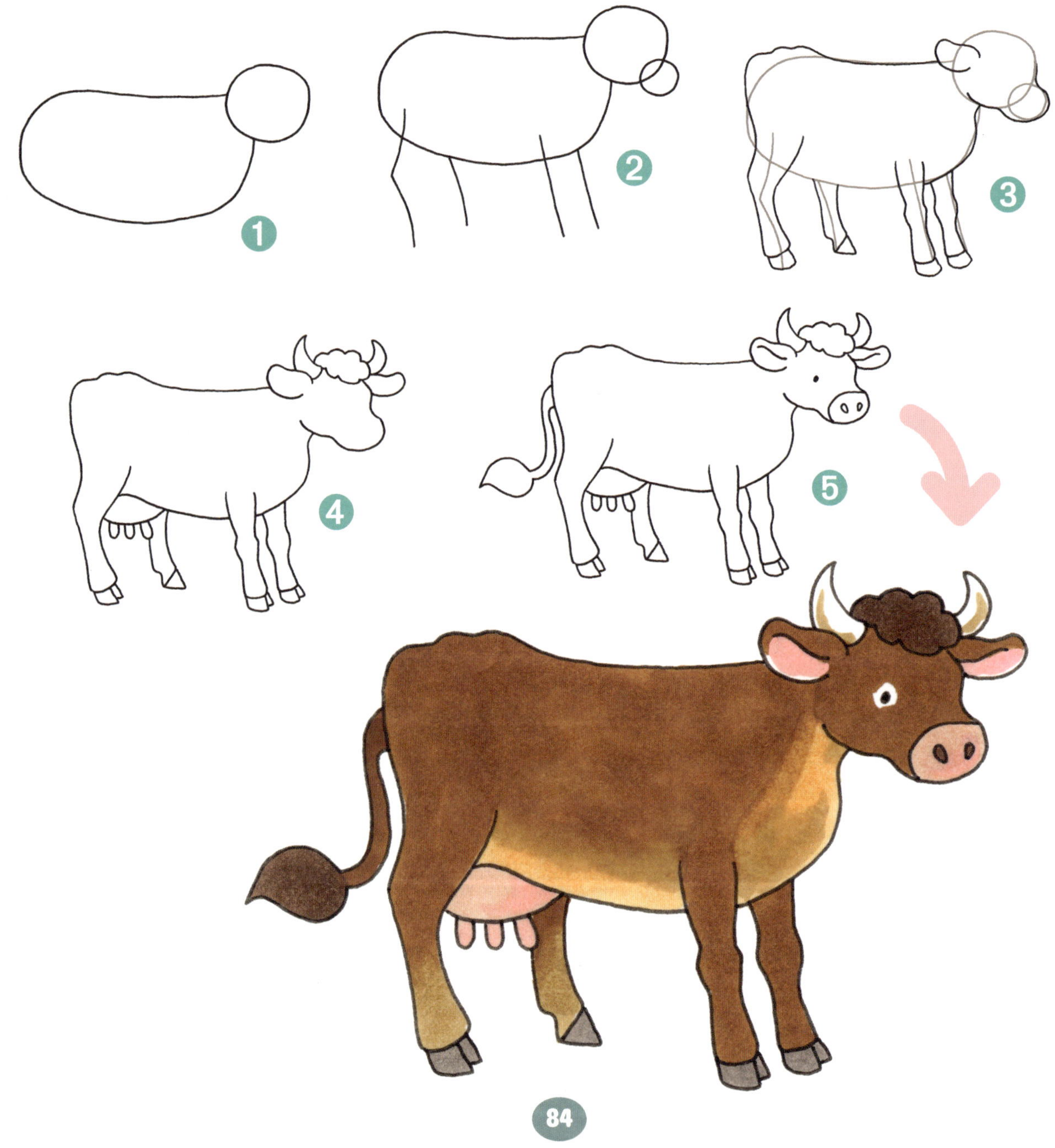

Donkey

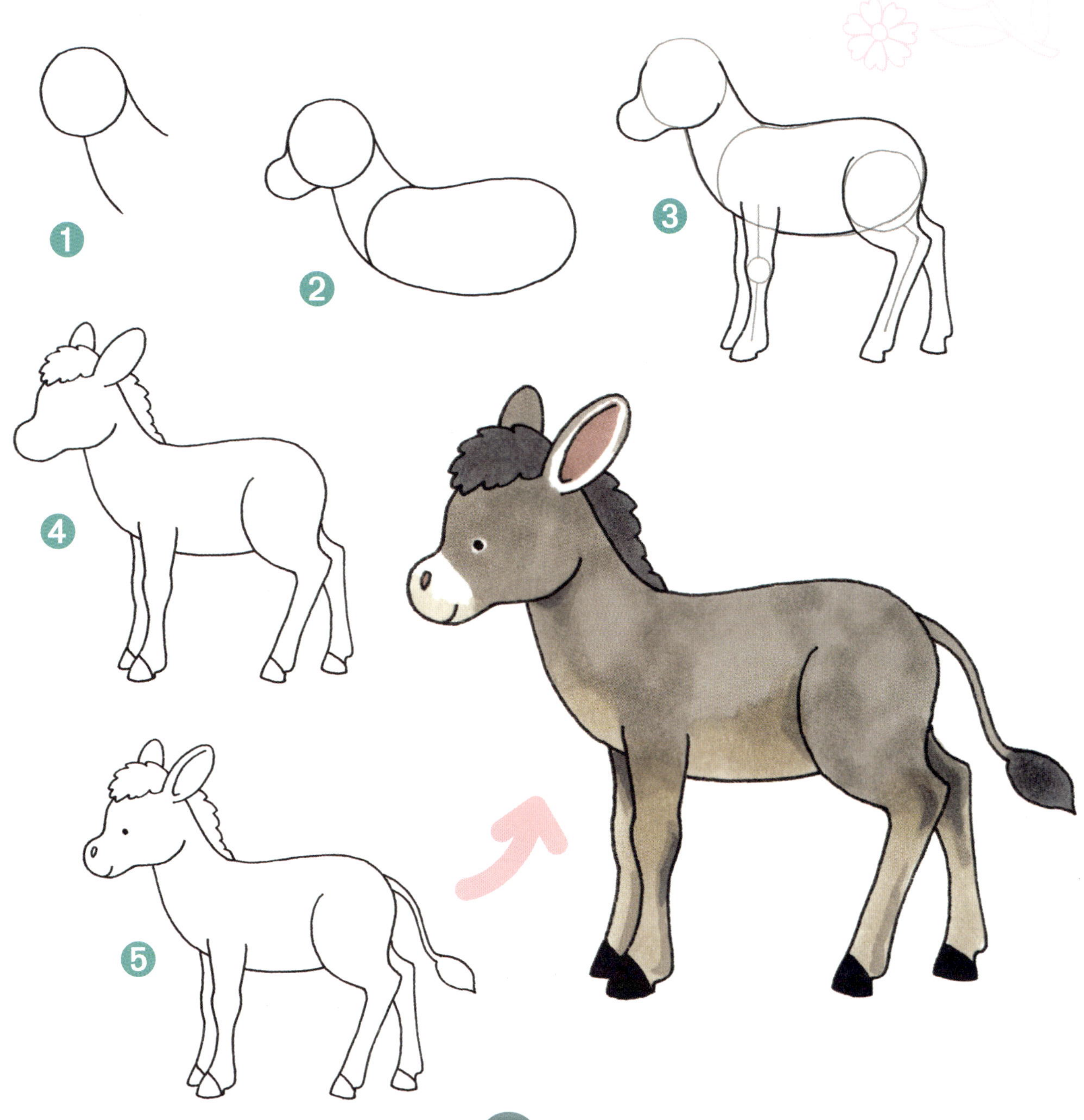

Goat

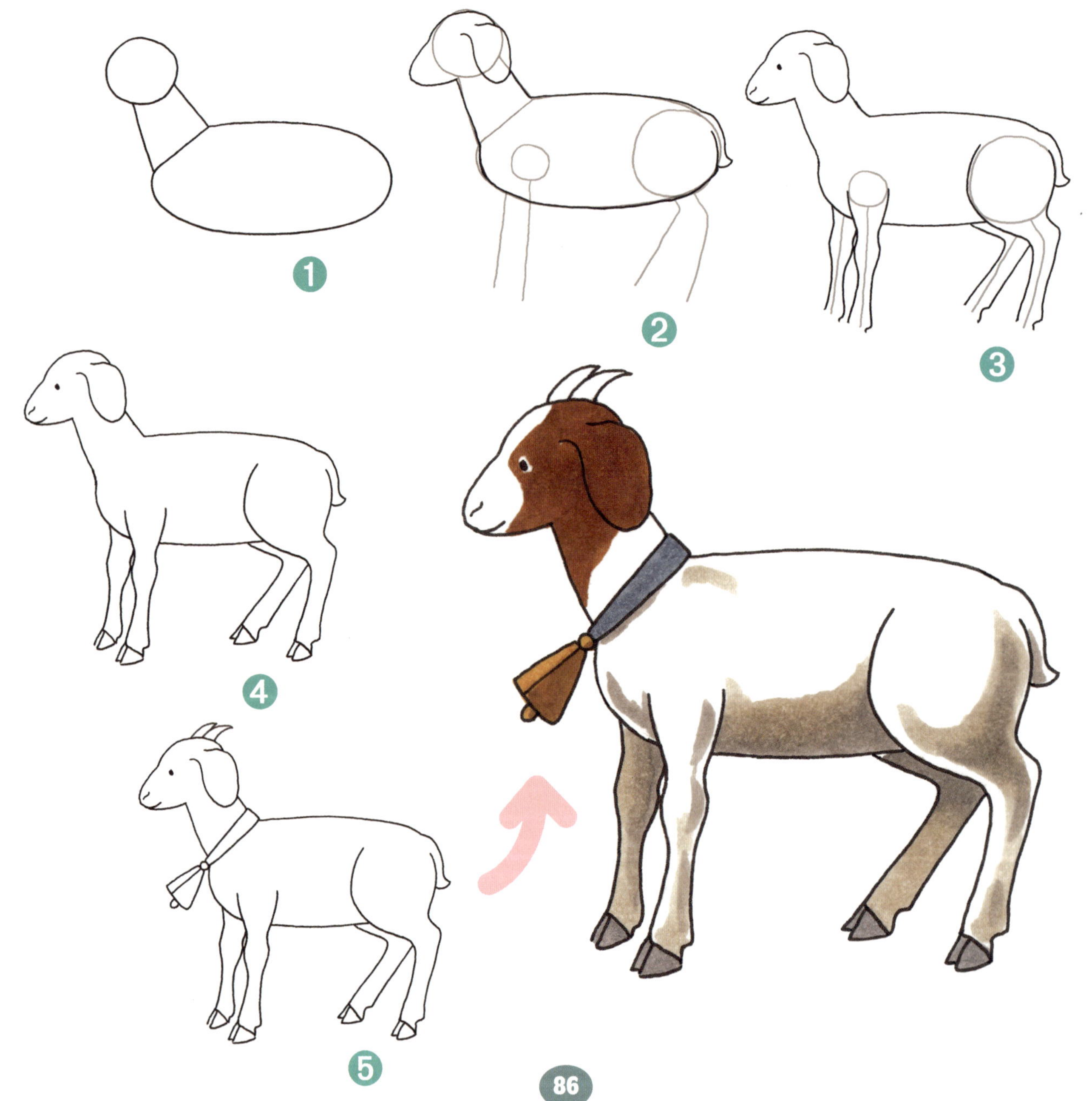

Llama

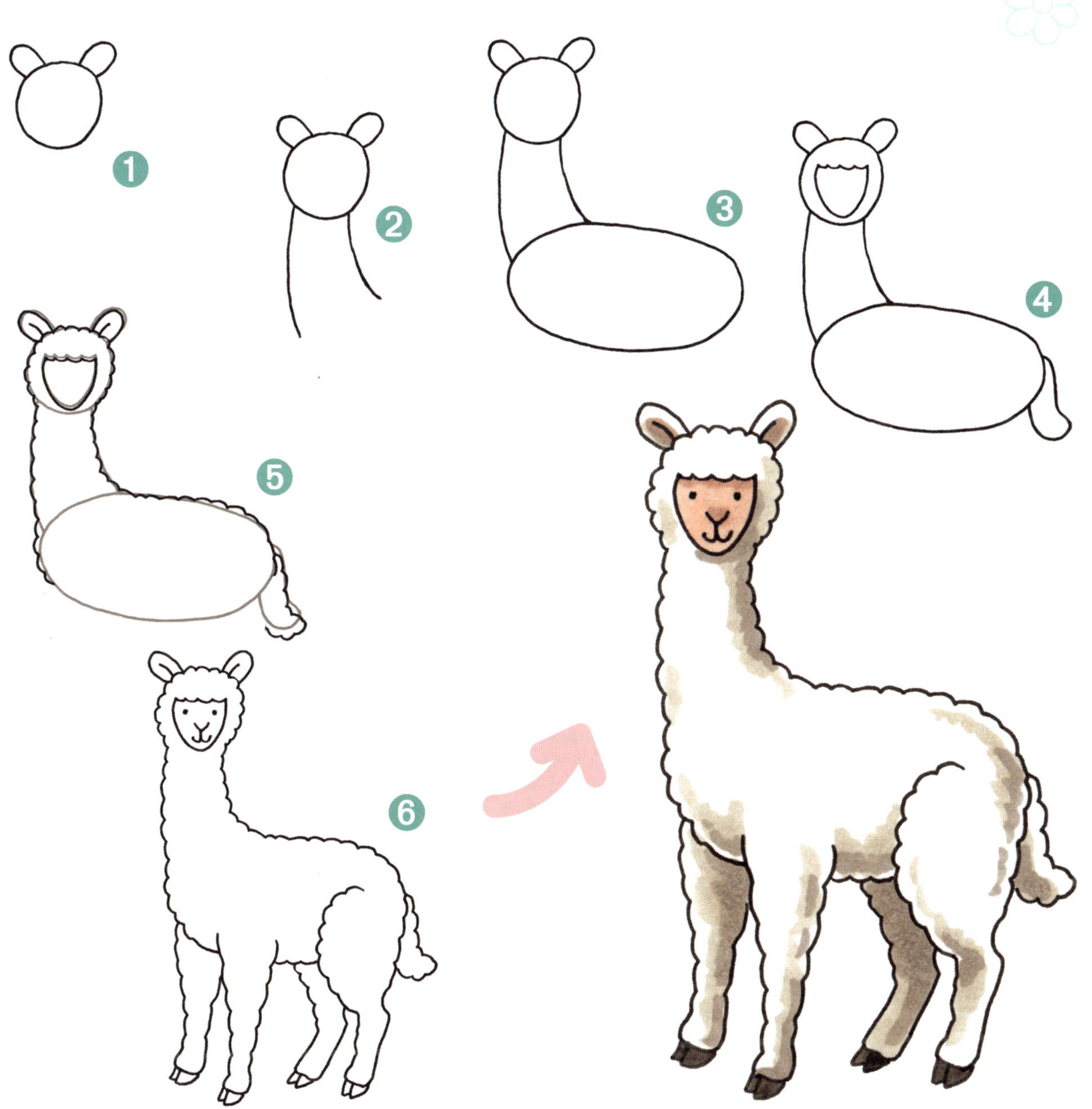

Rooster

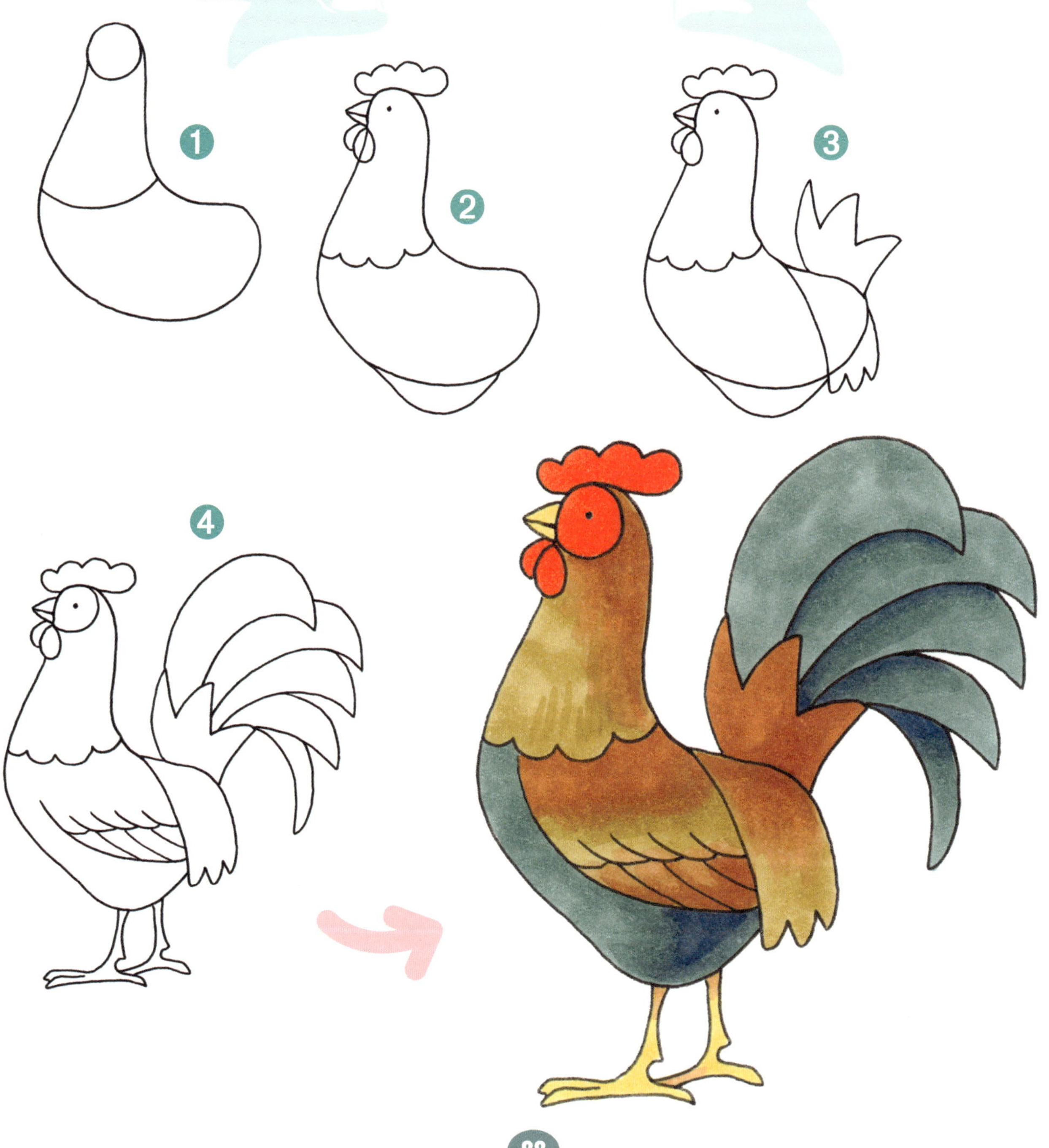

Chicken

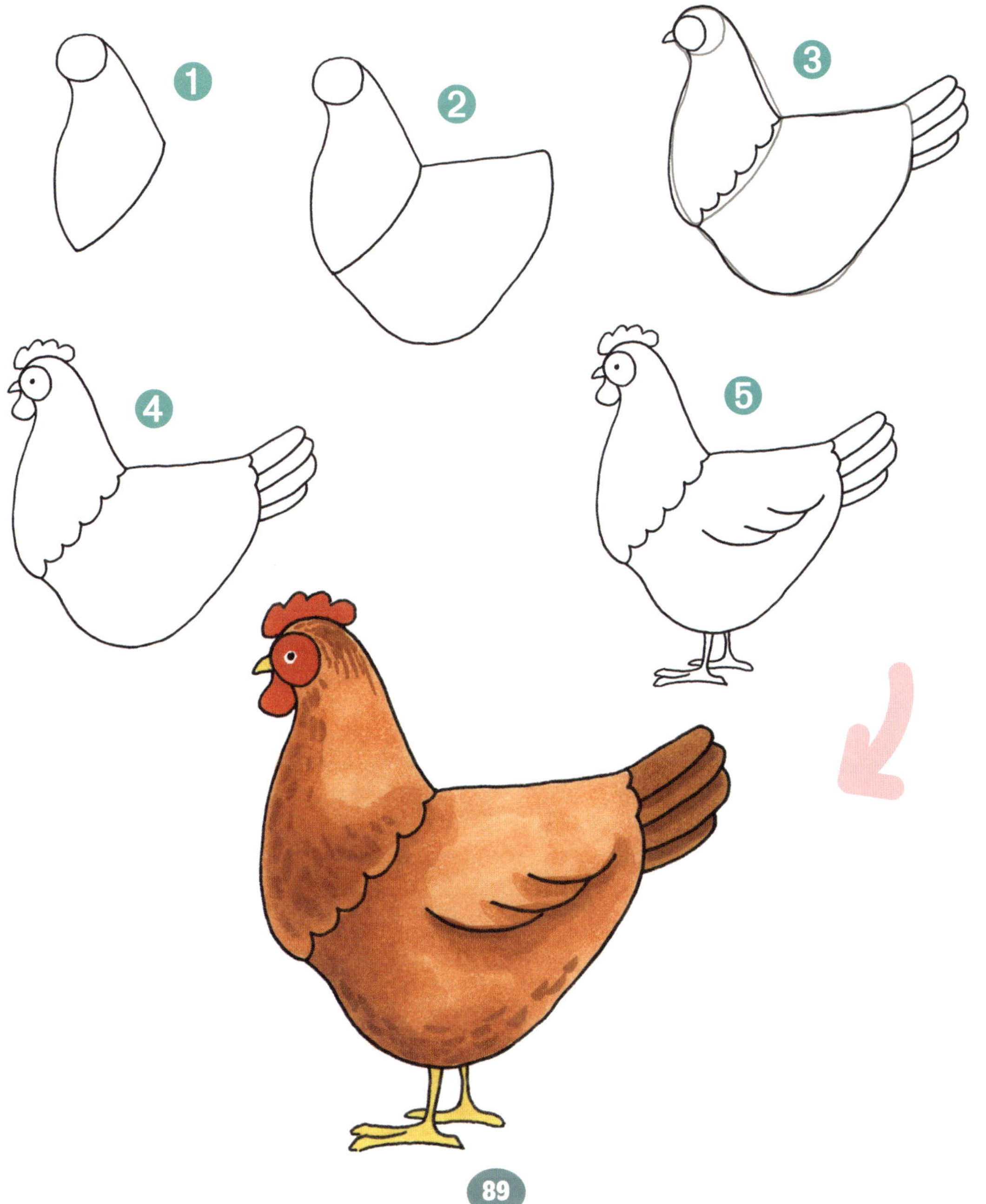

Sheep

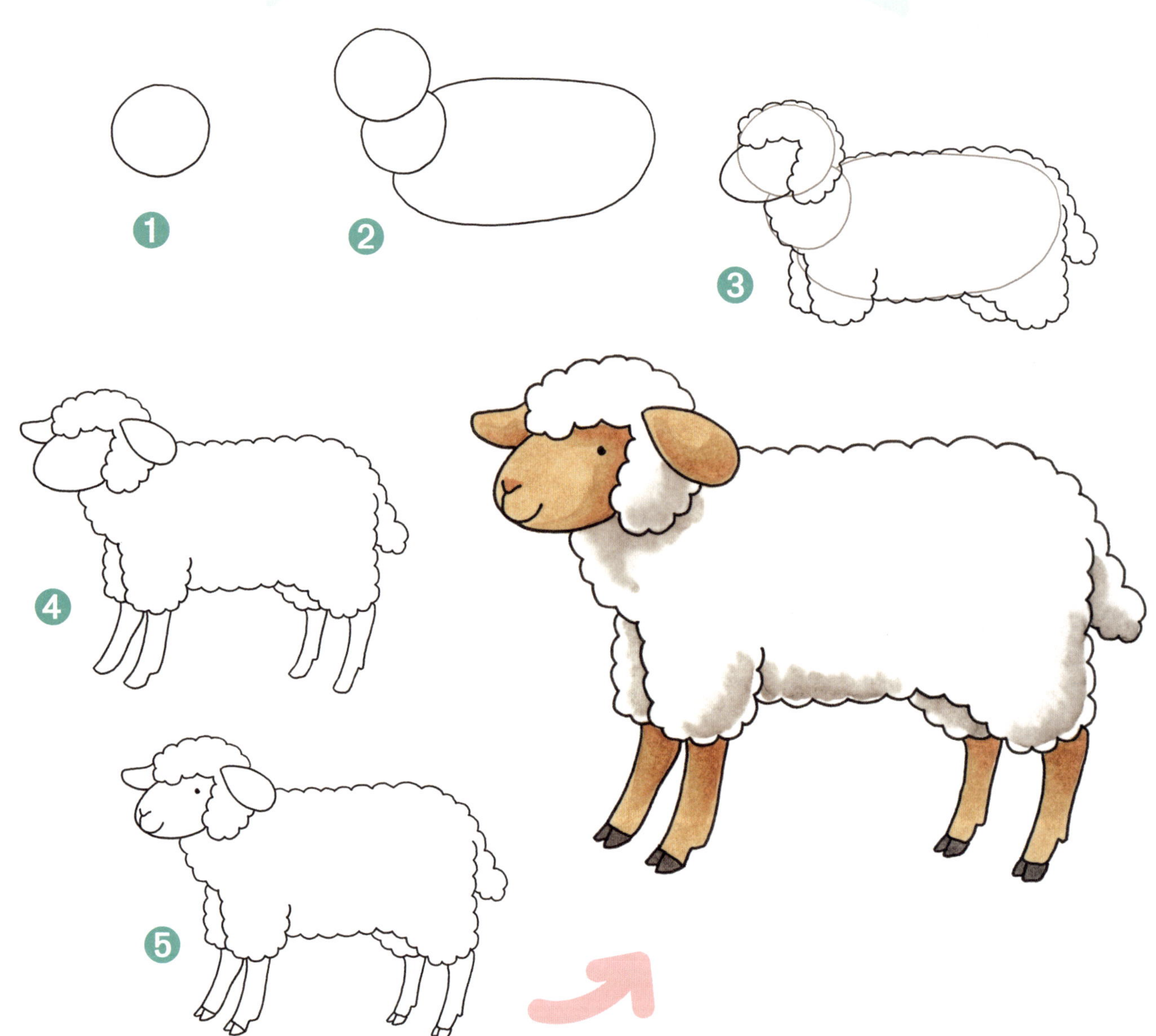

Pig

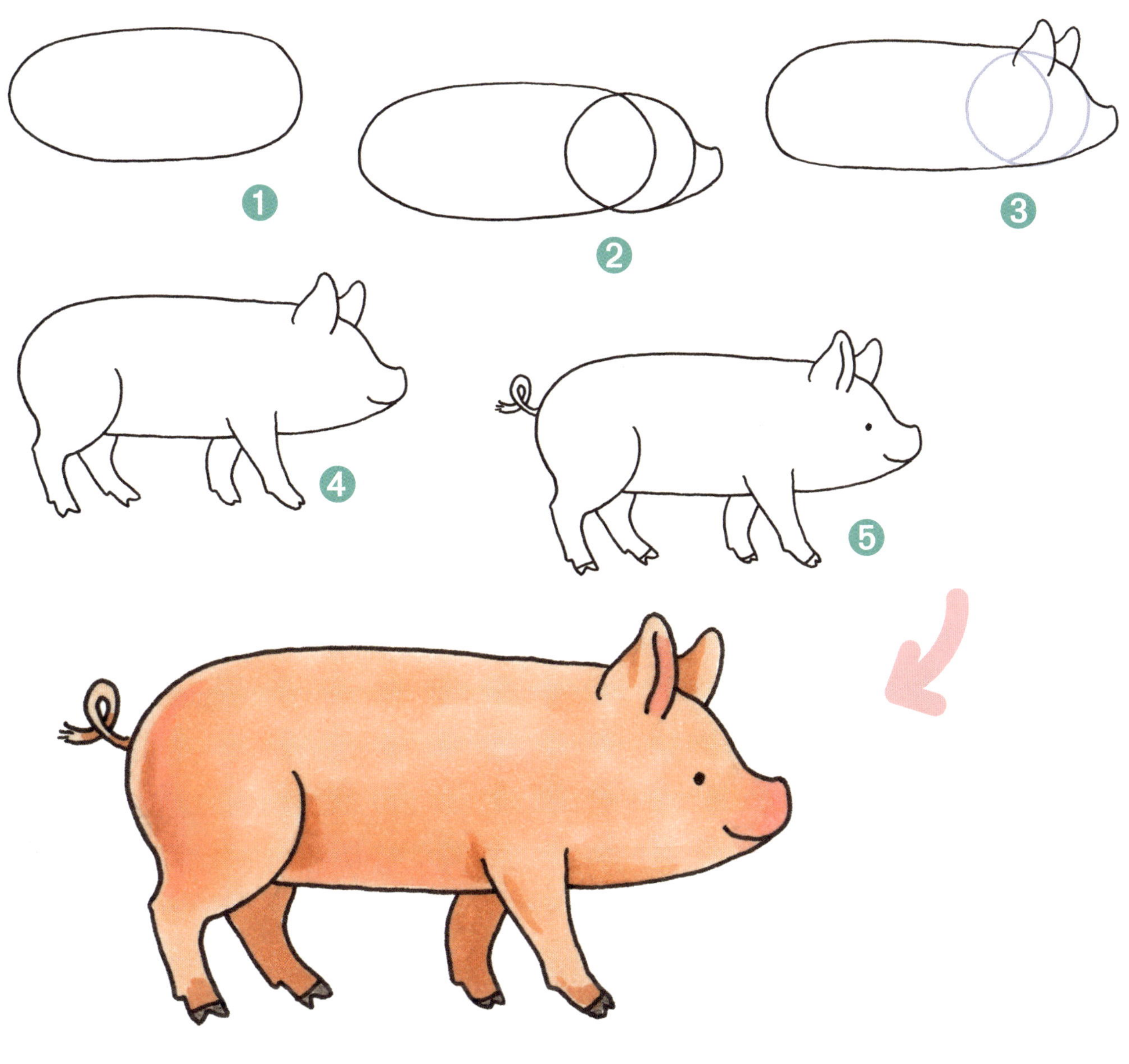

Kitty

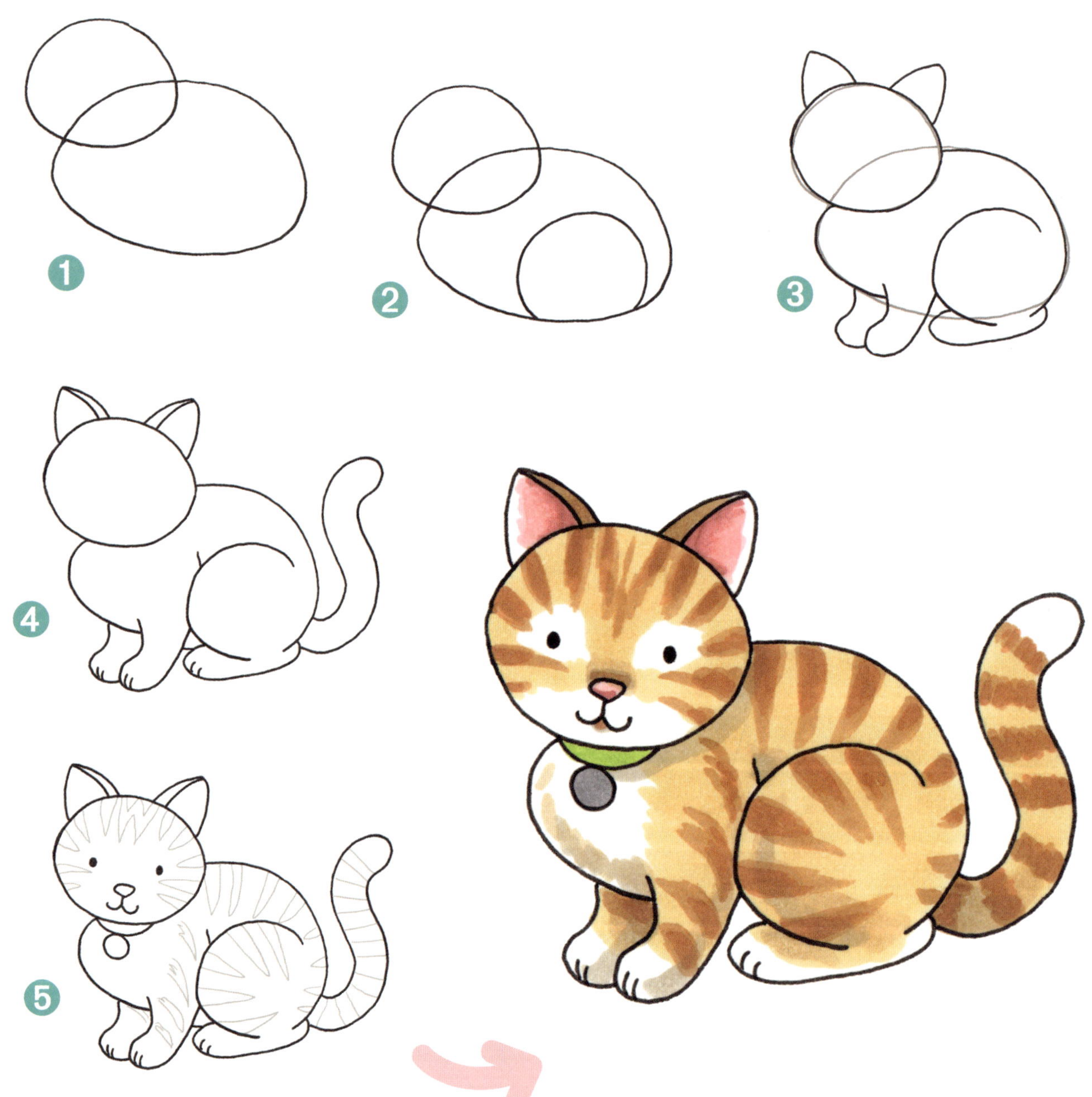

Dog

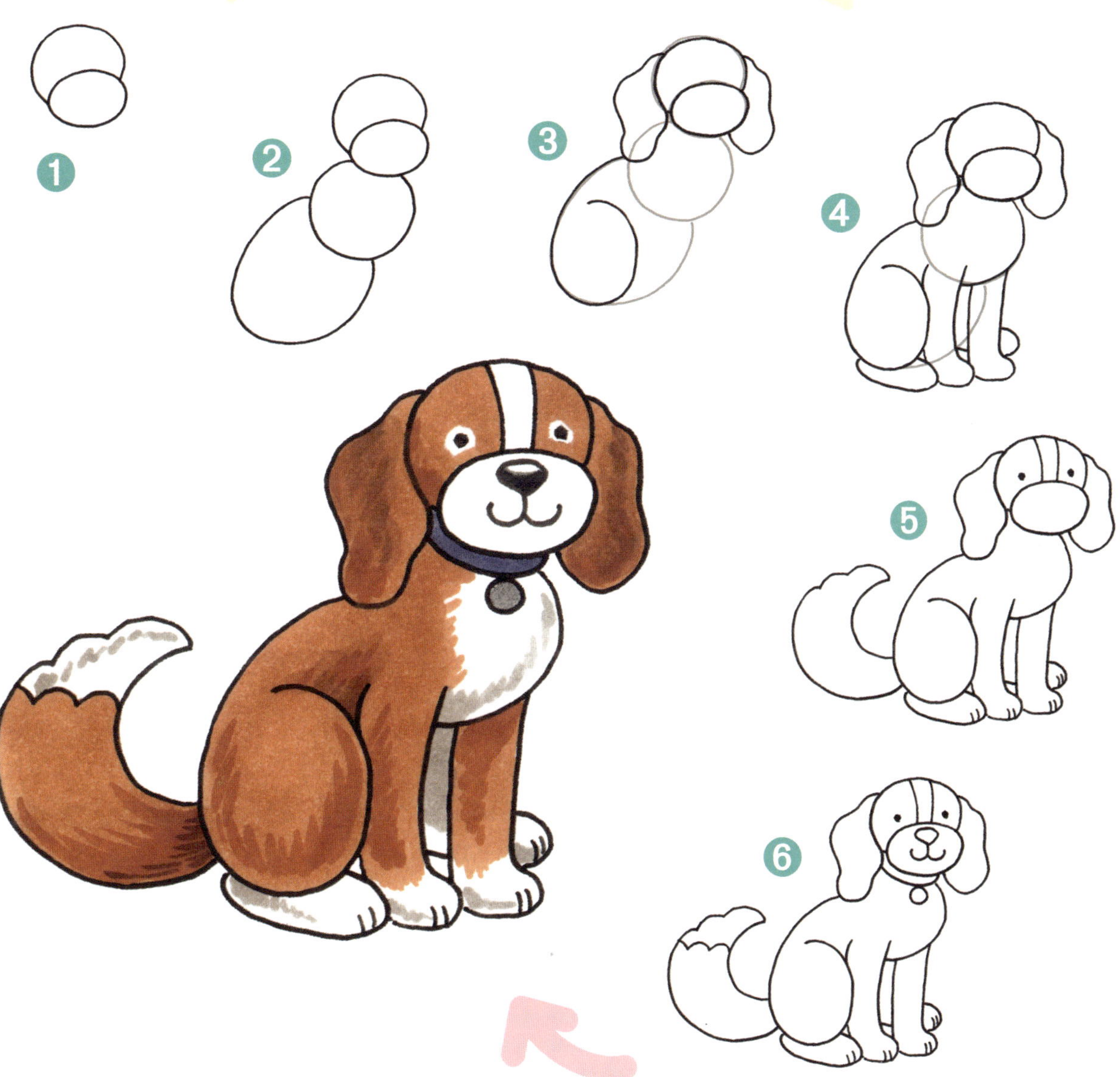

Goldfish

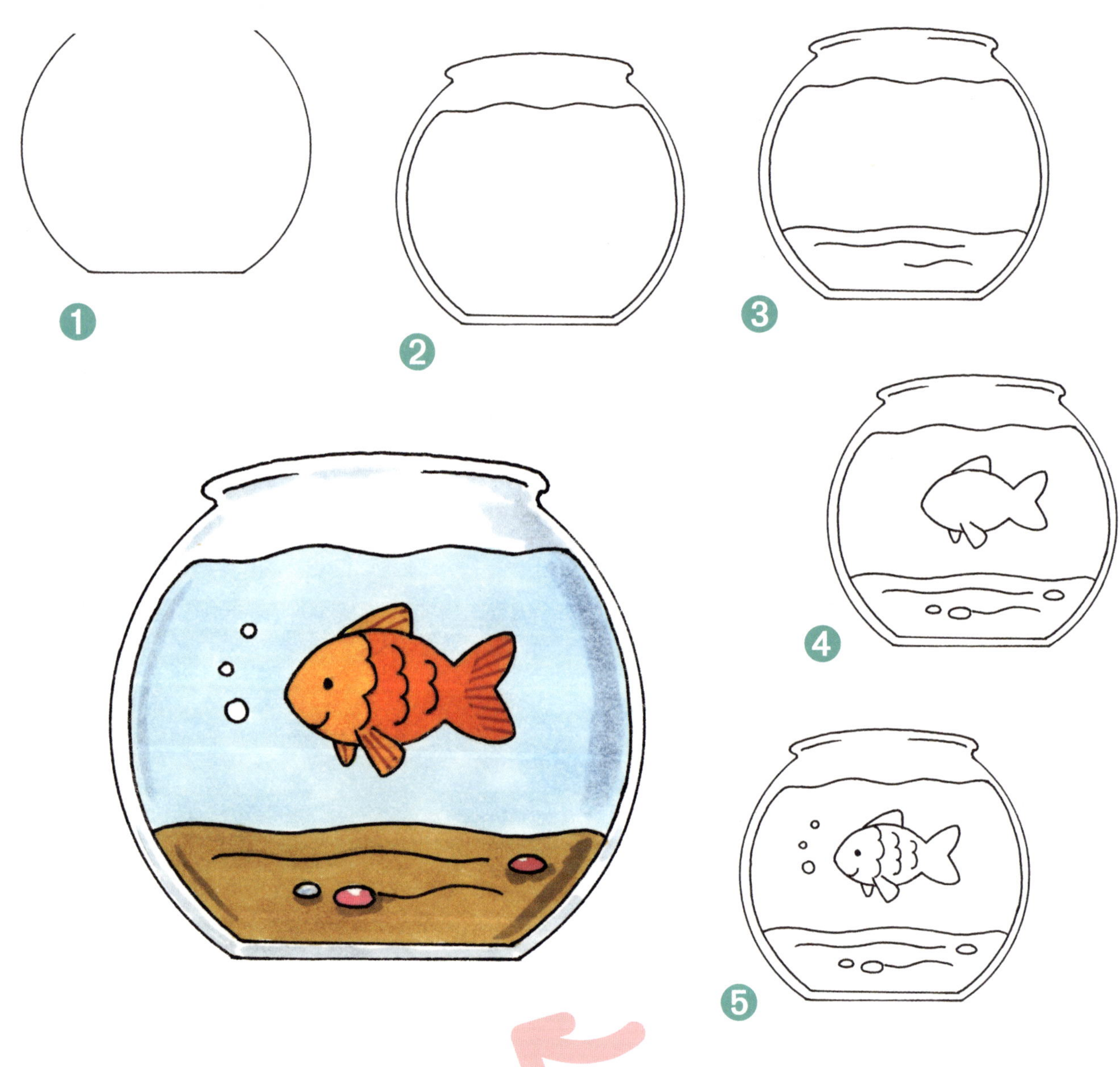

Birdcage

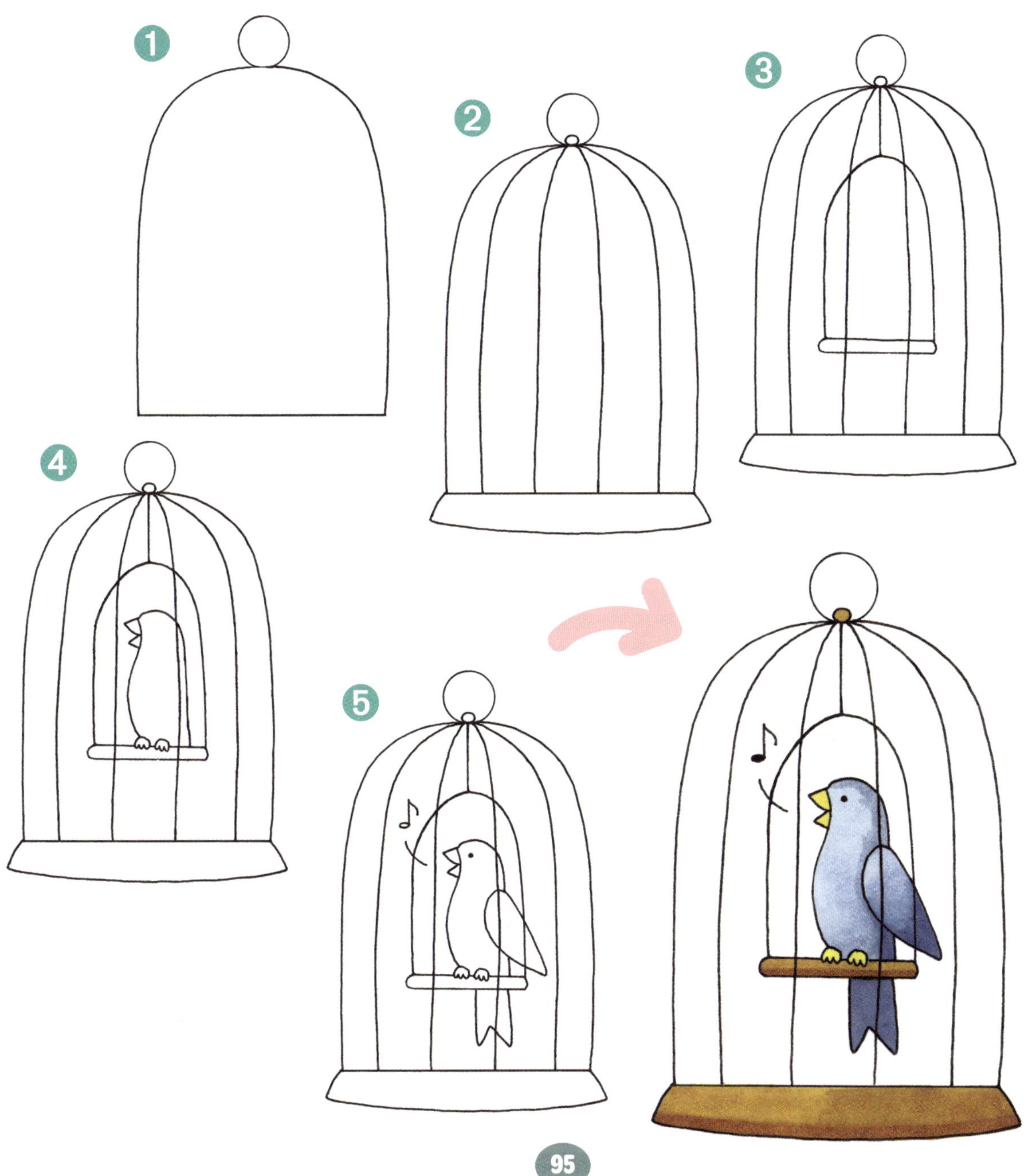

Teatime

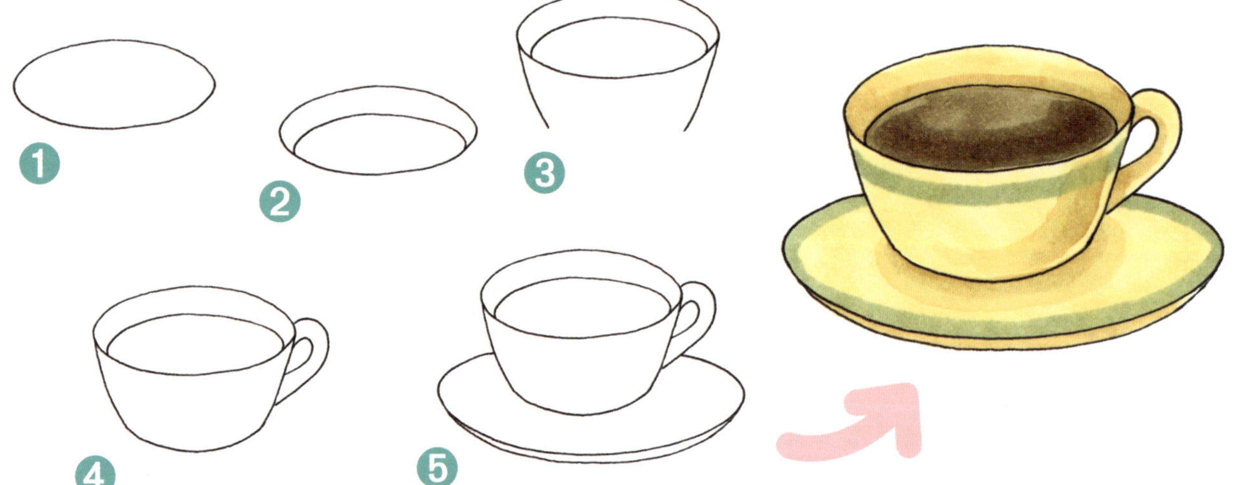

Coffee Break

COFFEEPOT

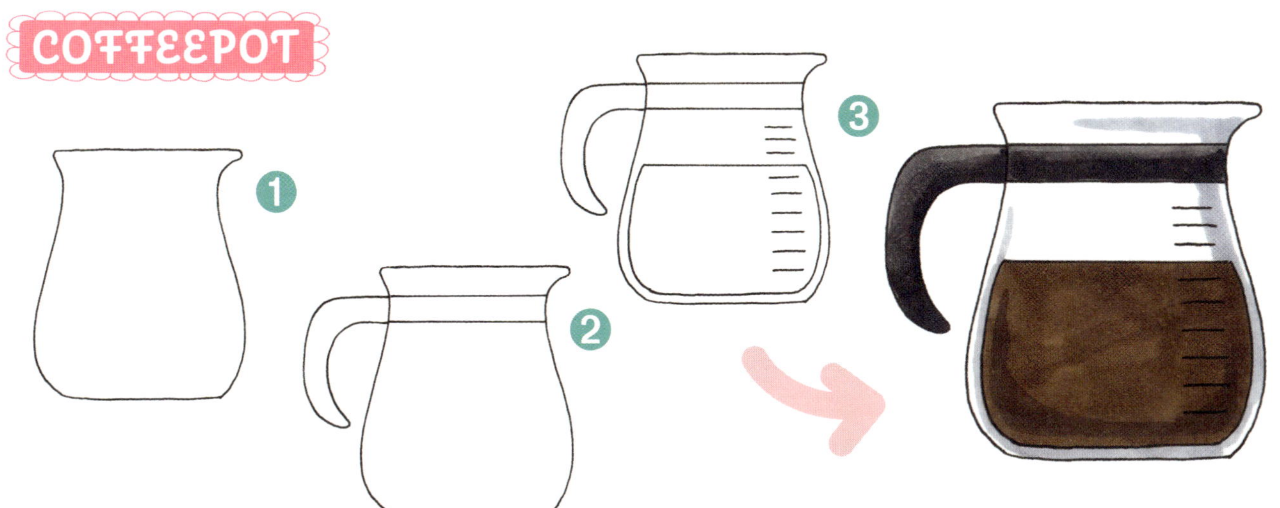

COFFEE CUP

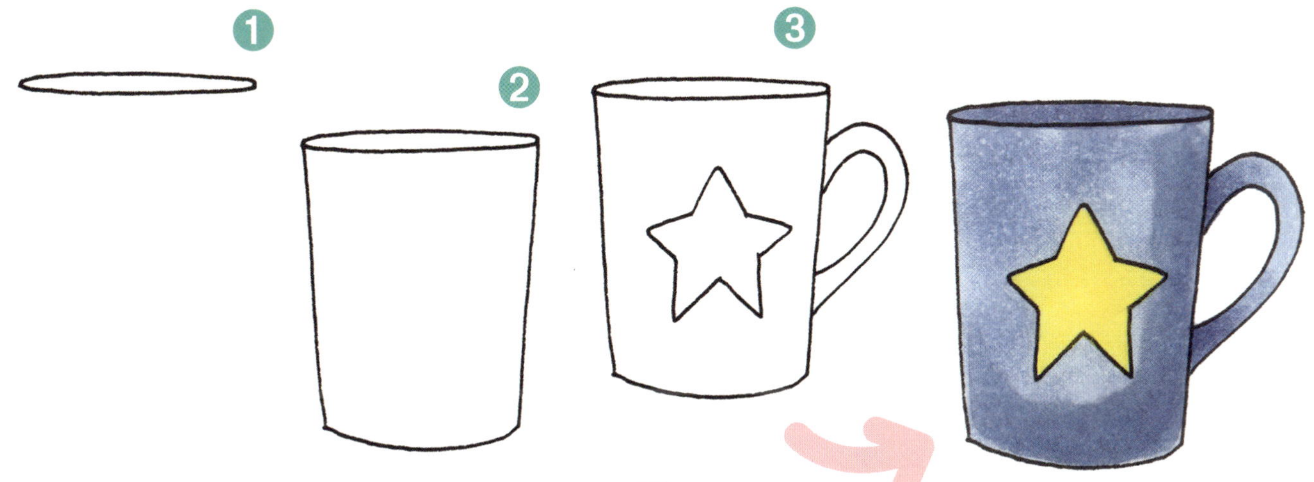

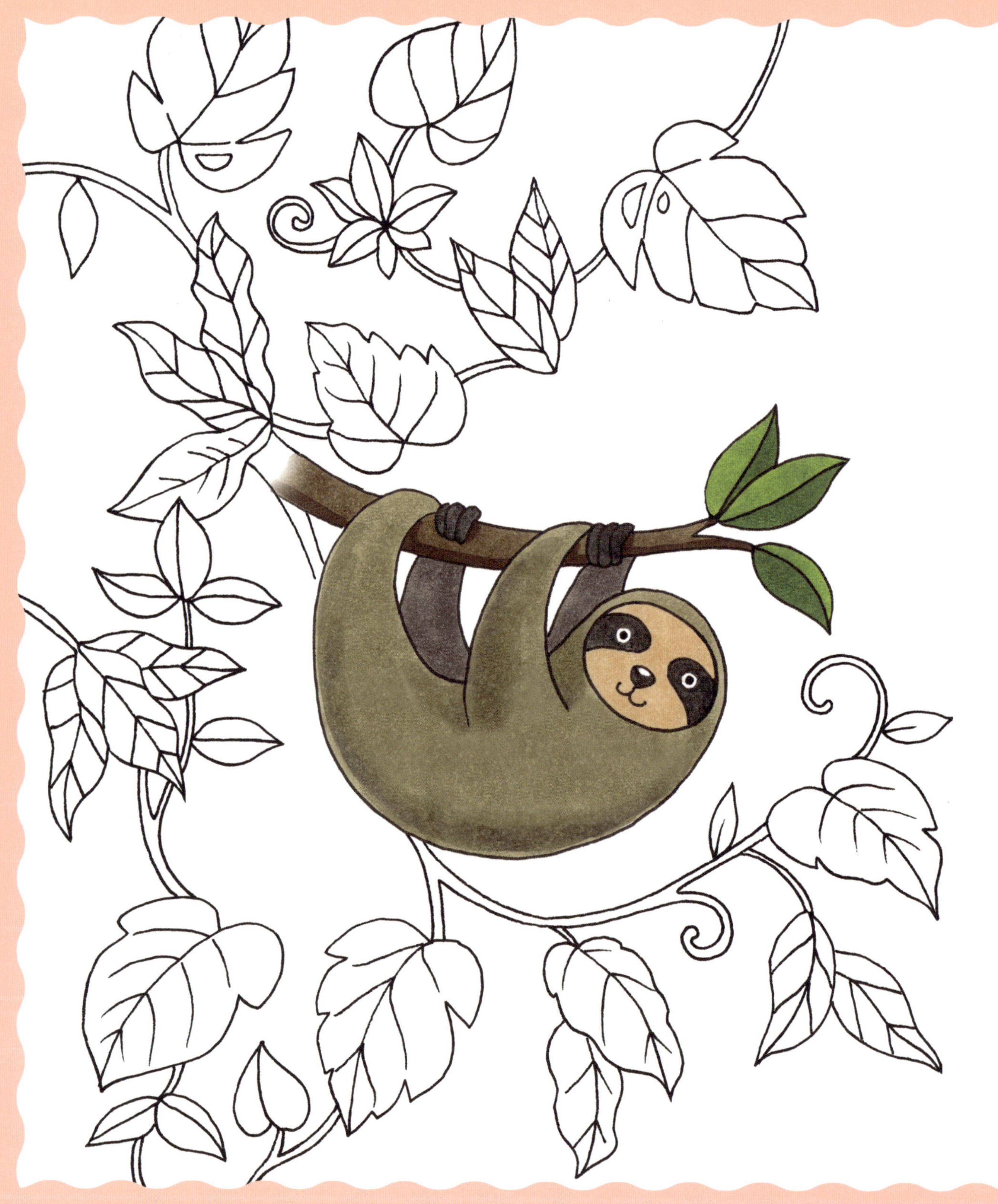

CHAPTER

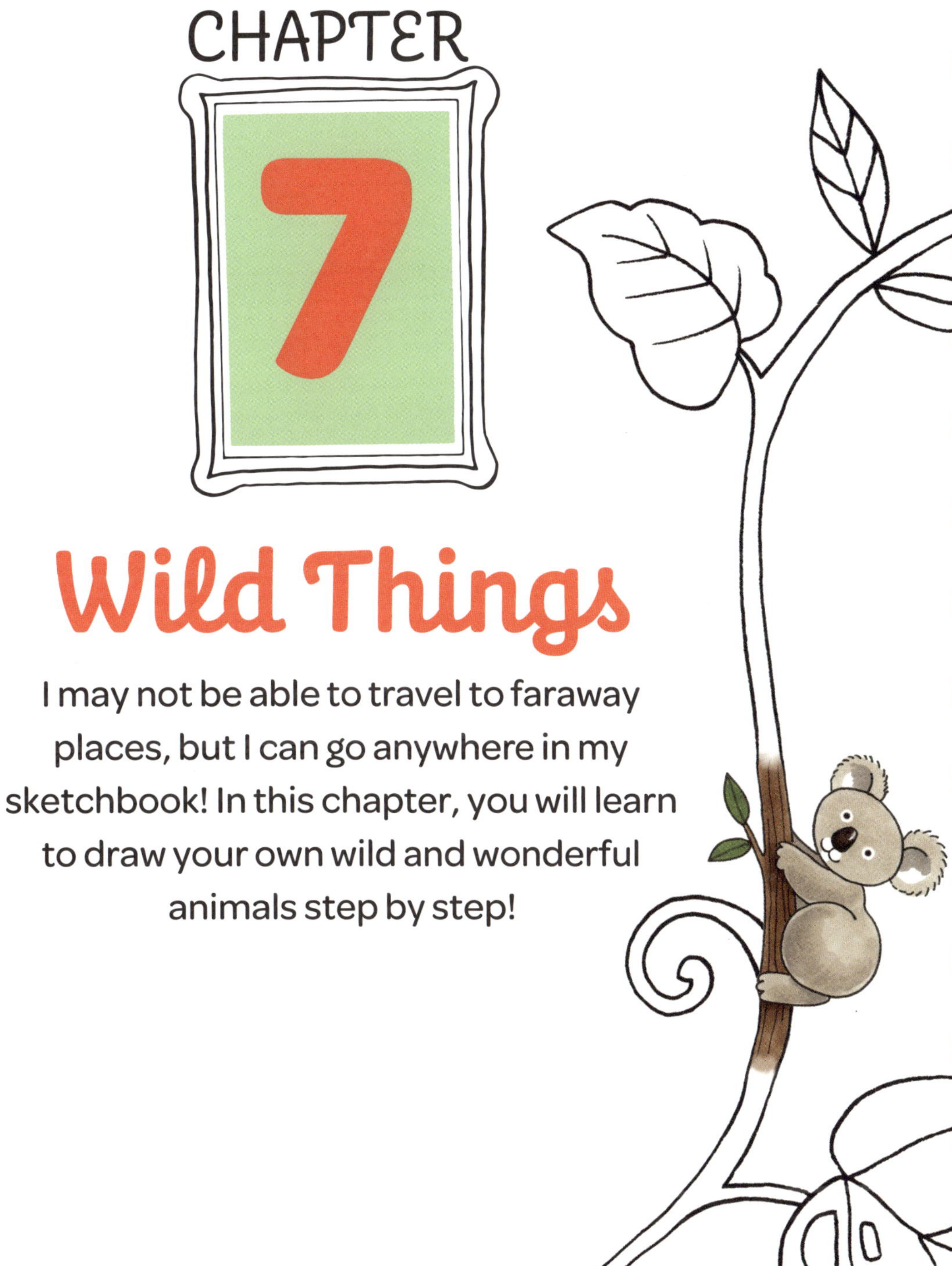

7

Wild Things

I may not be able to travel to faraway places, but I can go anywhere in my sketchbook! In this chapter, you will learn to draw your own wild and wonderful animals step by step!

Lion

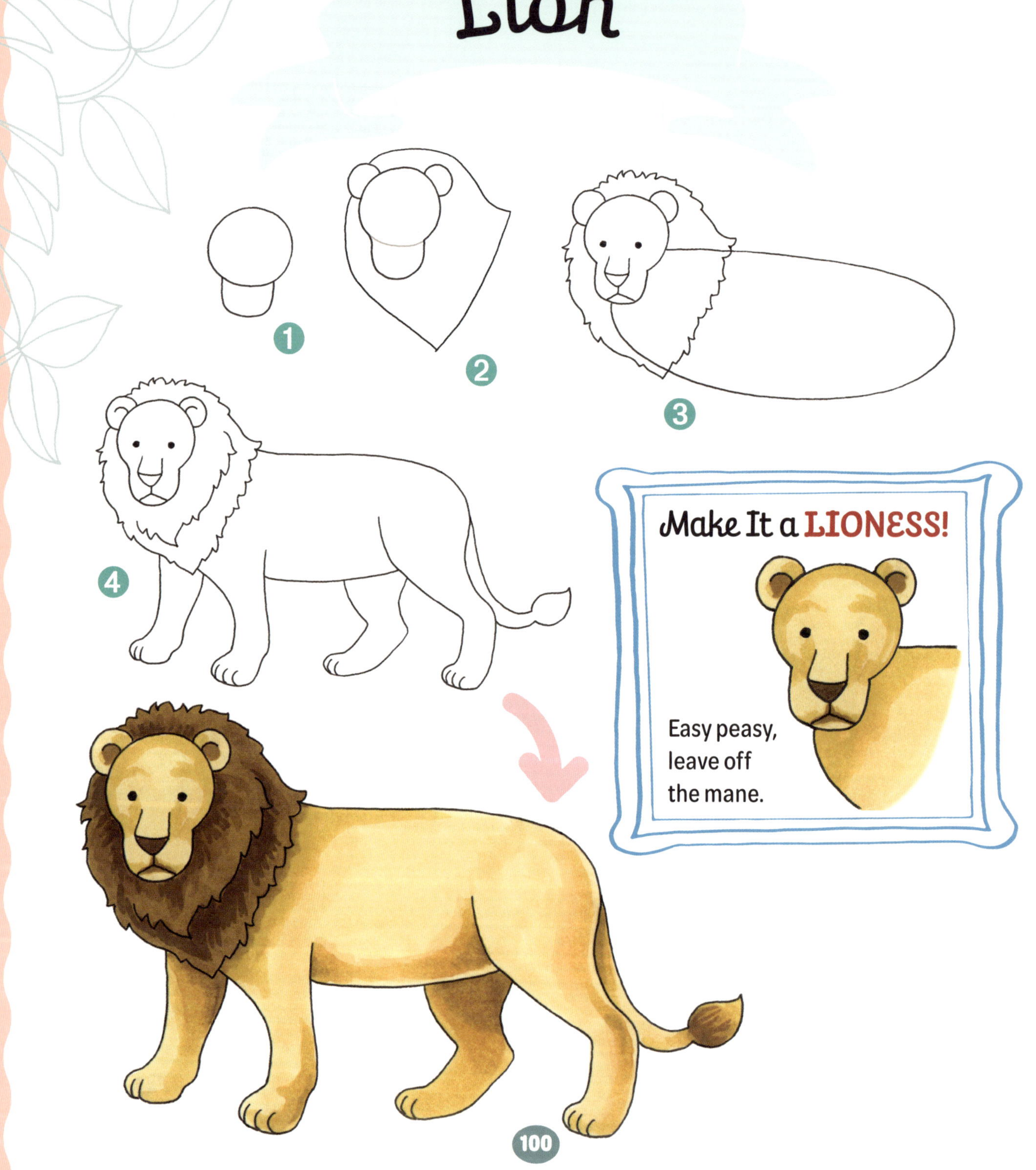

Hippopotamus

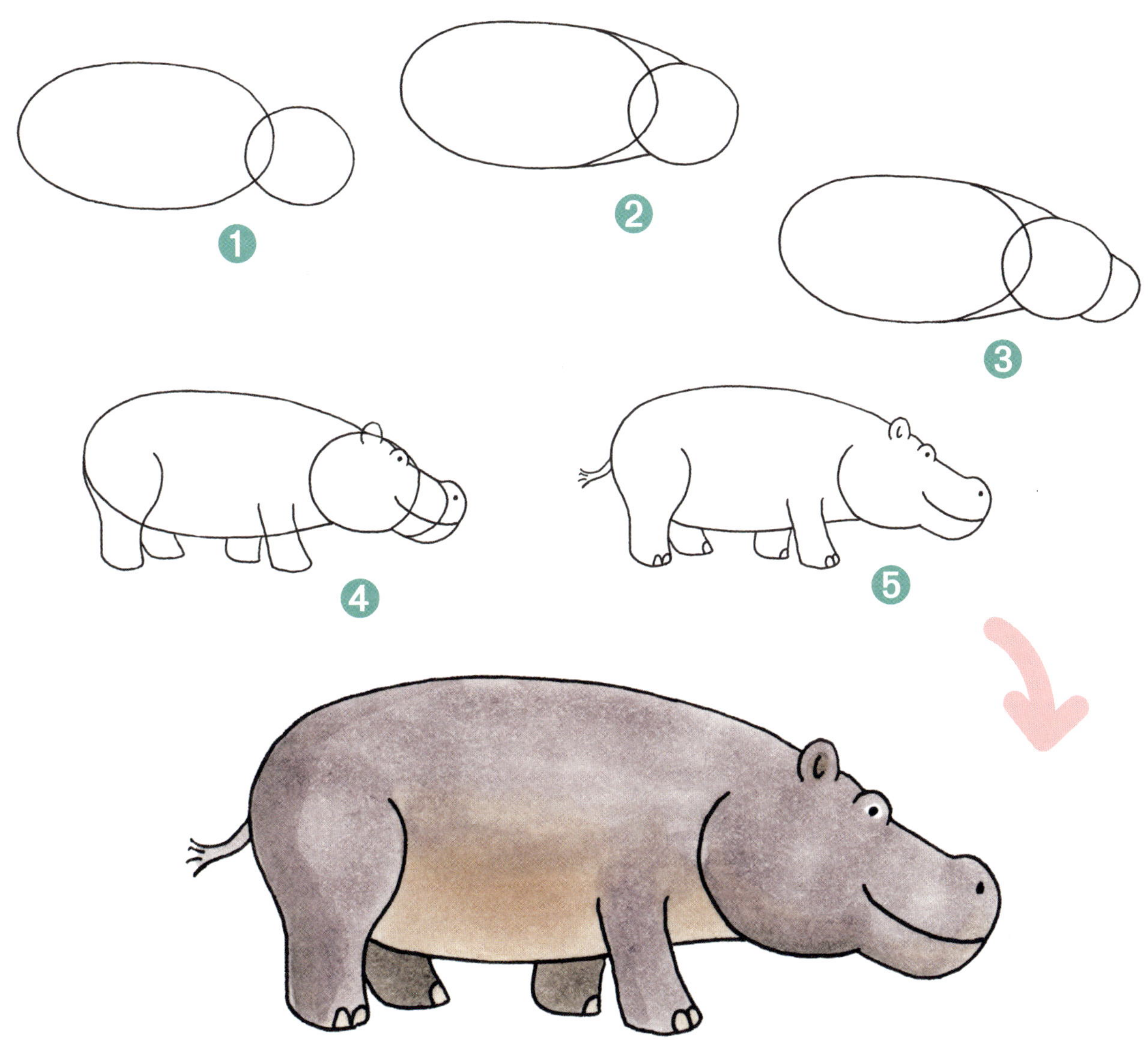

Camel

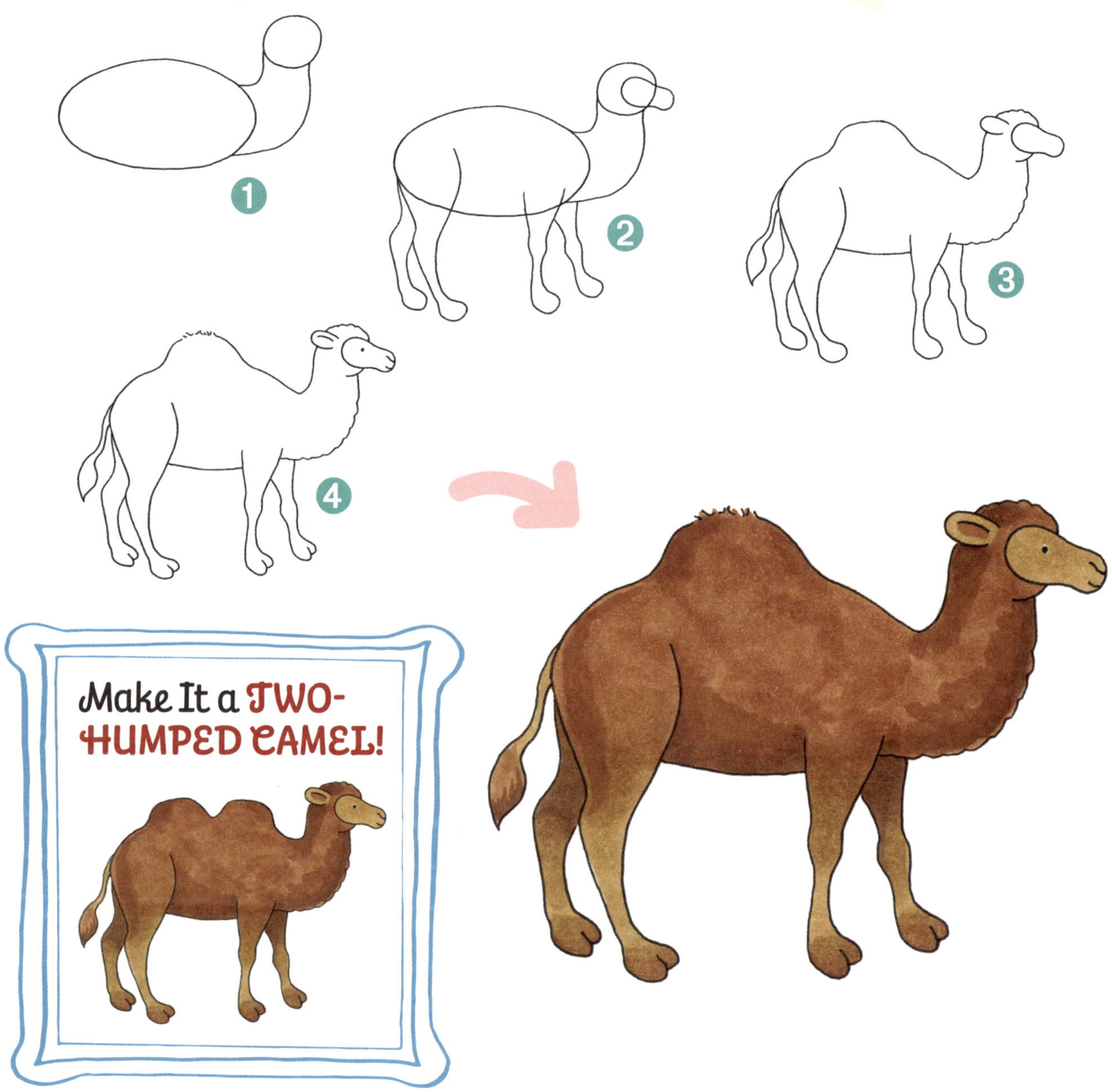

Zebra

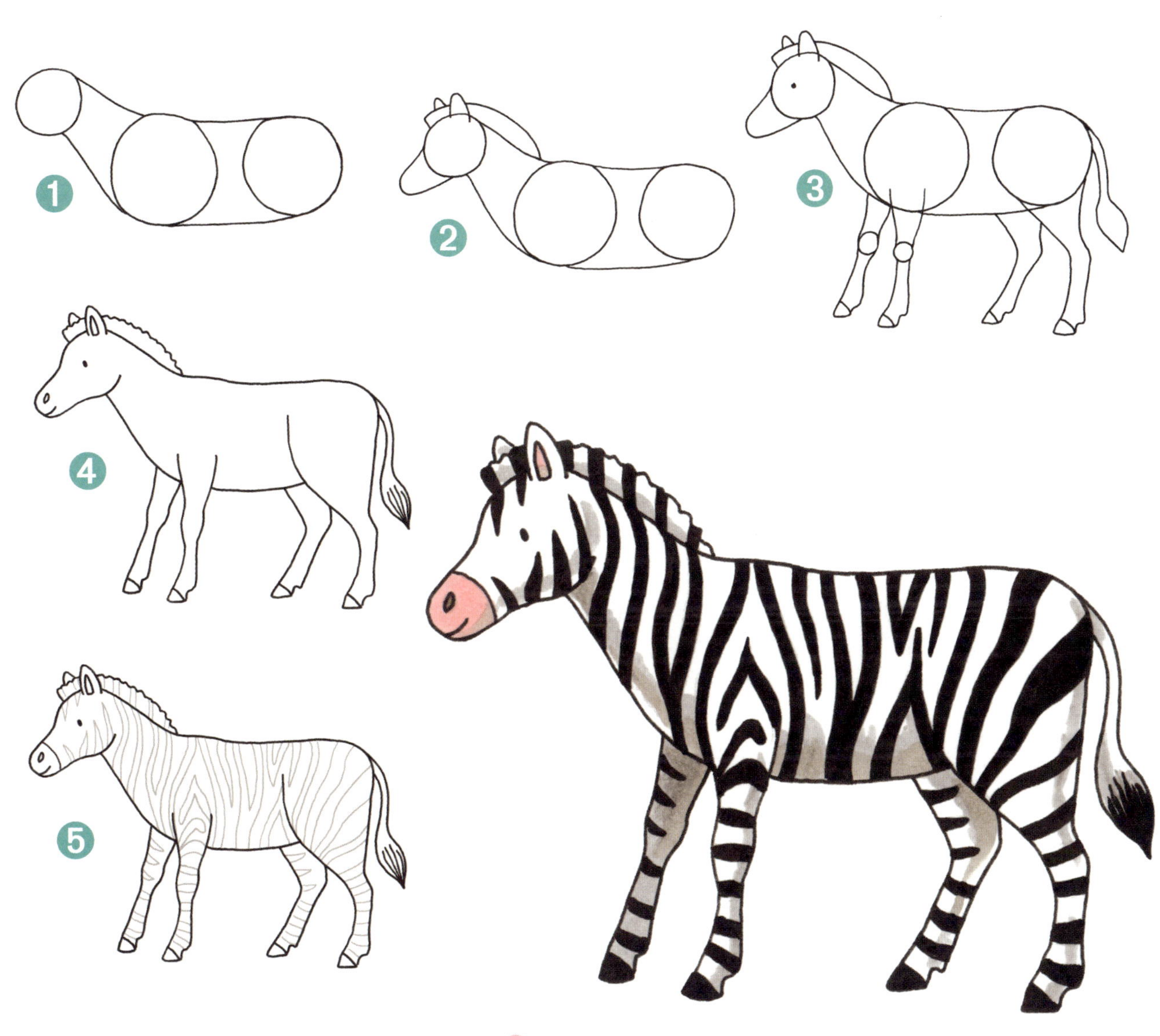

Red Panda

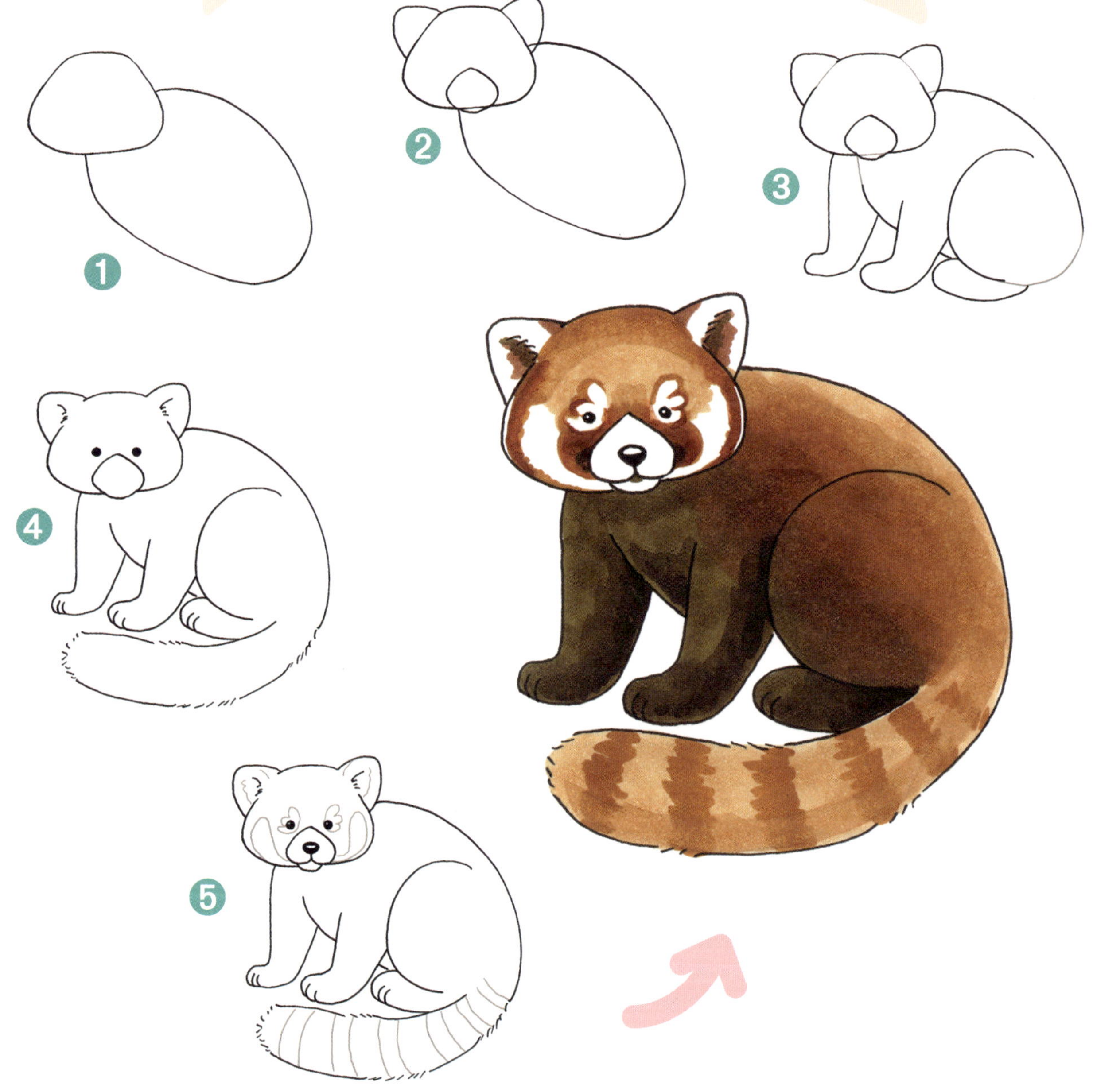

Rhinoceros

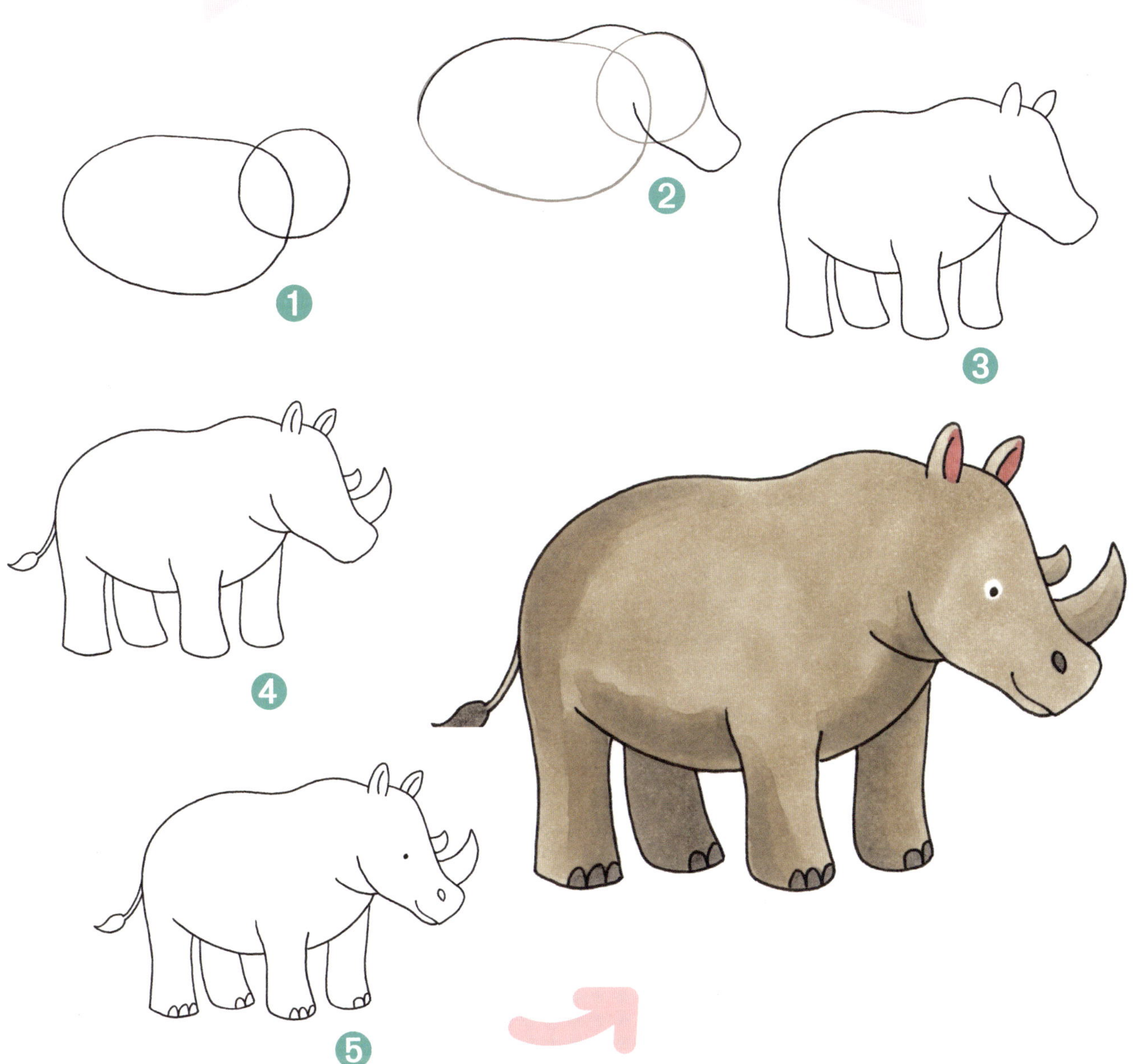

Koala

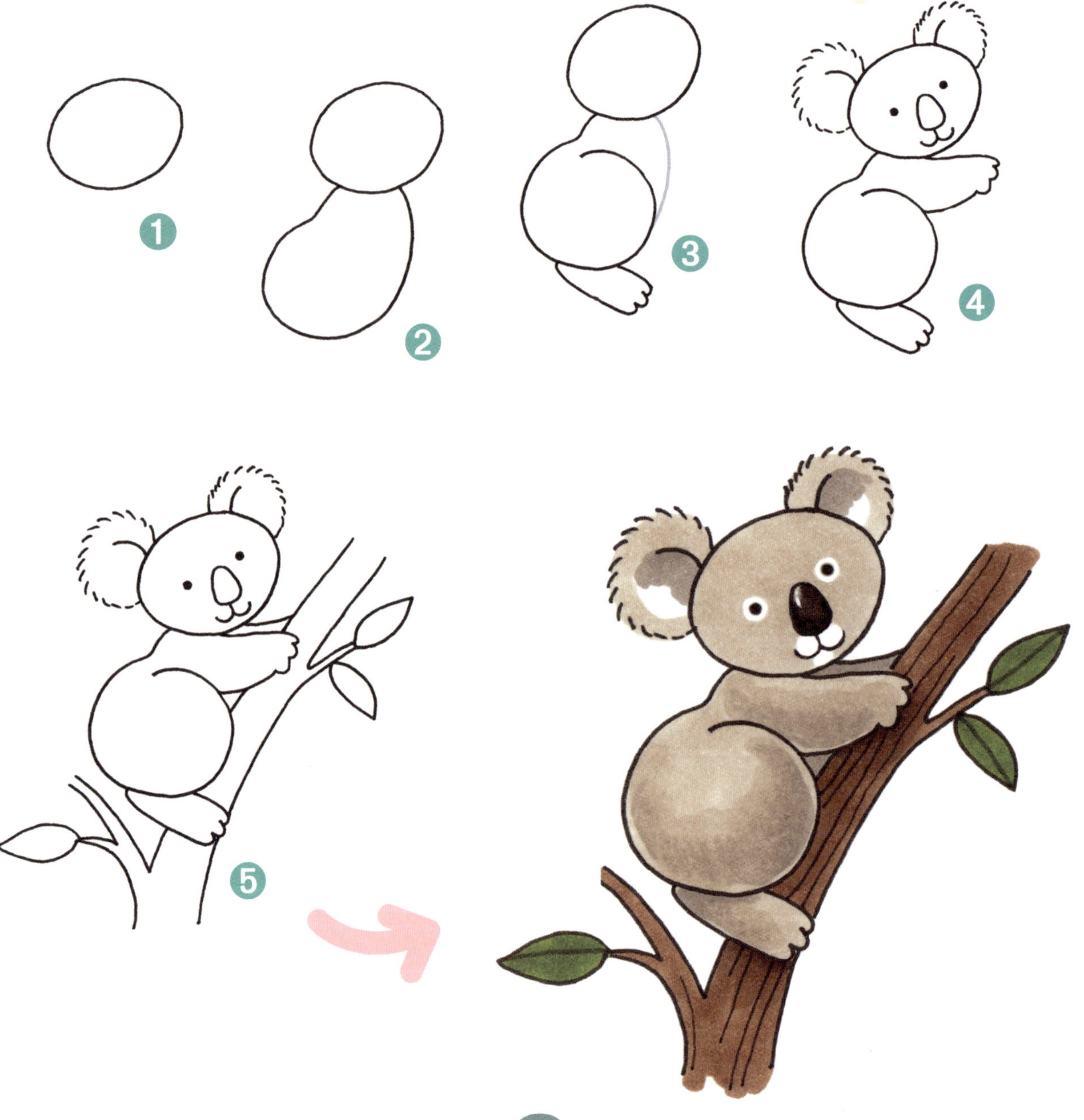

Sloth

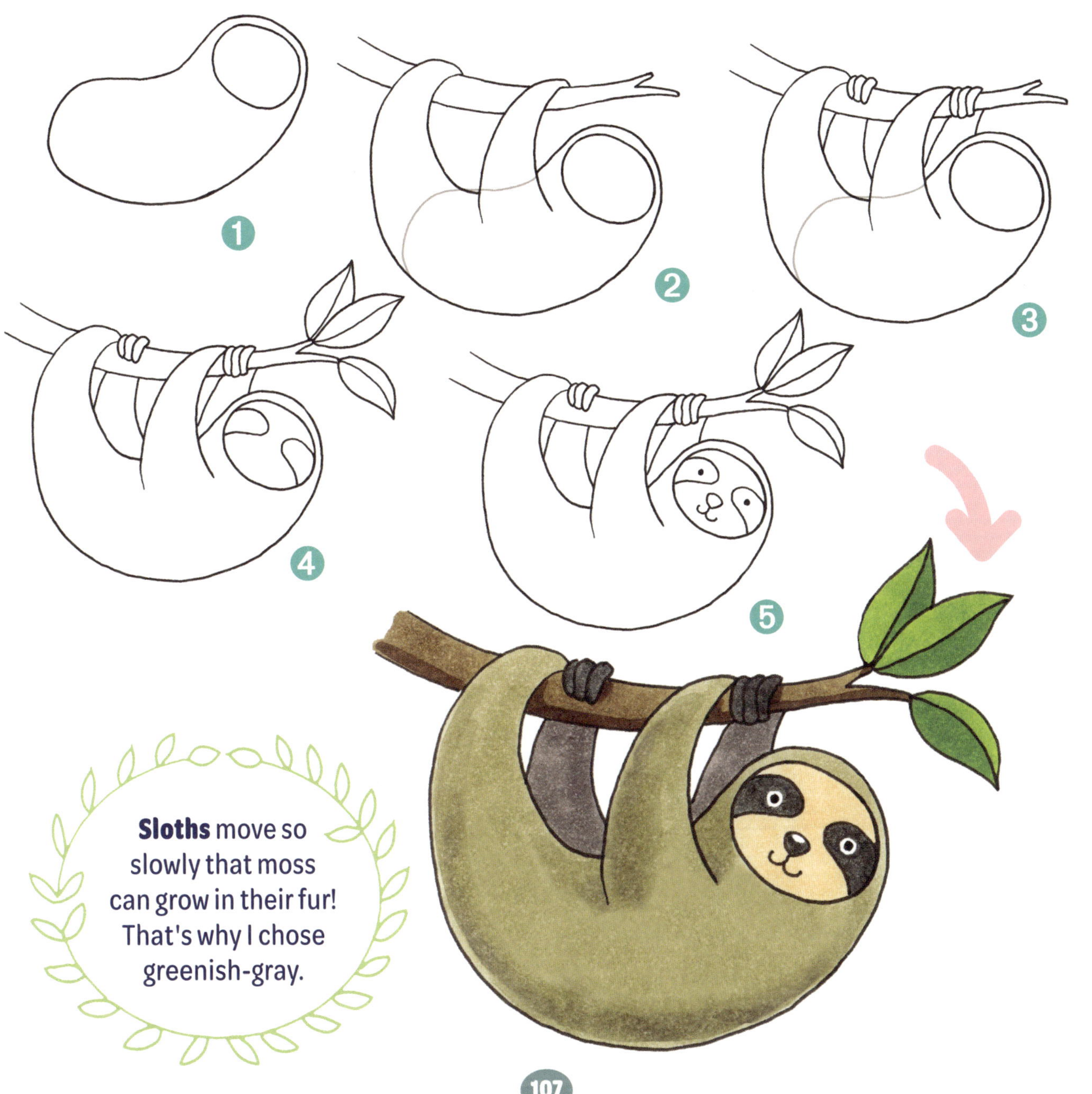

Sloths move so slowly that moss can grow in their fur! That's why I chose greenish-gray.

Wolf

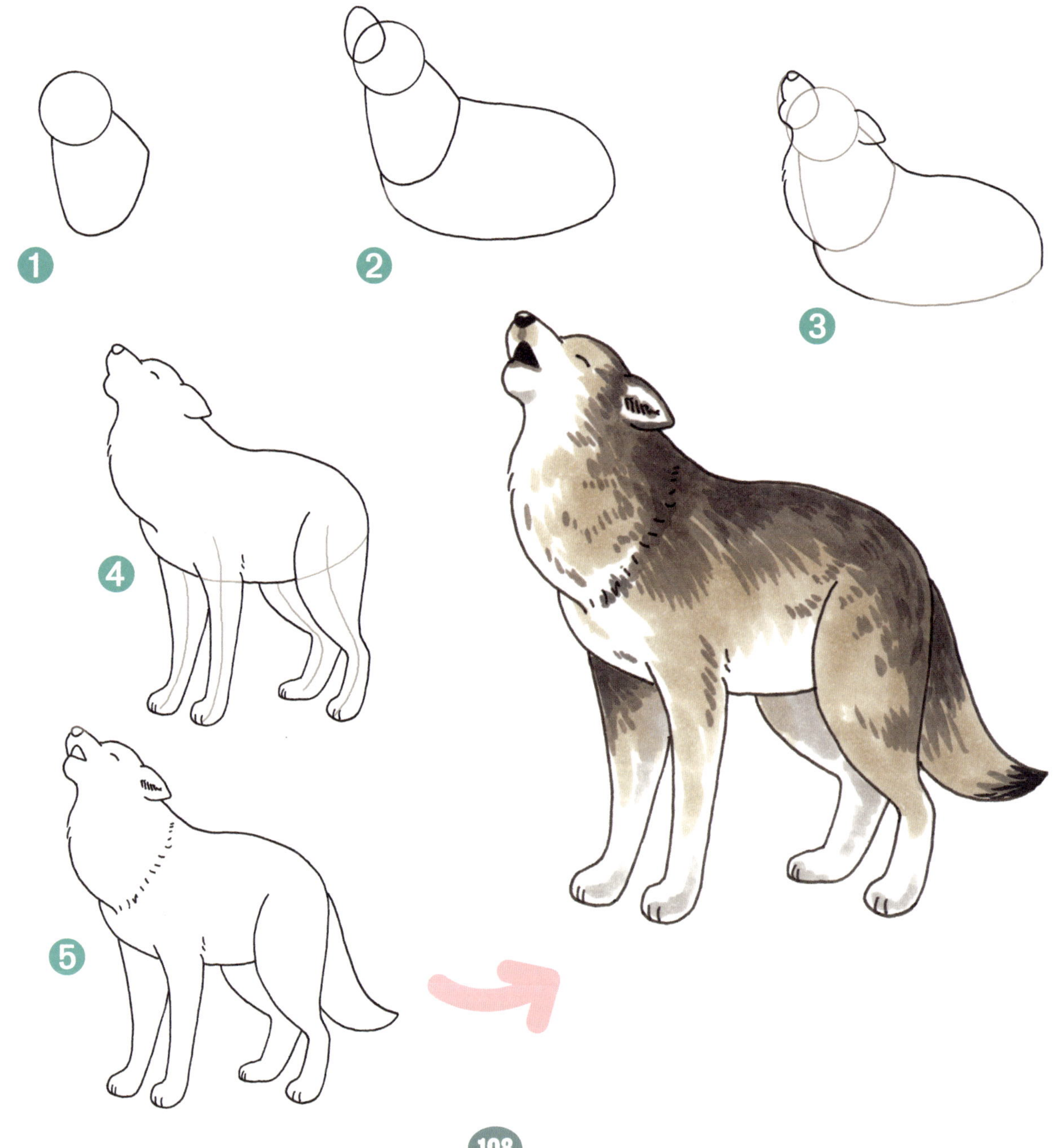

Monkey

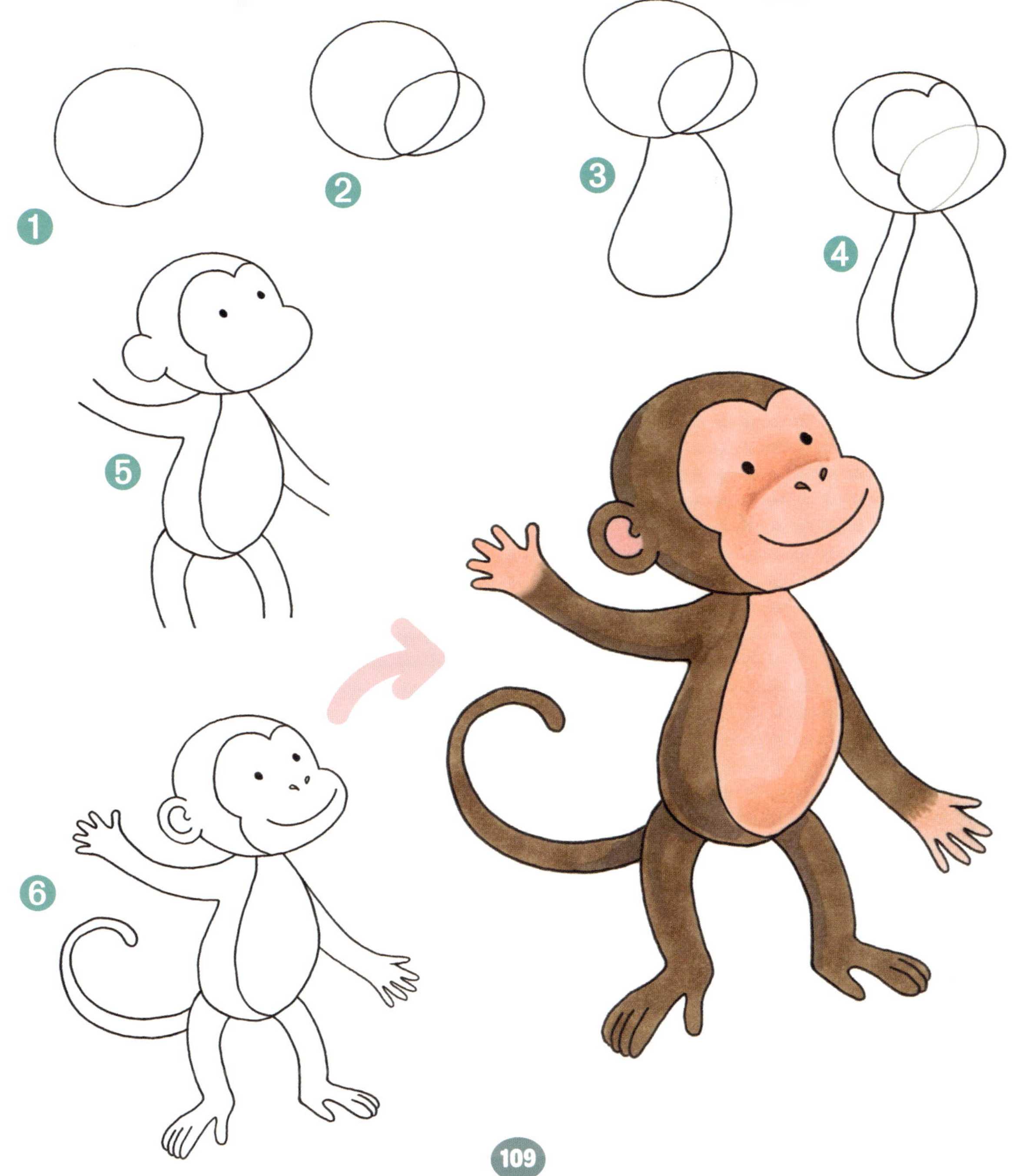

Bison

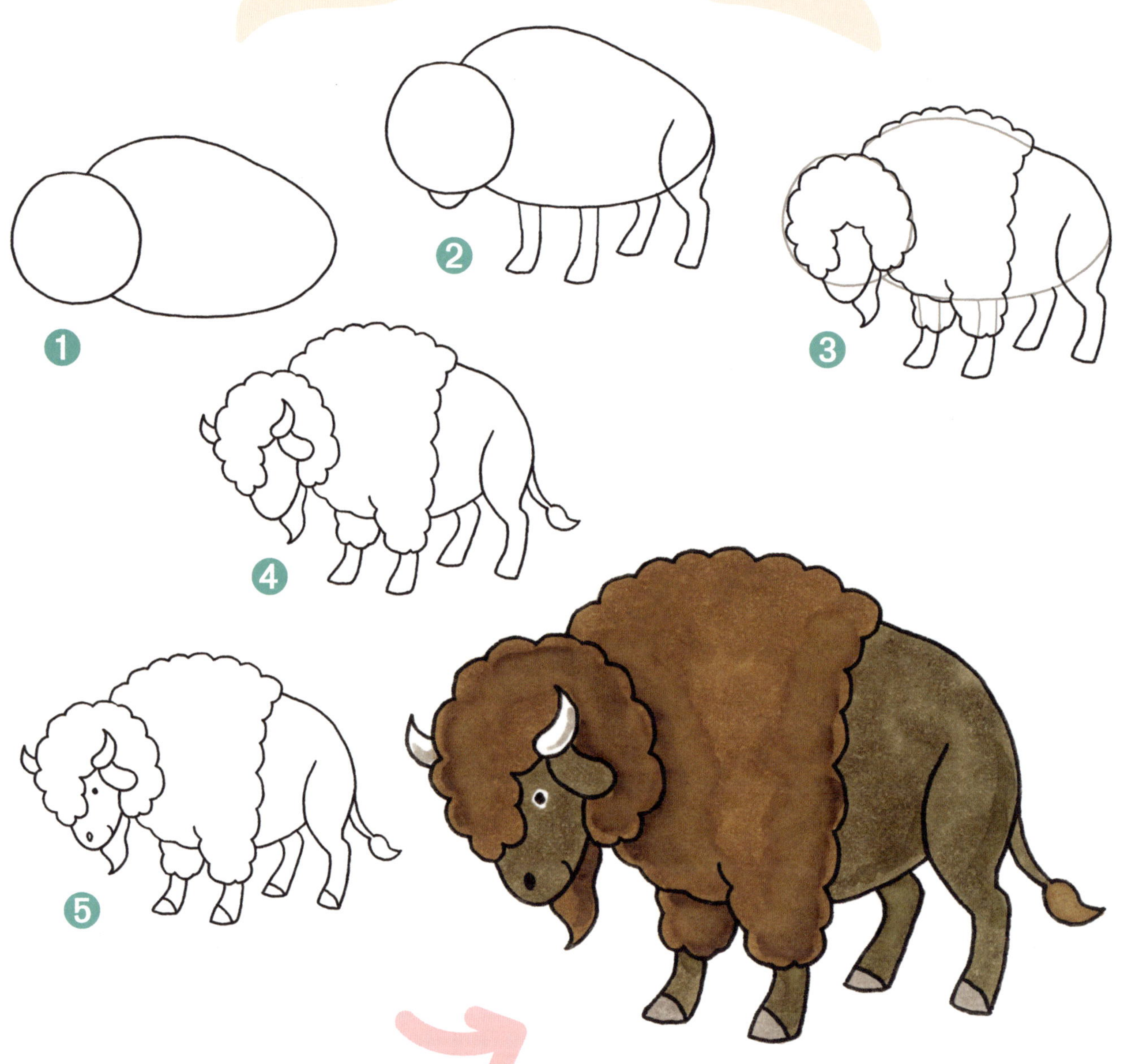

Platypus

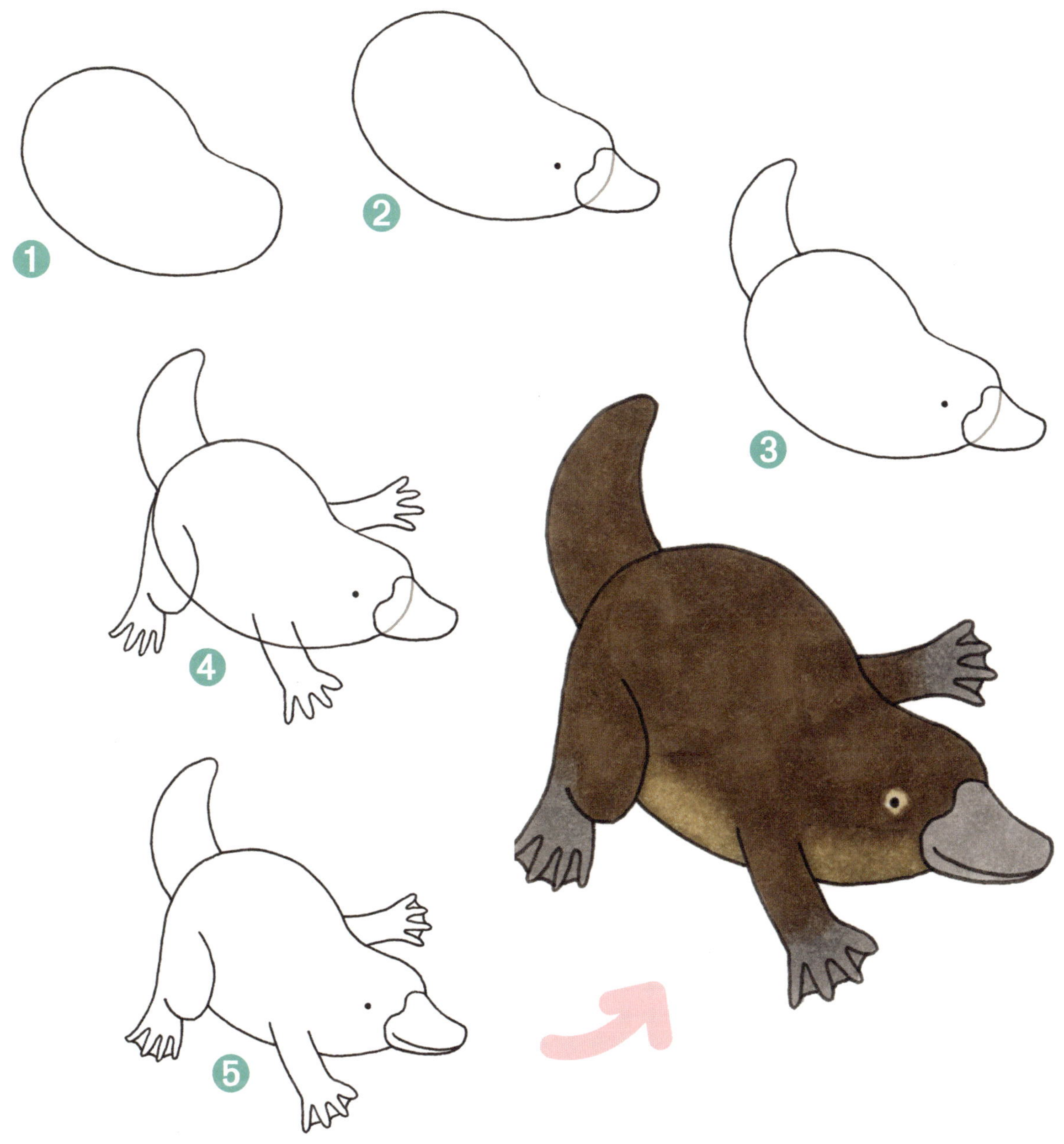

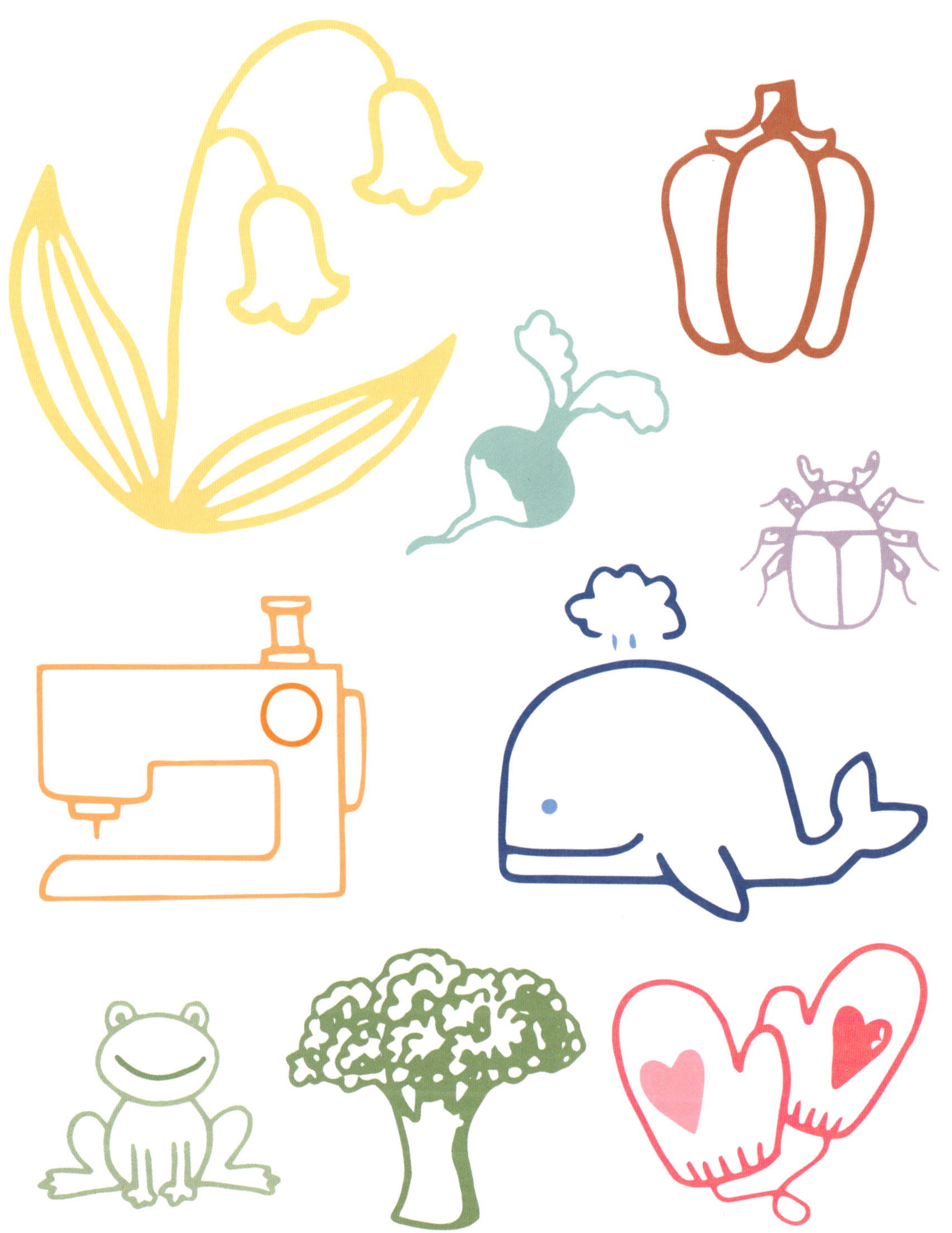

CHAPTER

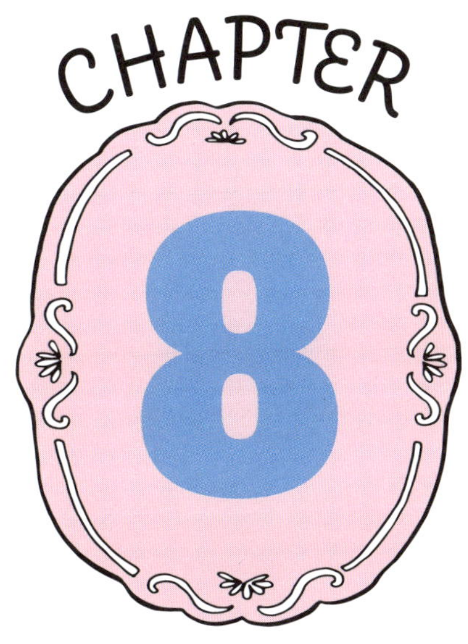

Super Cute, Super Easy Worksheets

In this section each page features super easy step-by-step instructions, with a final space for you to try it yourself! The worksheets are divided into themes, fun for developing your skills, adding artwork to journal pages, and just doodling around!

Draw Here

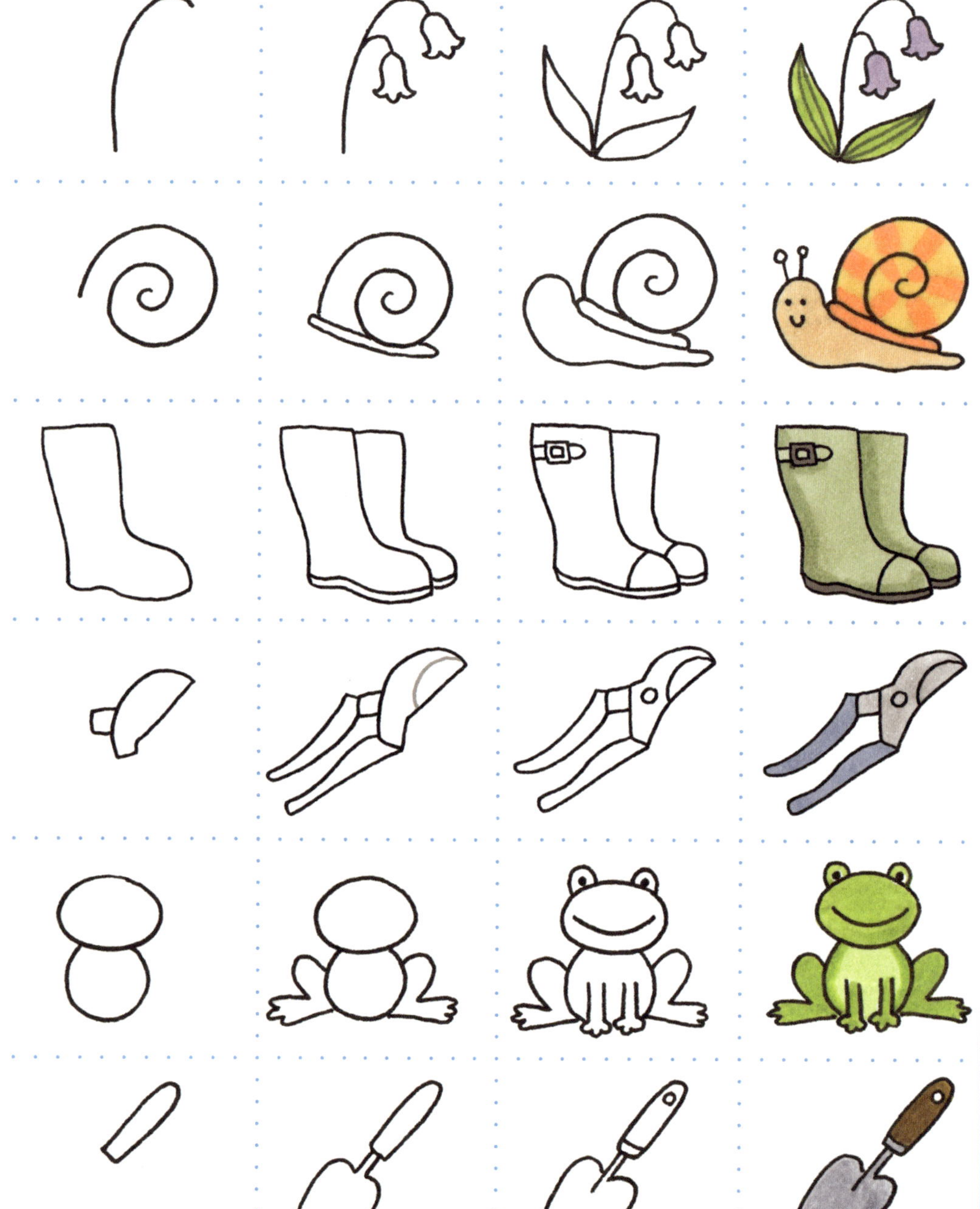

Nature's Delights

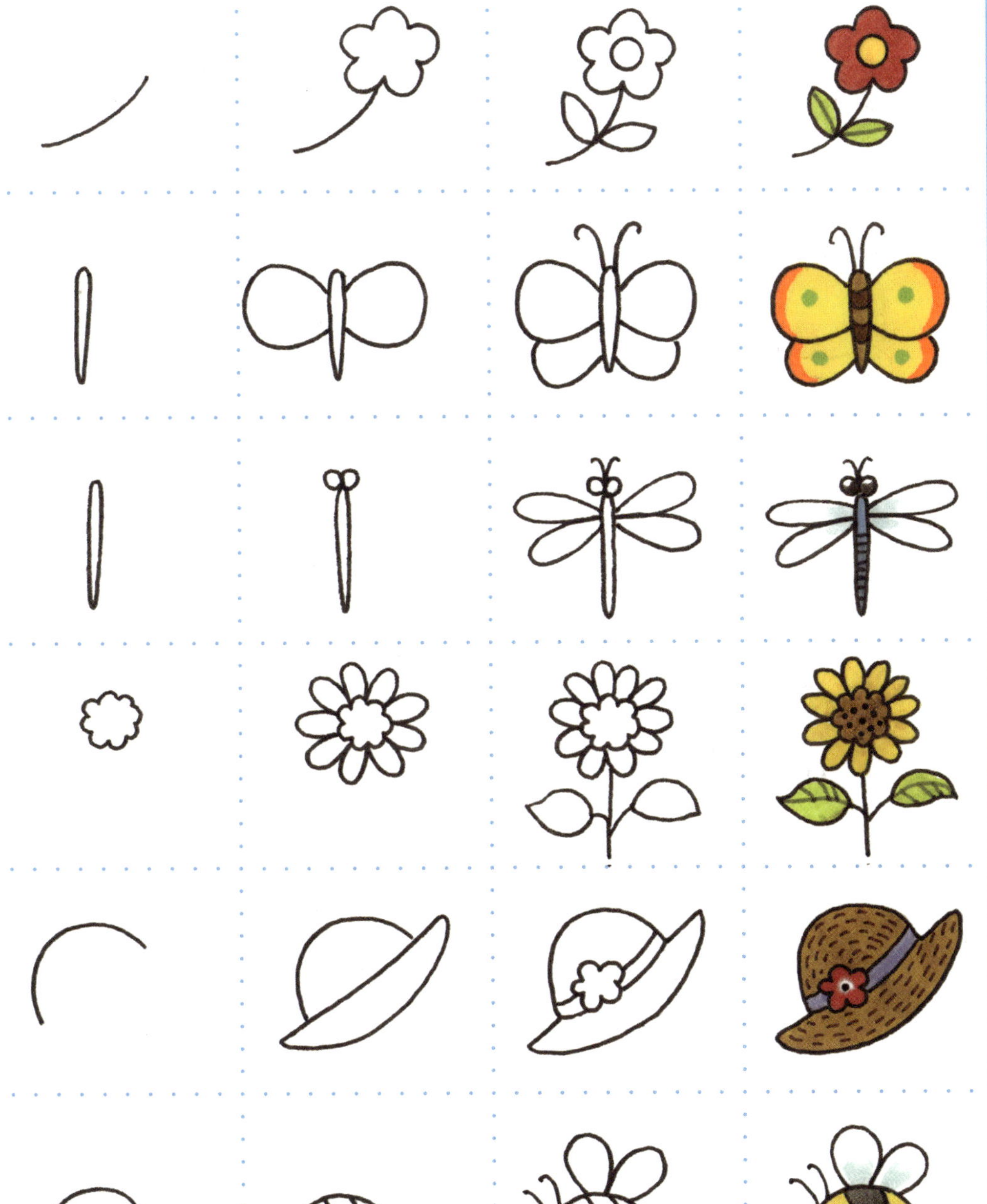

Little Critters

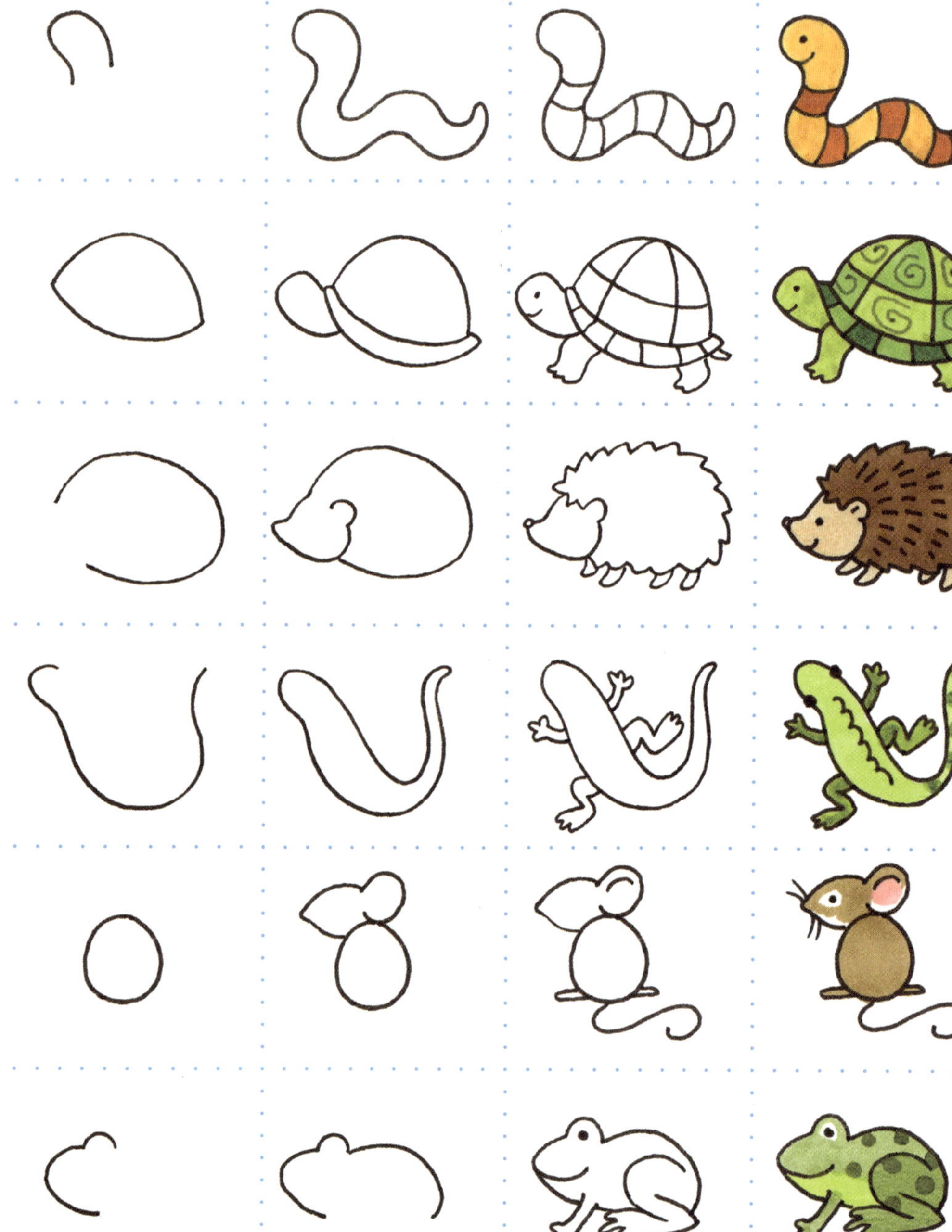

Bugs & Such

Draw Here

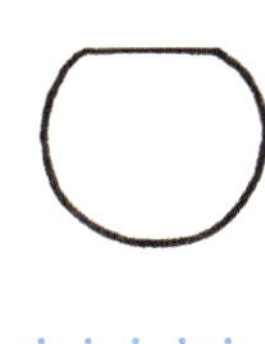 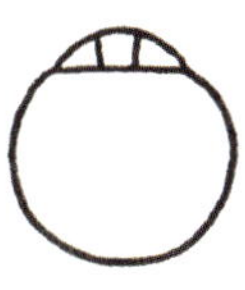 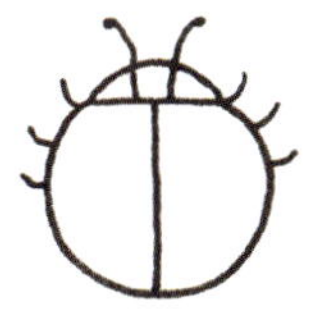 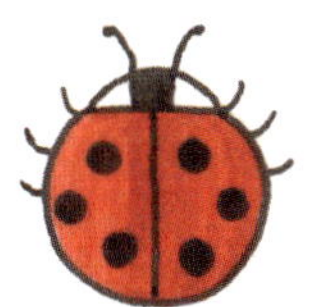

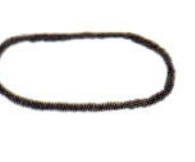 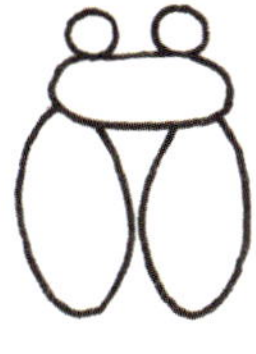 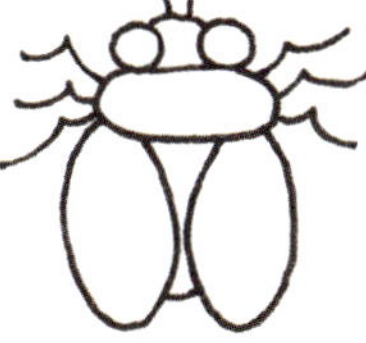 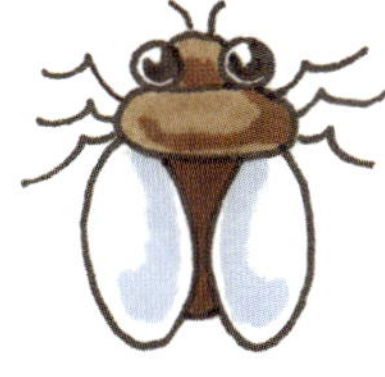

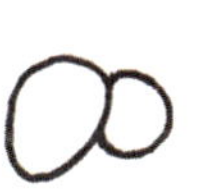  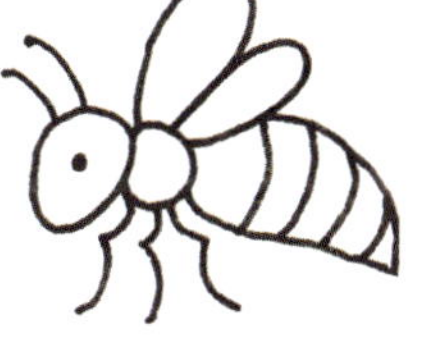 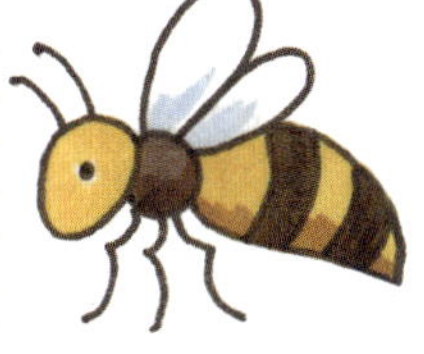

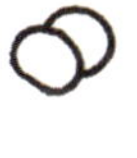 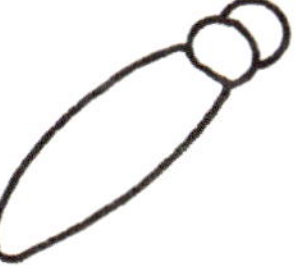 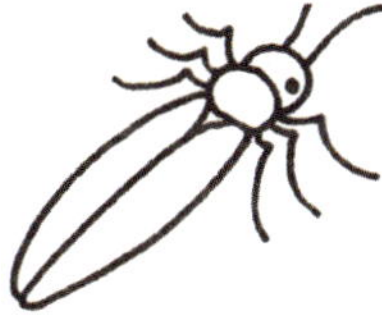 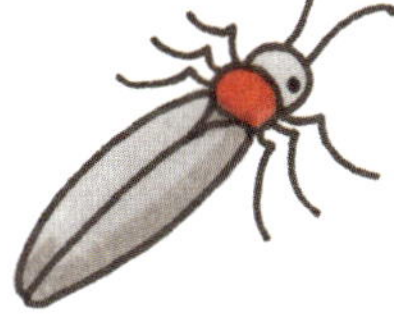

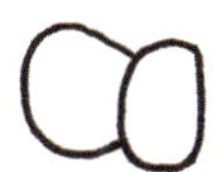 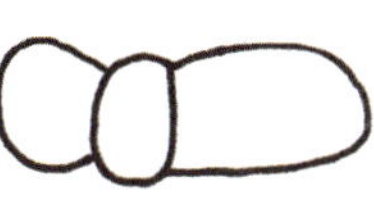 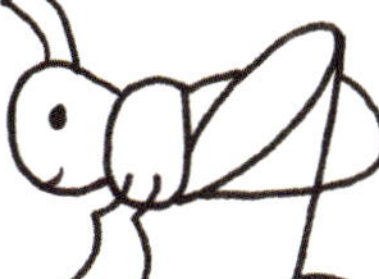 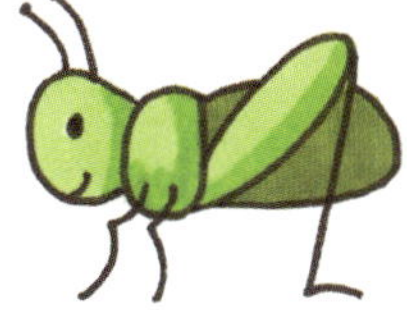

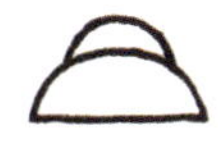 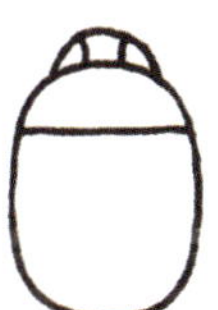 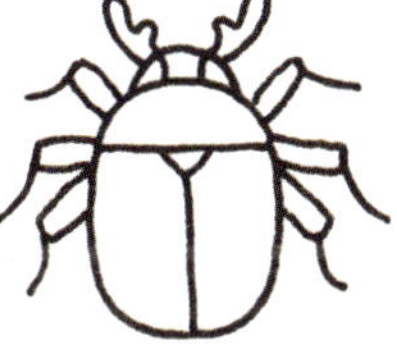 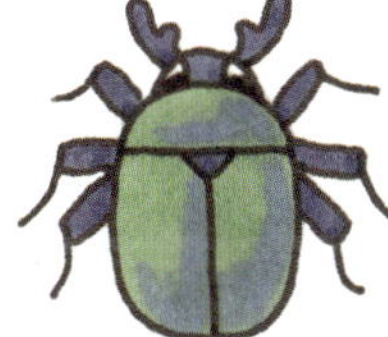

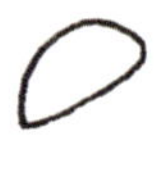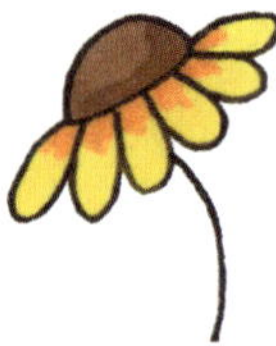

Draw Here

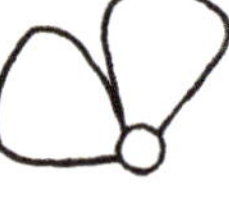

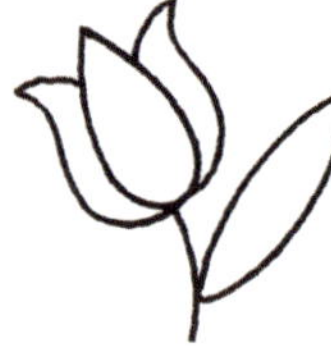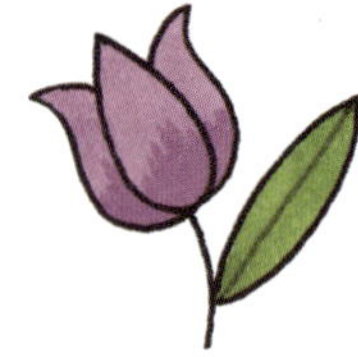

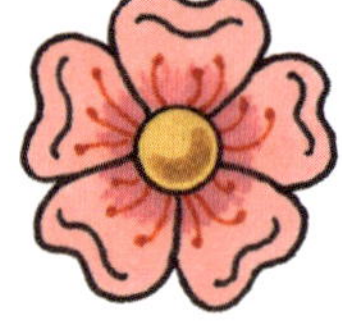

Draw Here

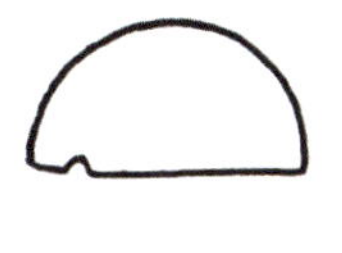 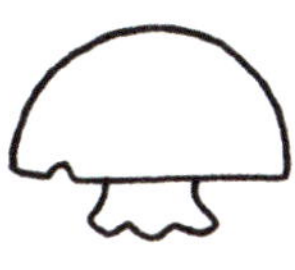 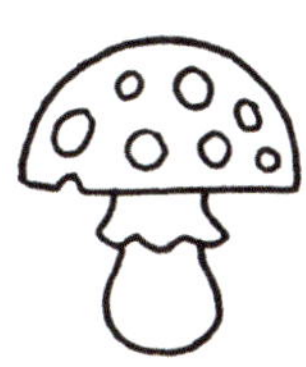 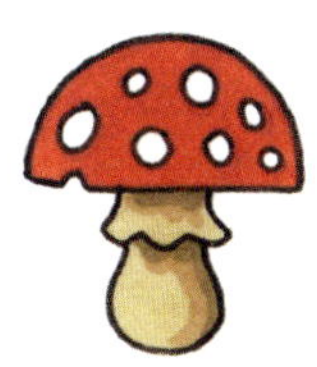

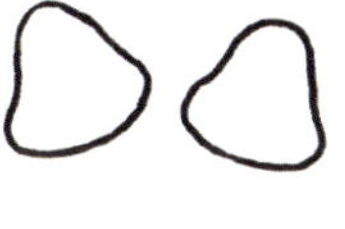 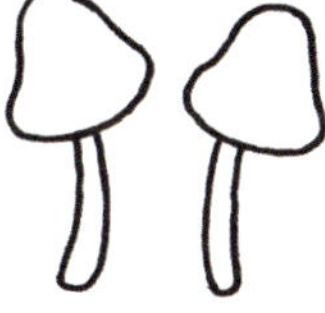 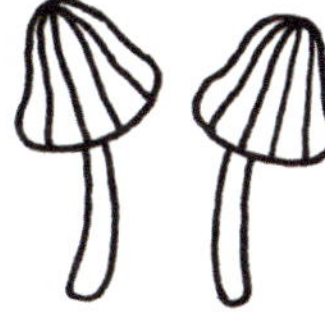 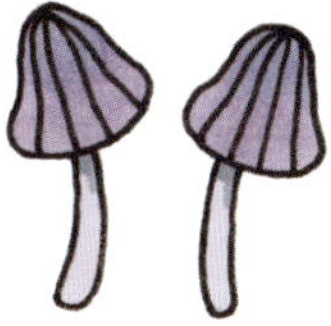

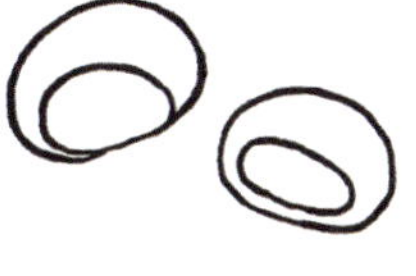 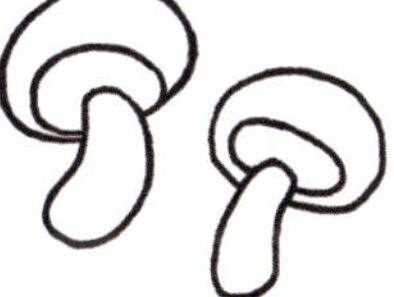 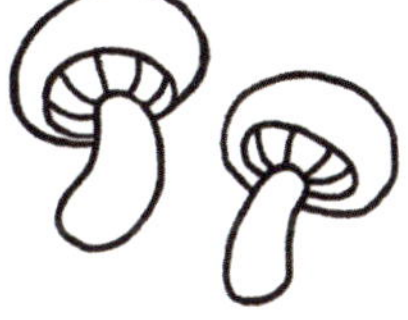 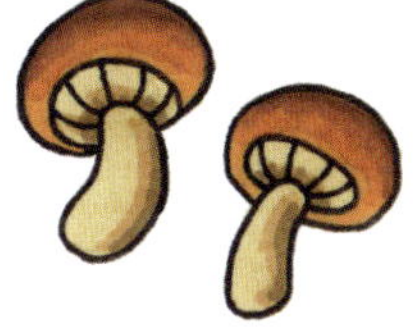

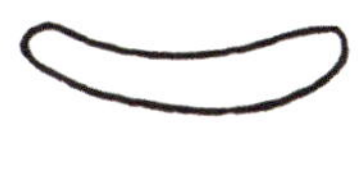 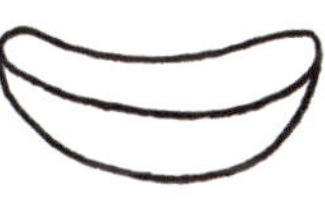 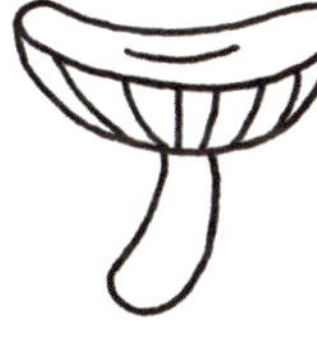 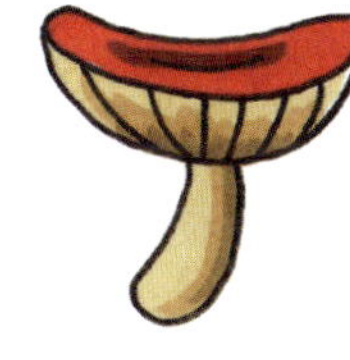

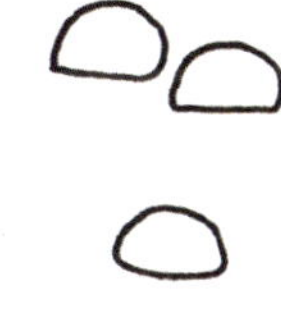 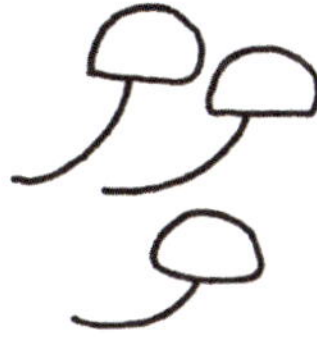 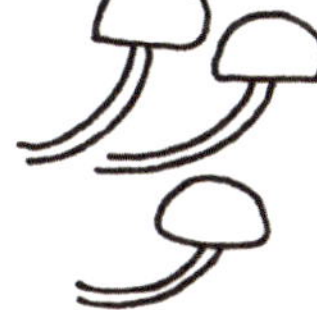 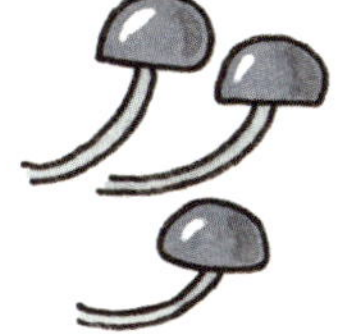

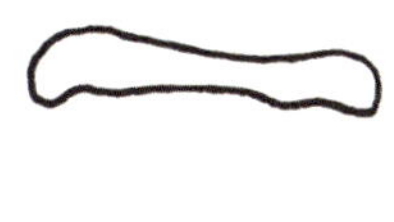 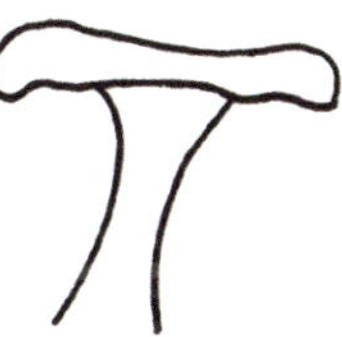 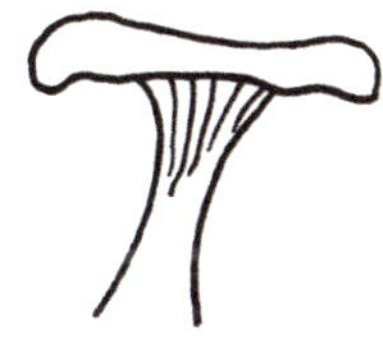 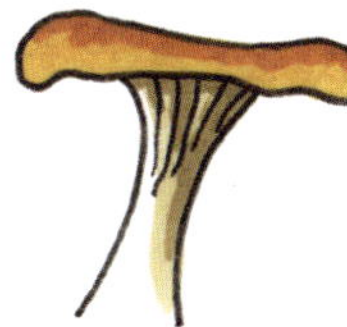

Fruits & Berries

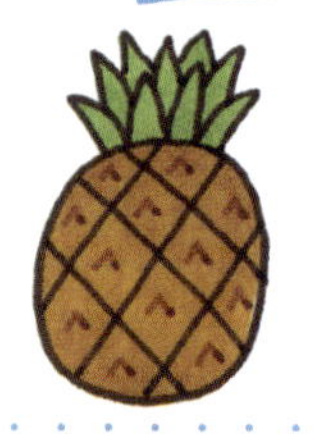

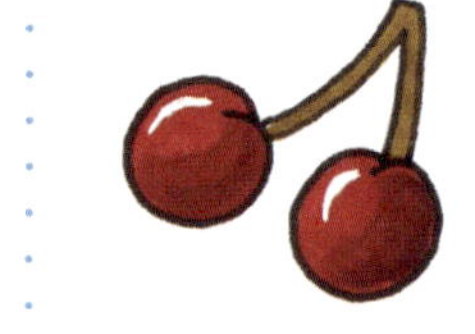

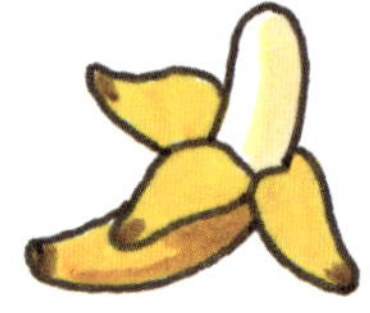
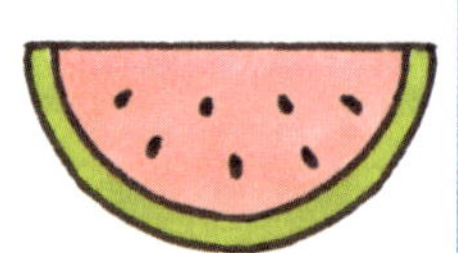
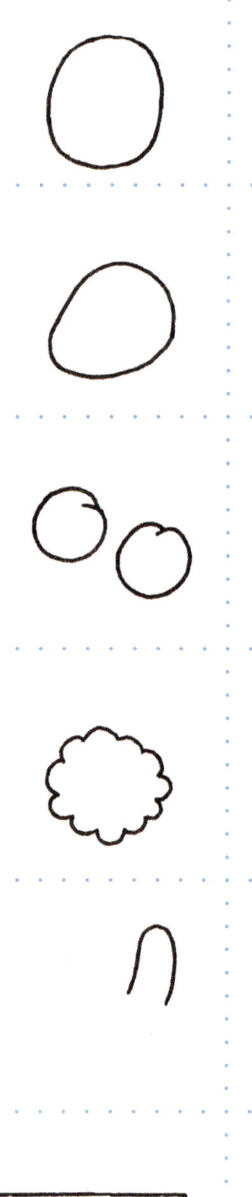
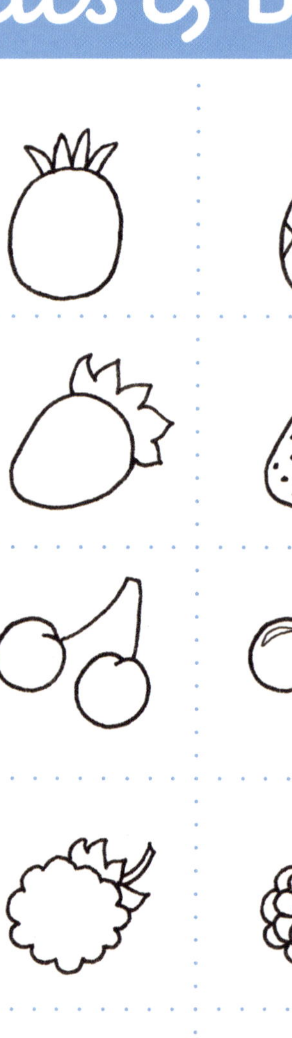
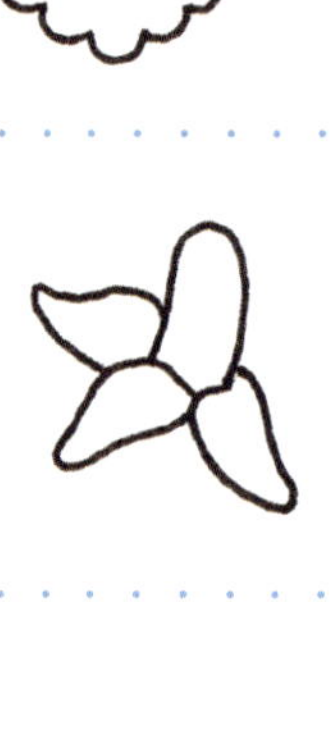
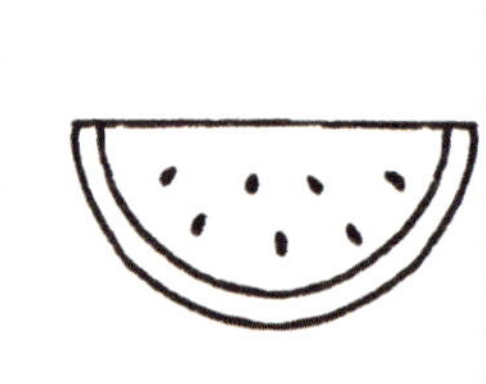

Vegetables

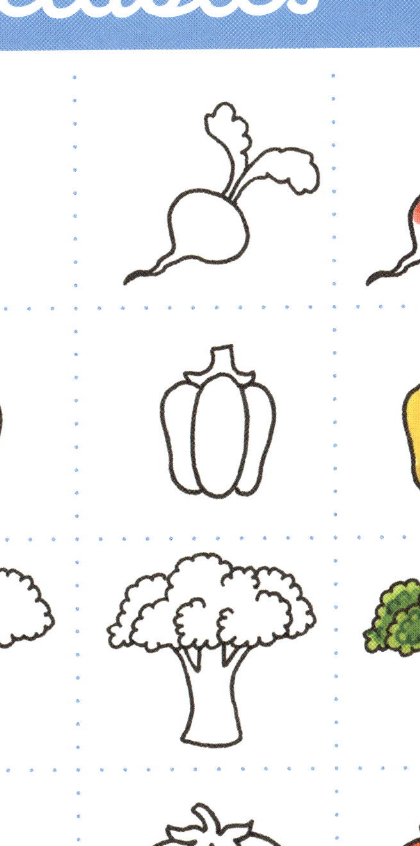

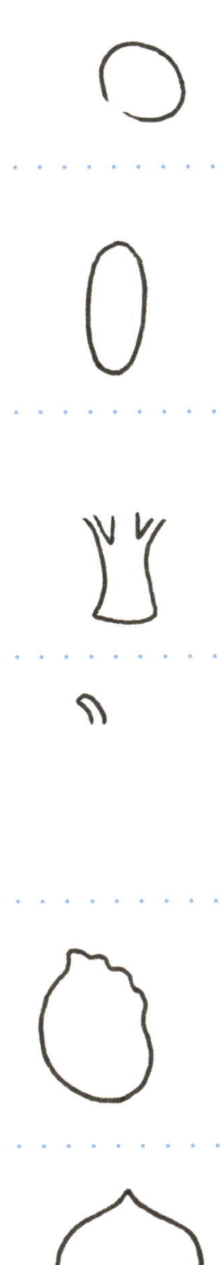

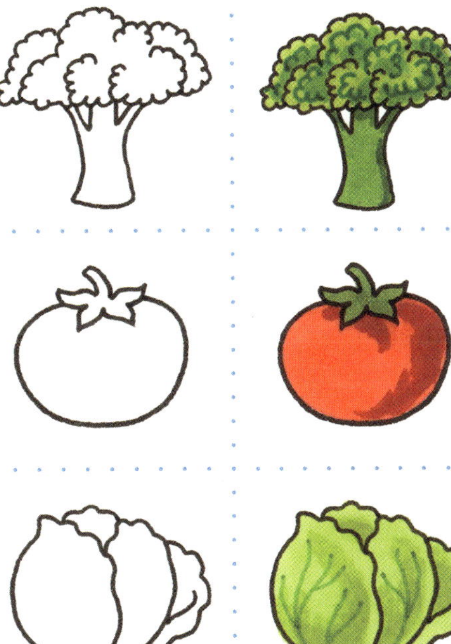

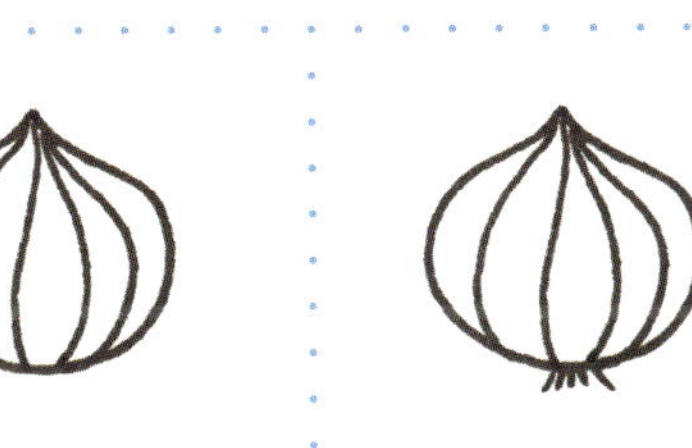

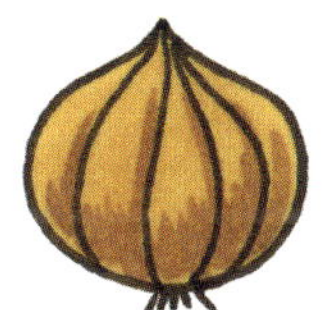

Succulents & Cacti

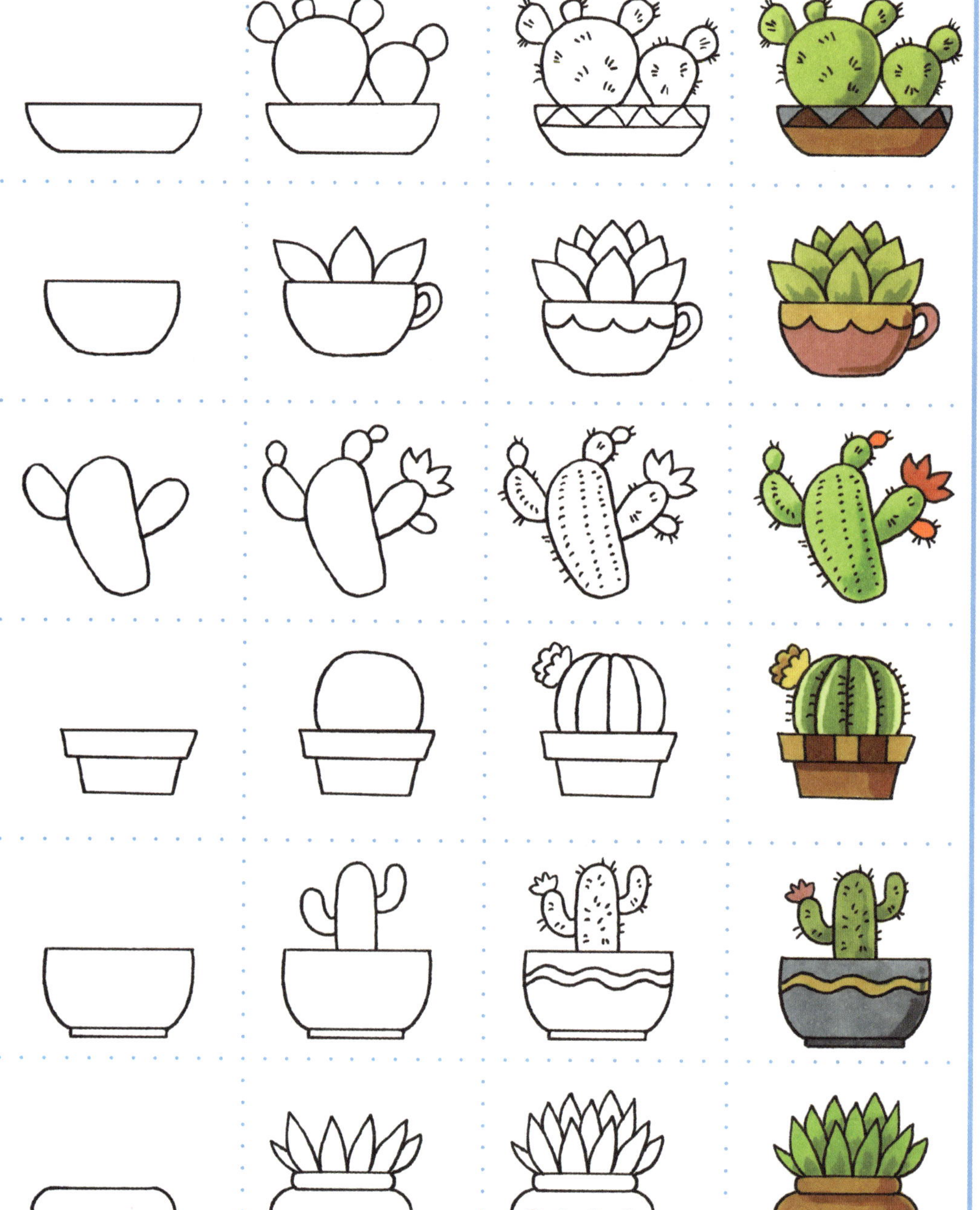

Wild & Western

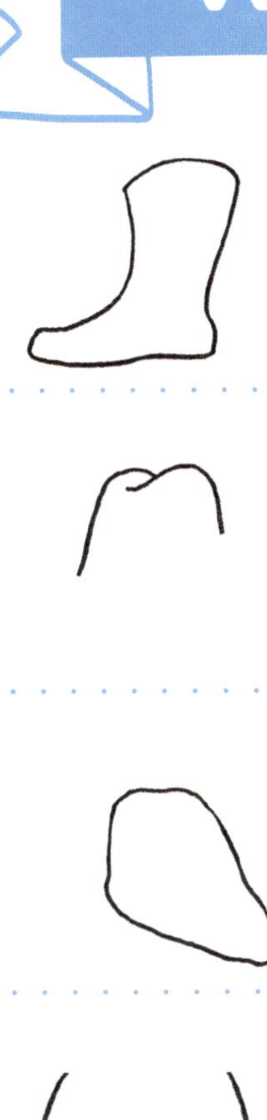
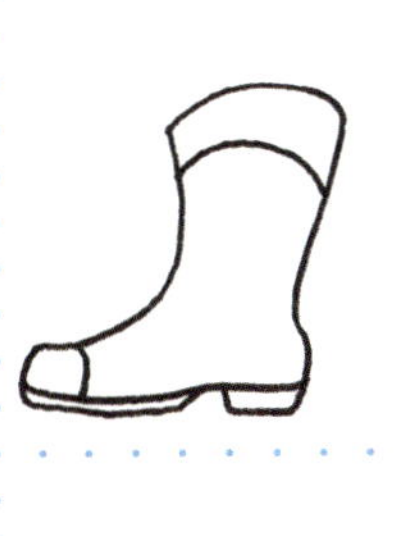
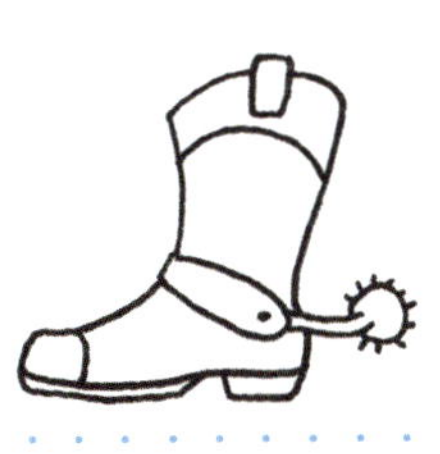
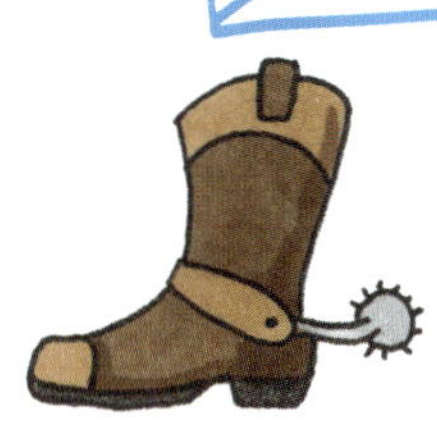
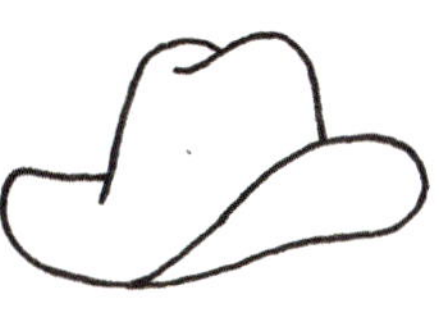
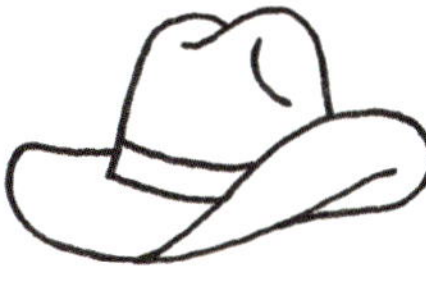
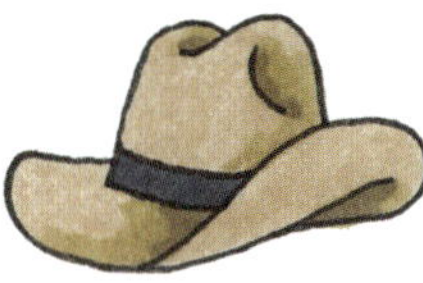
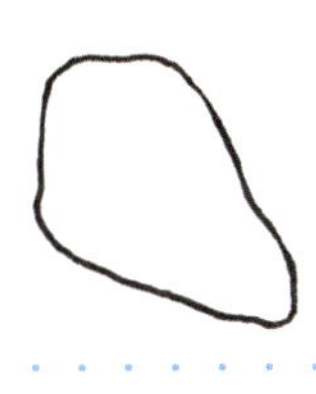
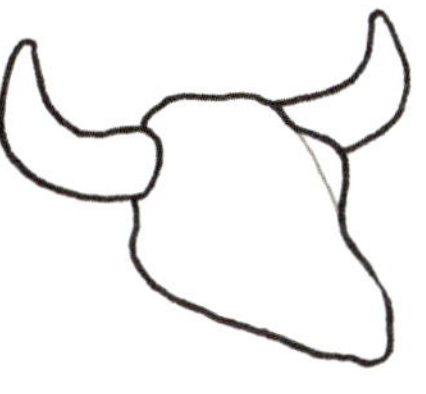
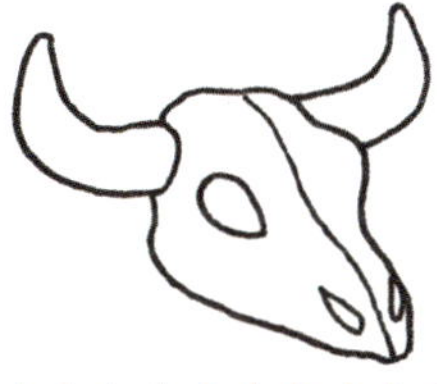
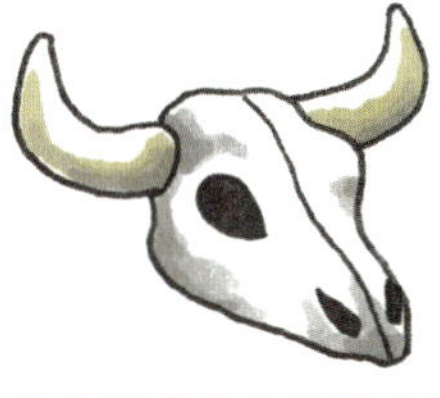
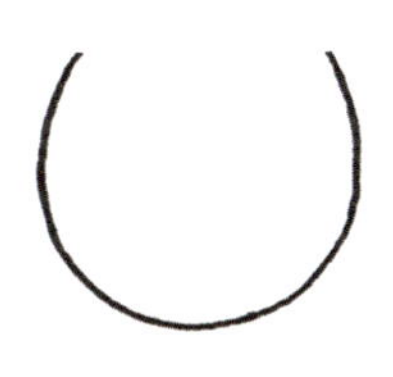
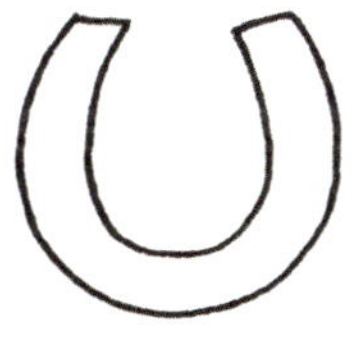
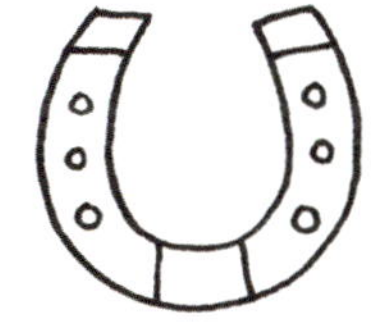
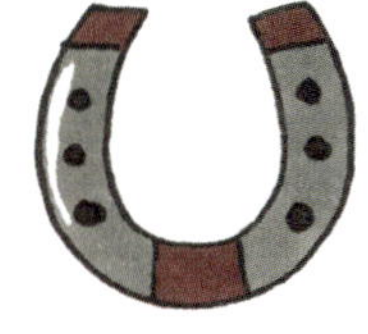
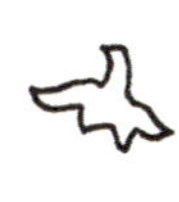
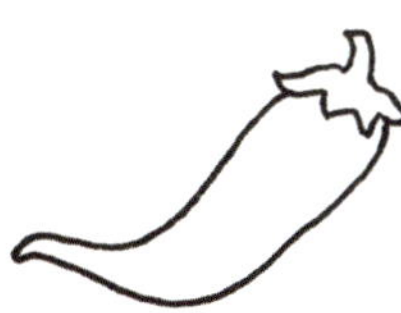
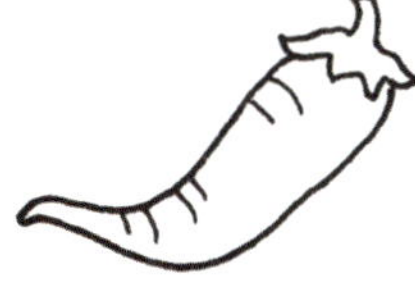
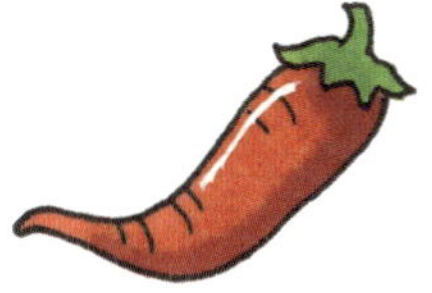
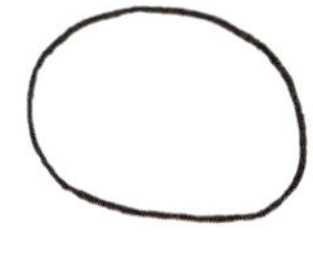
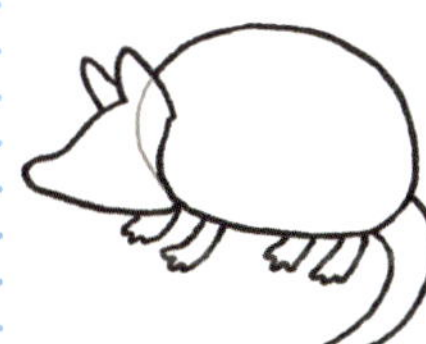
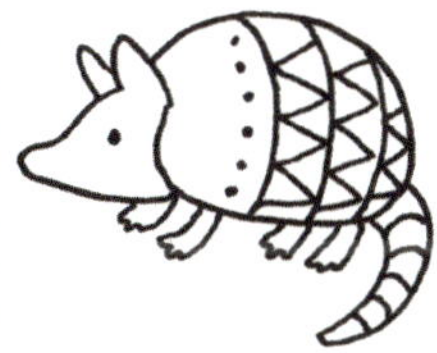
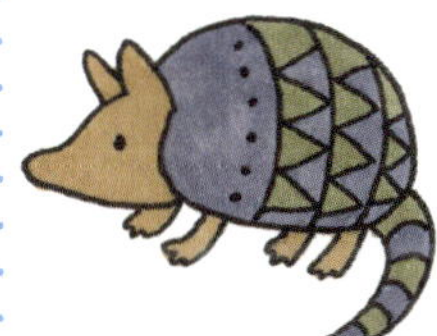

Making Music

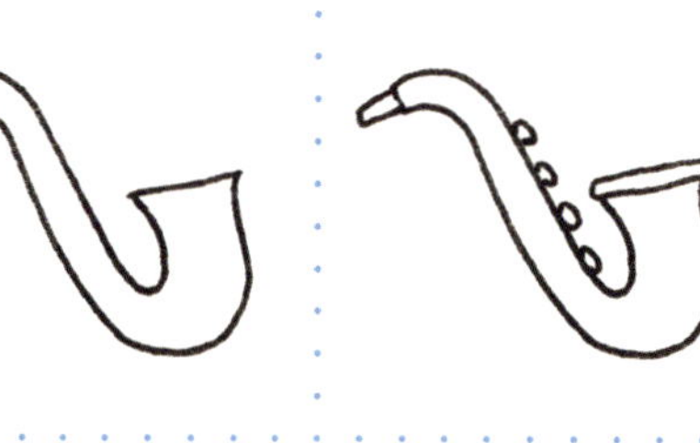
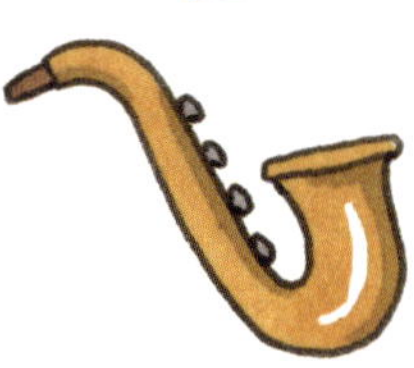

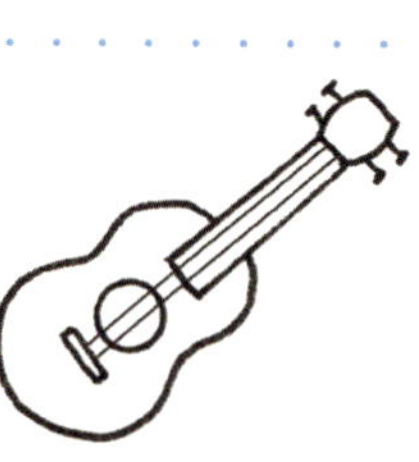
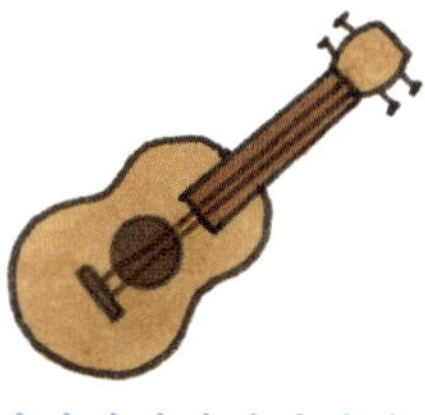

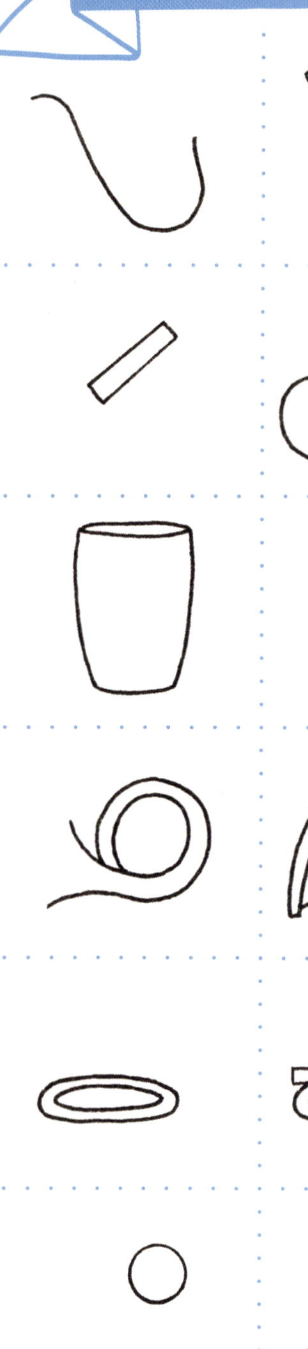
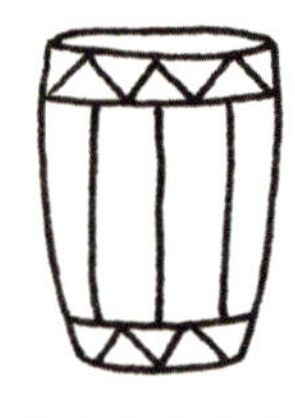
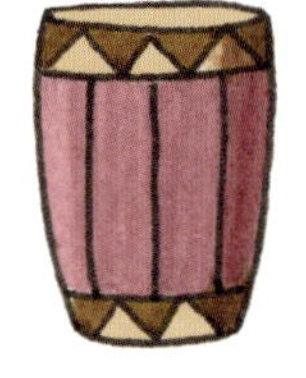

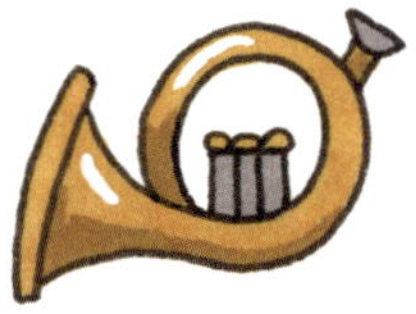

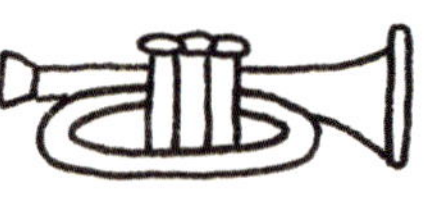
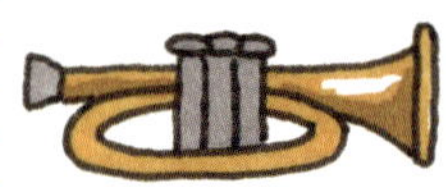

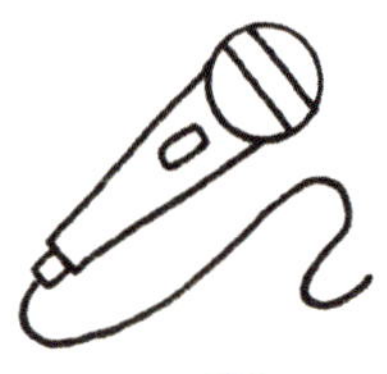
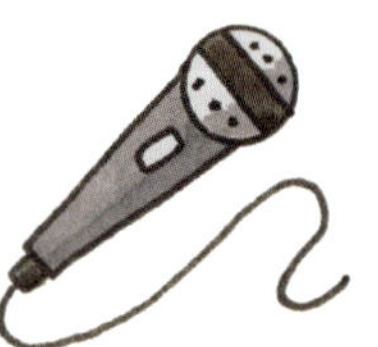

Tools

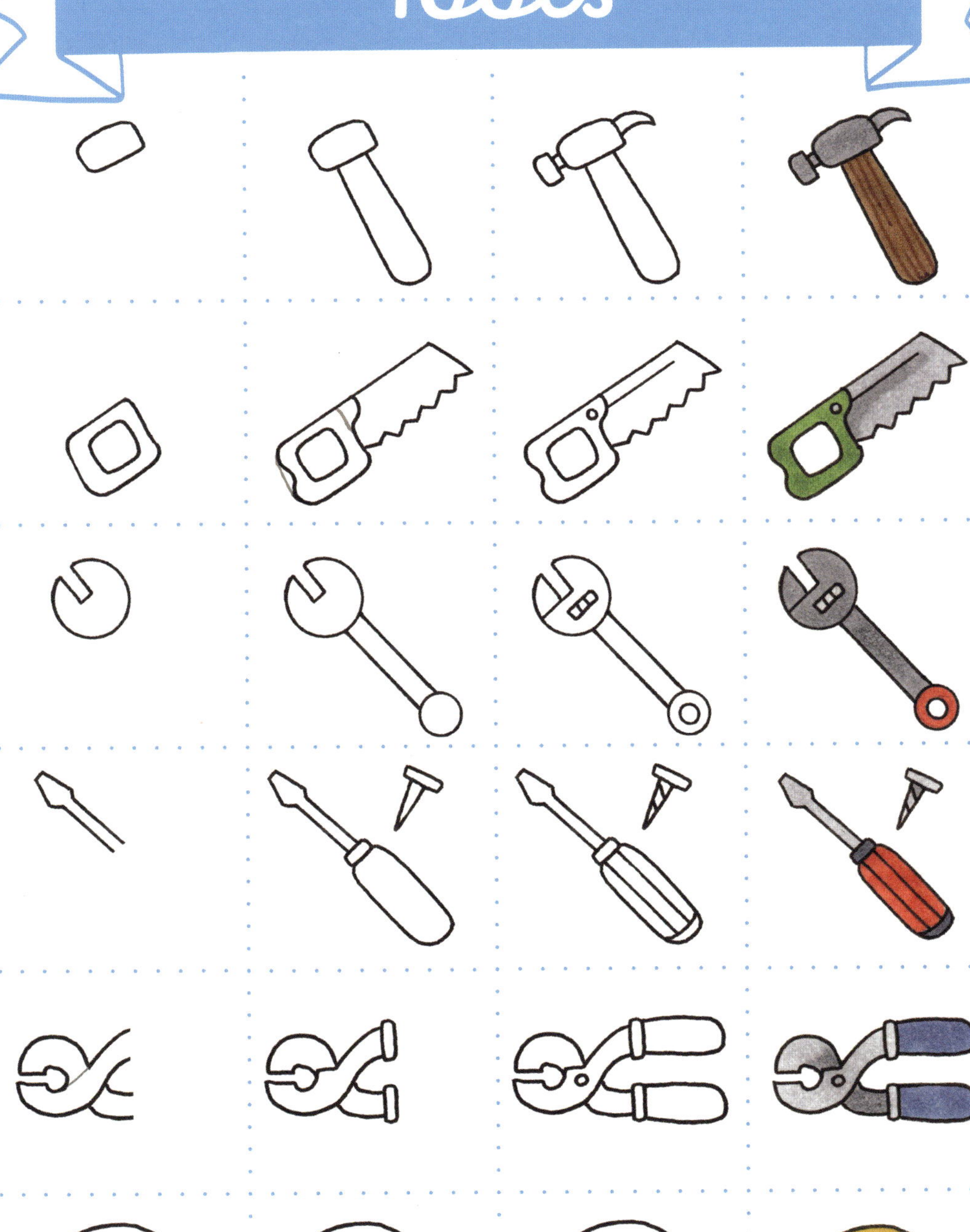

Draw Here

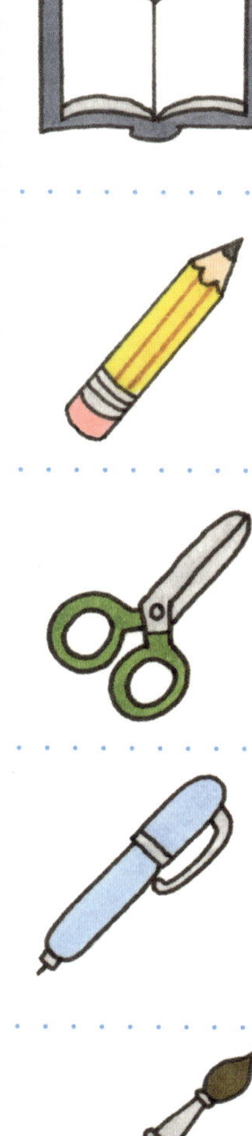

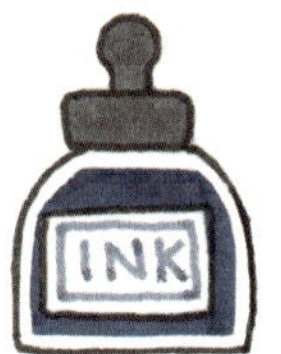
INK

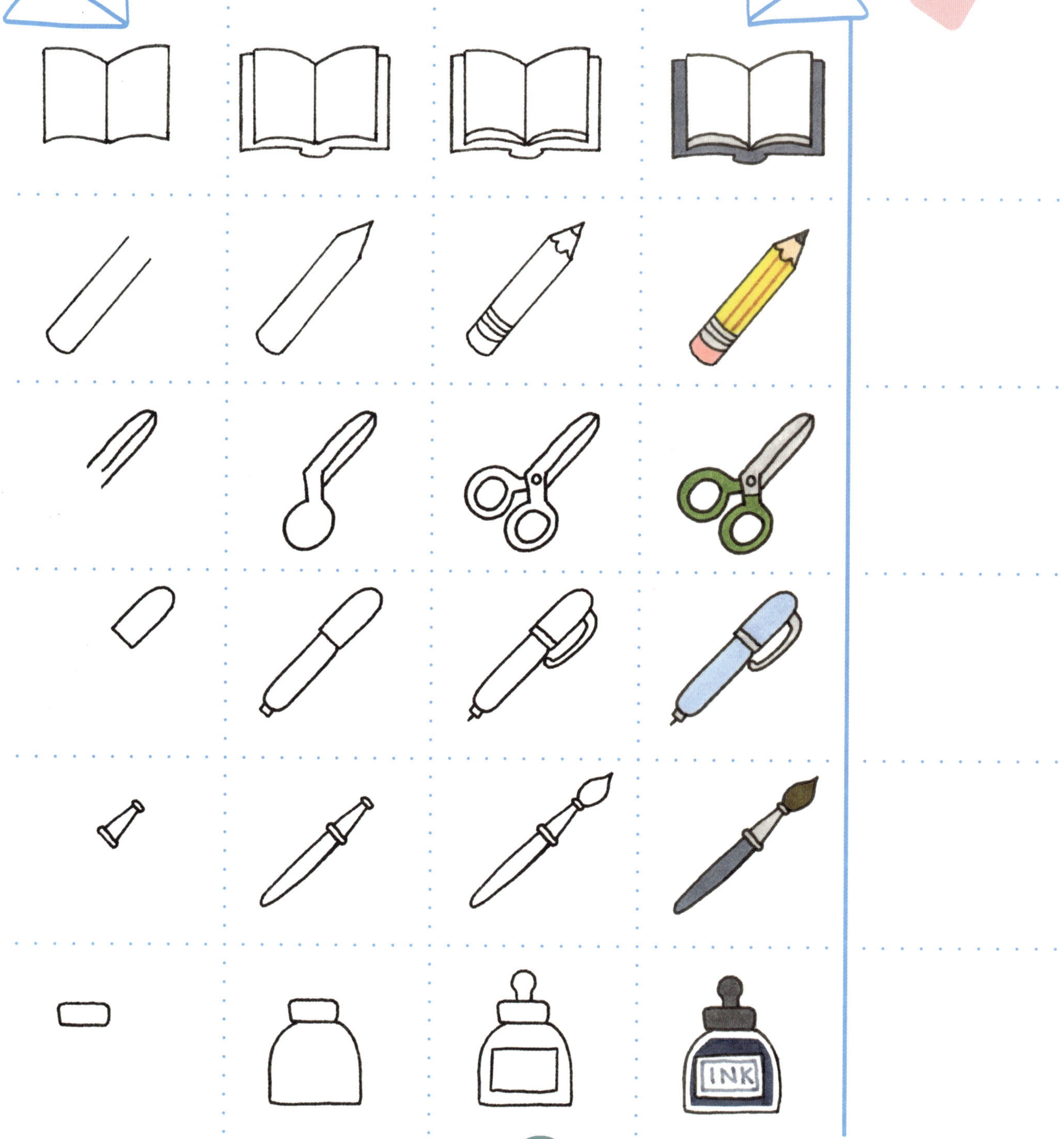

Draw Here

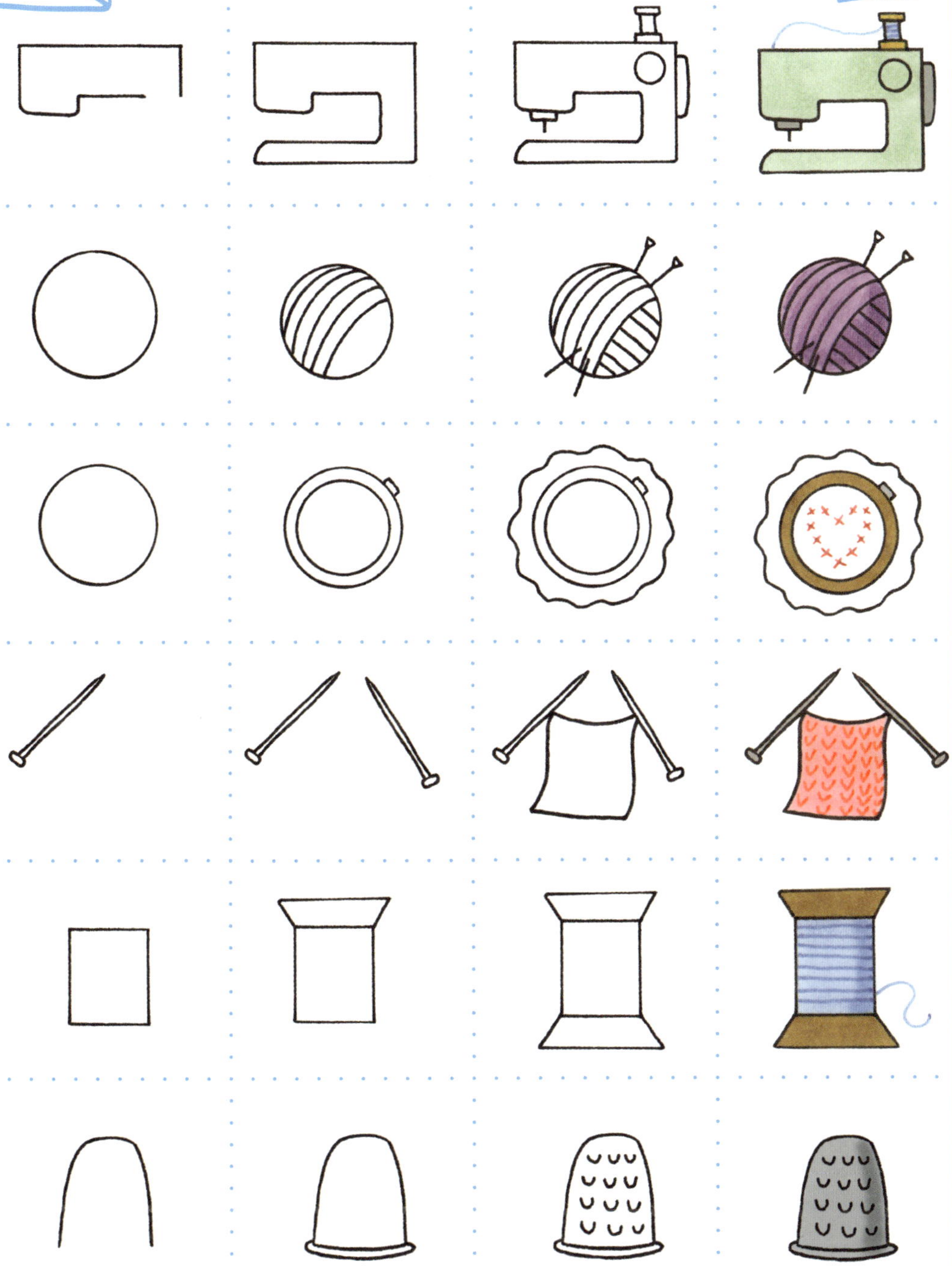

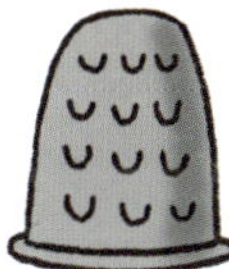

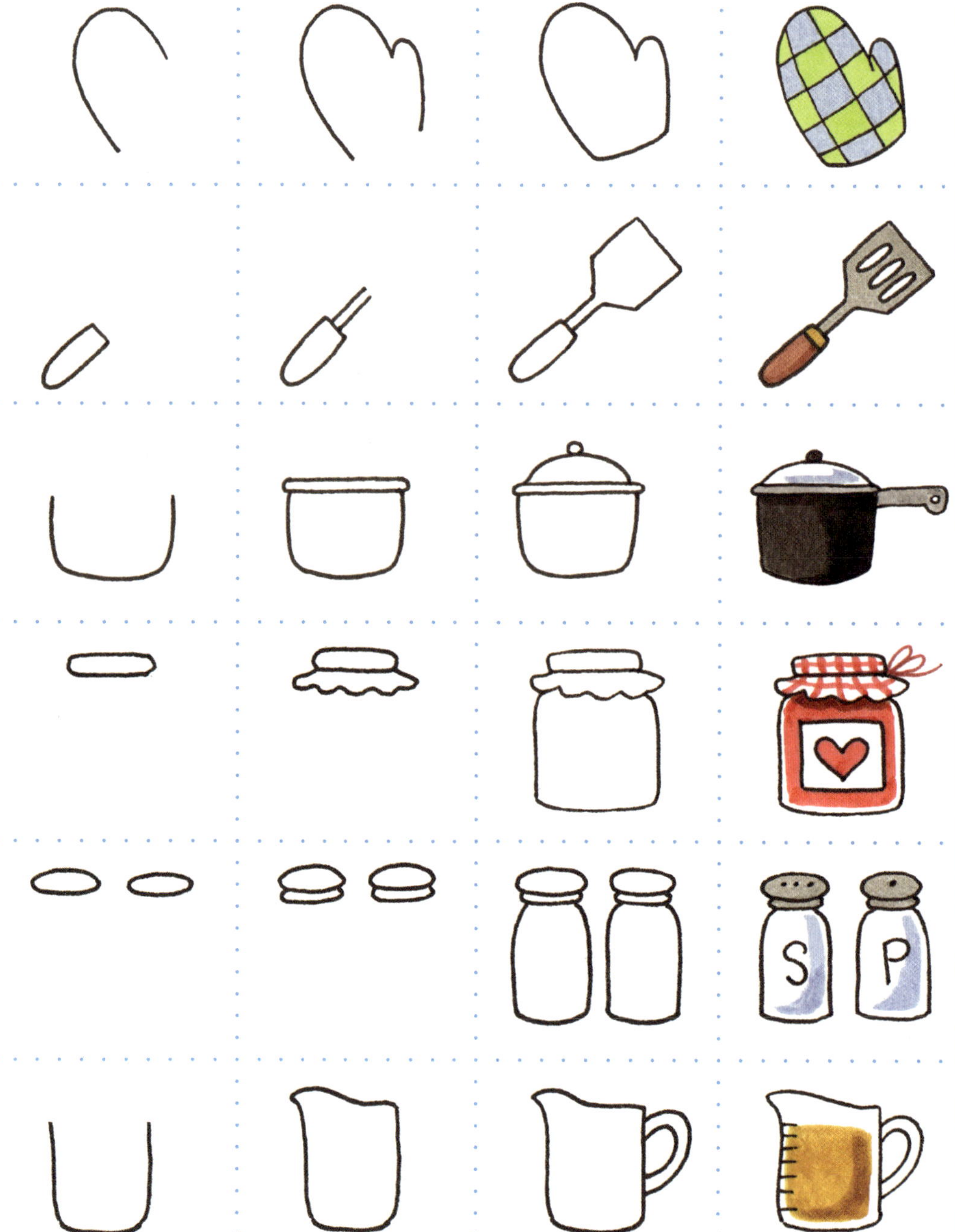
Draw Here

Food, Glorious Food!

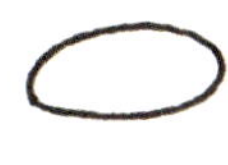 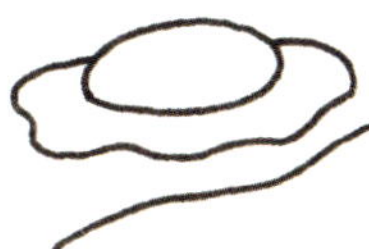 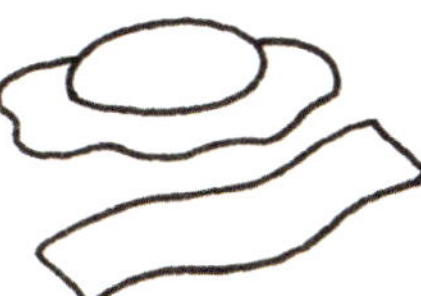 

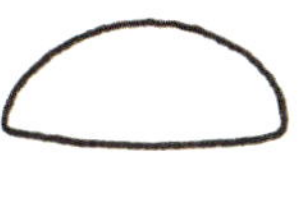 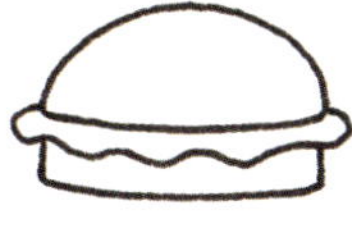 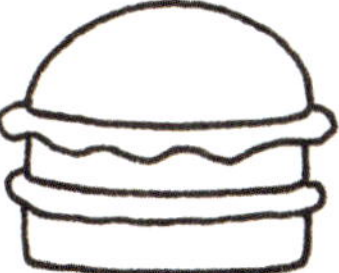 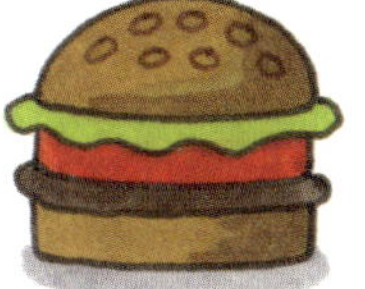

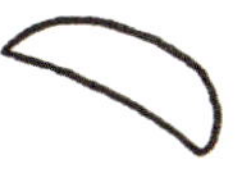 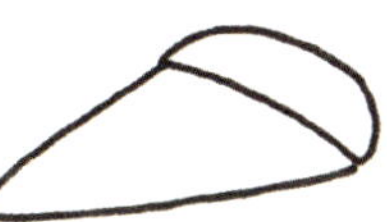 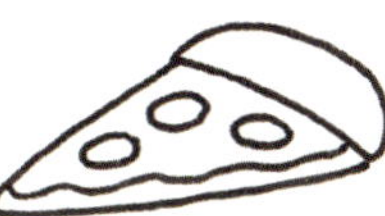 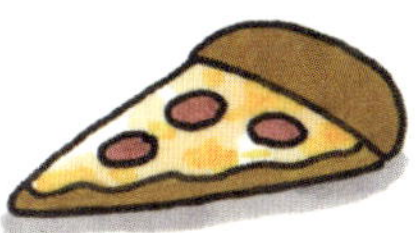

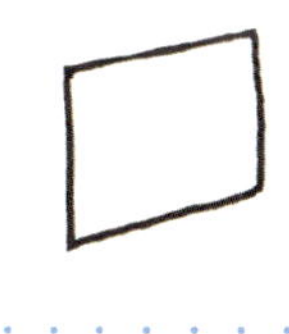 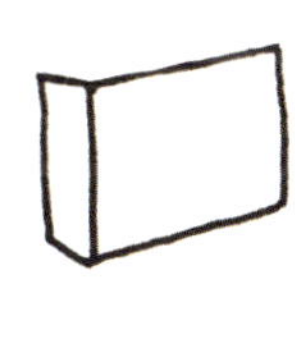 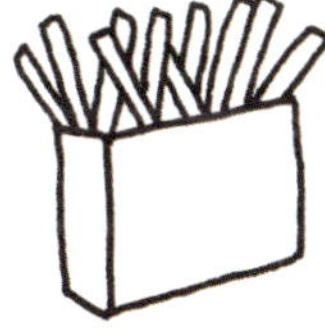 

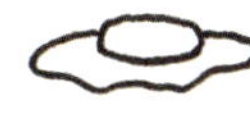 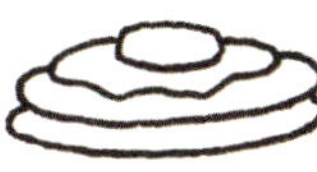 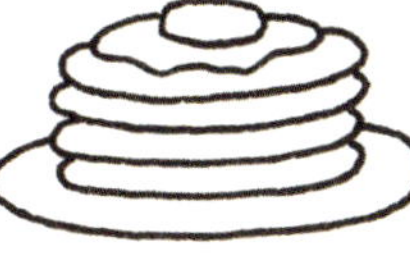 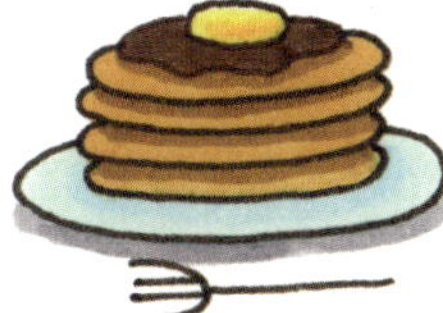

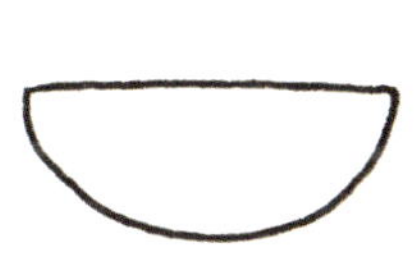 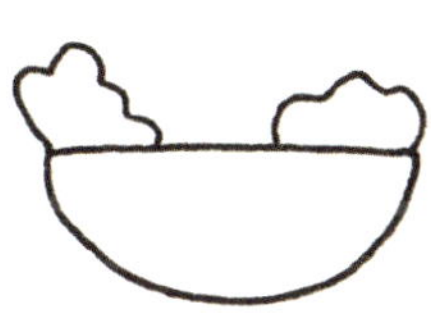 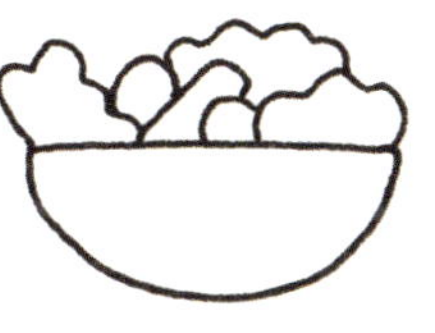 

Draw Here

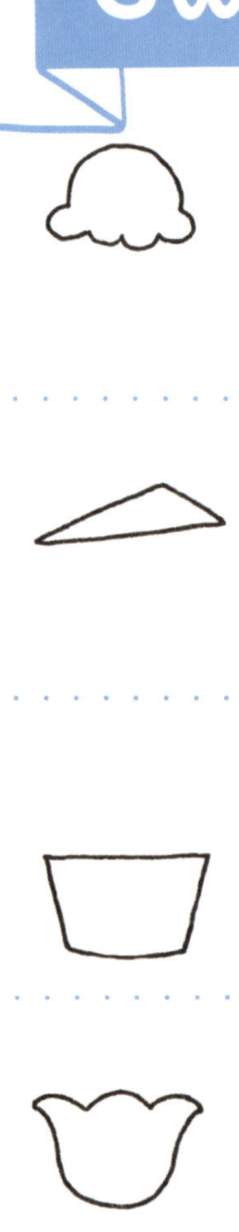   

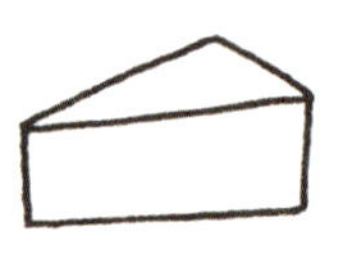 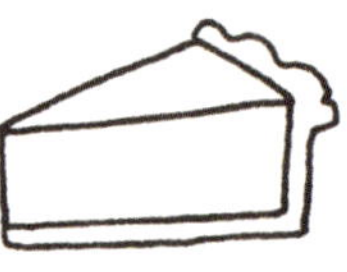 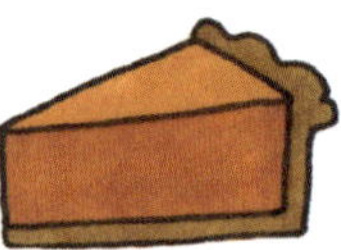

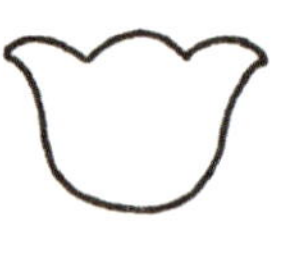 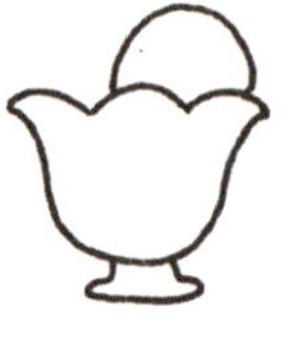 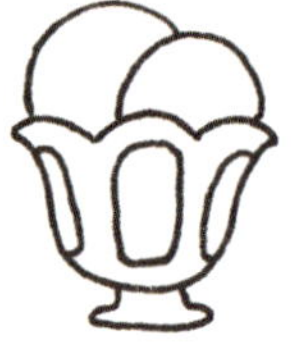 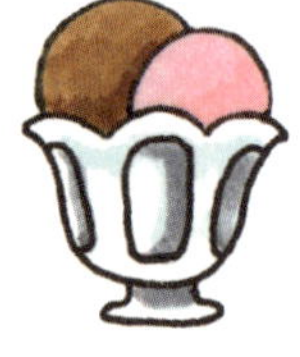

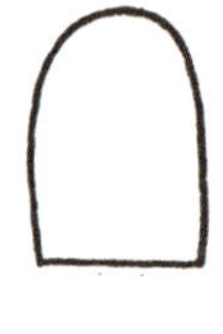 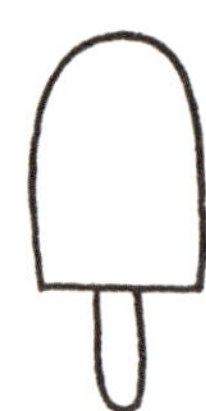 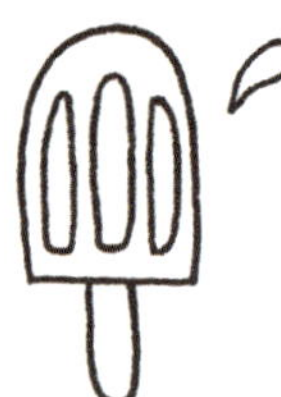 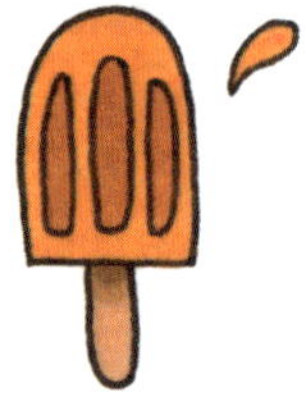

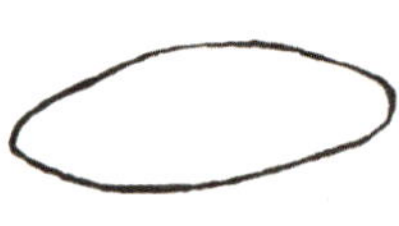 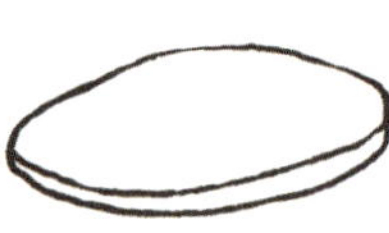 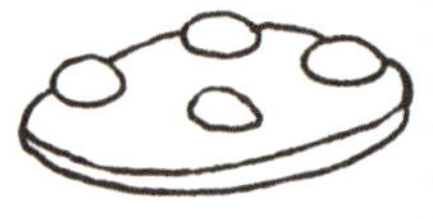 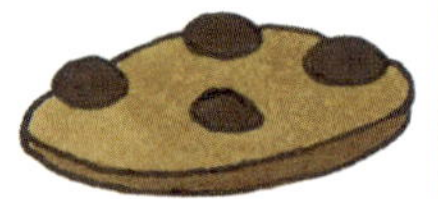

Baked In

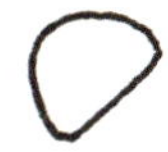 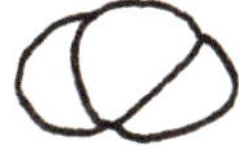  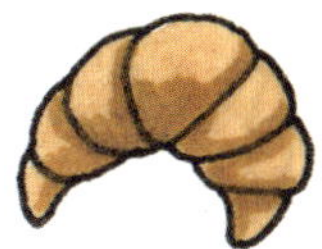

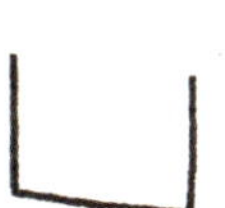  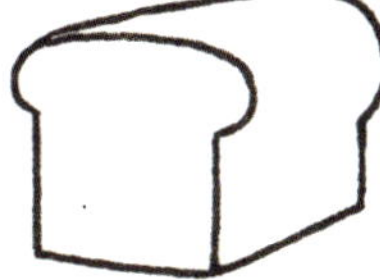 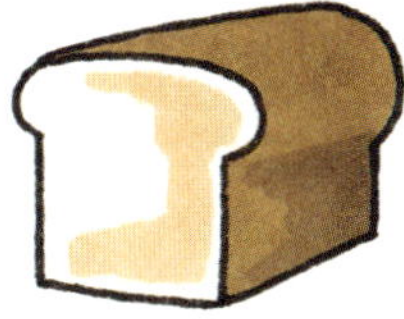

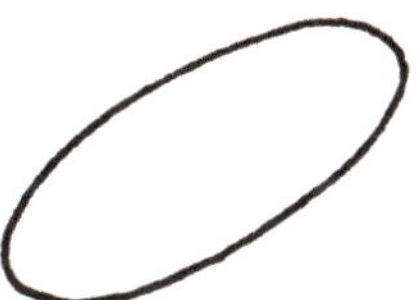 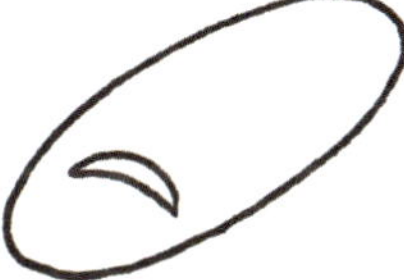 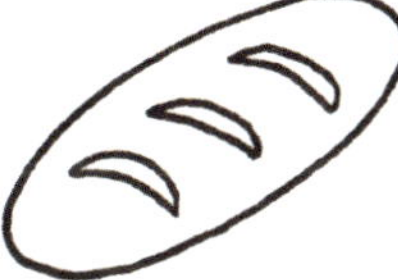 

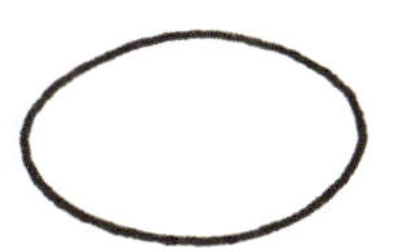 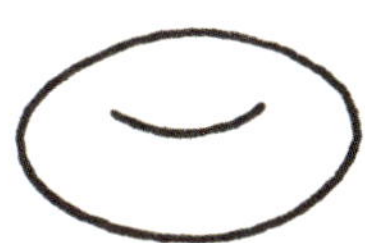 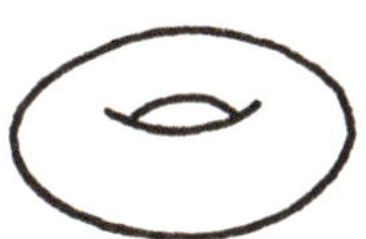 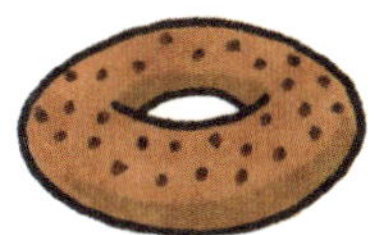

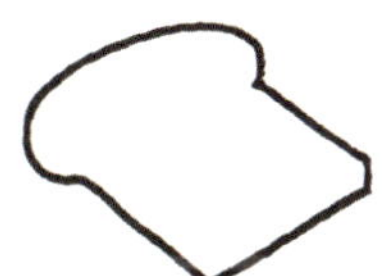 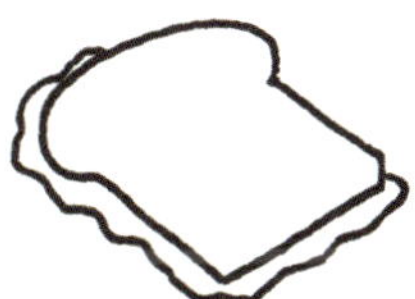 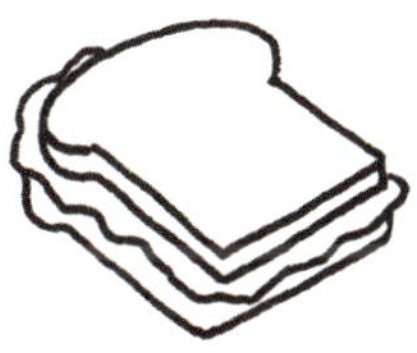 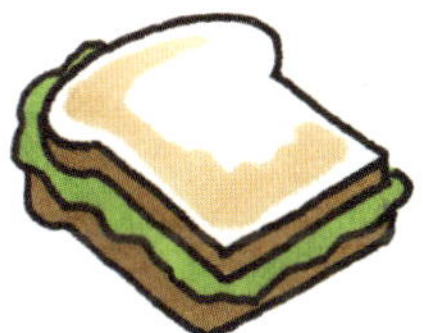

Sip & Savor!
Draw Here

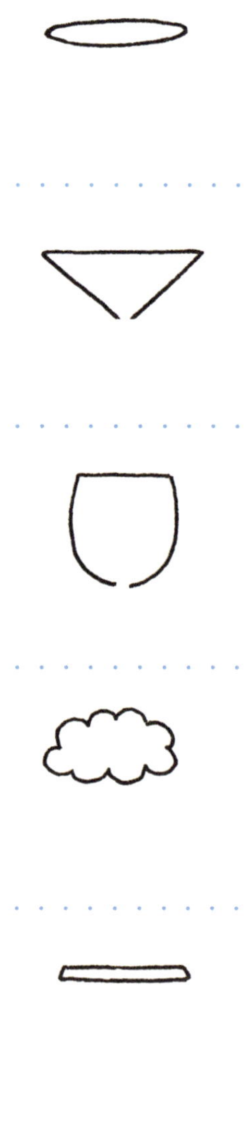
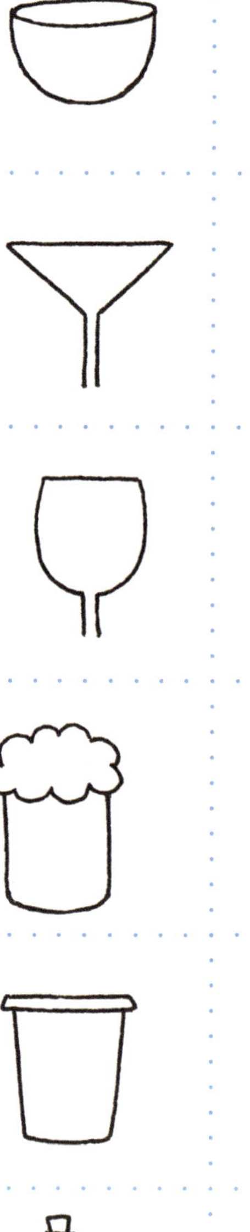
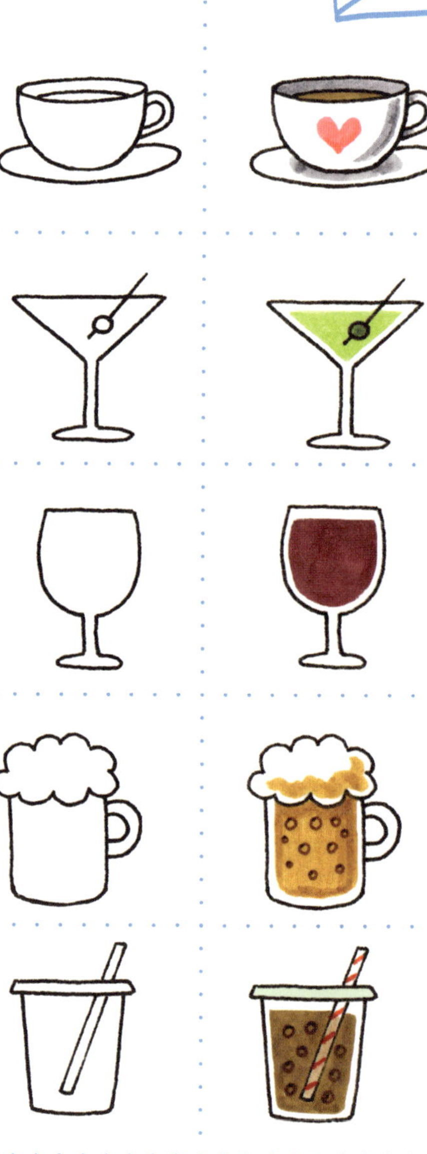
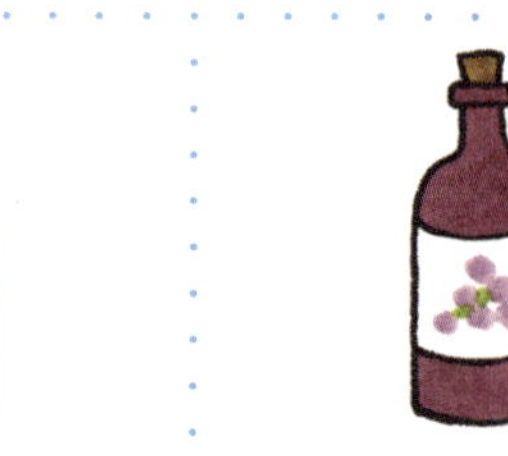

Draw Here

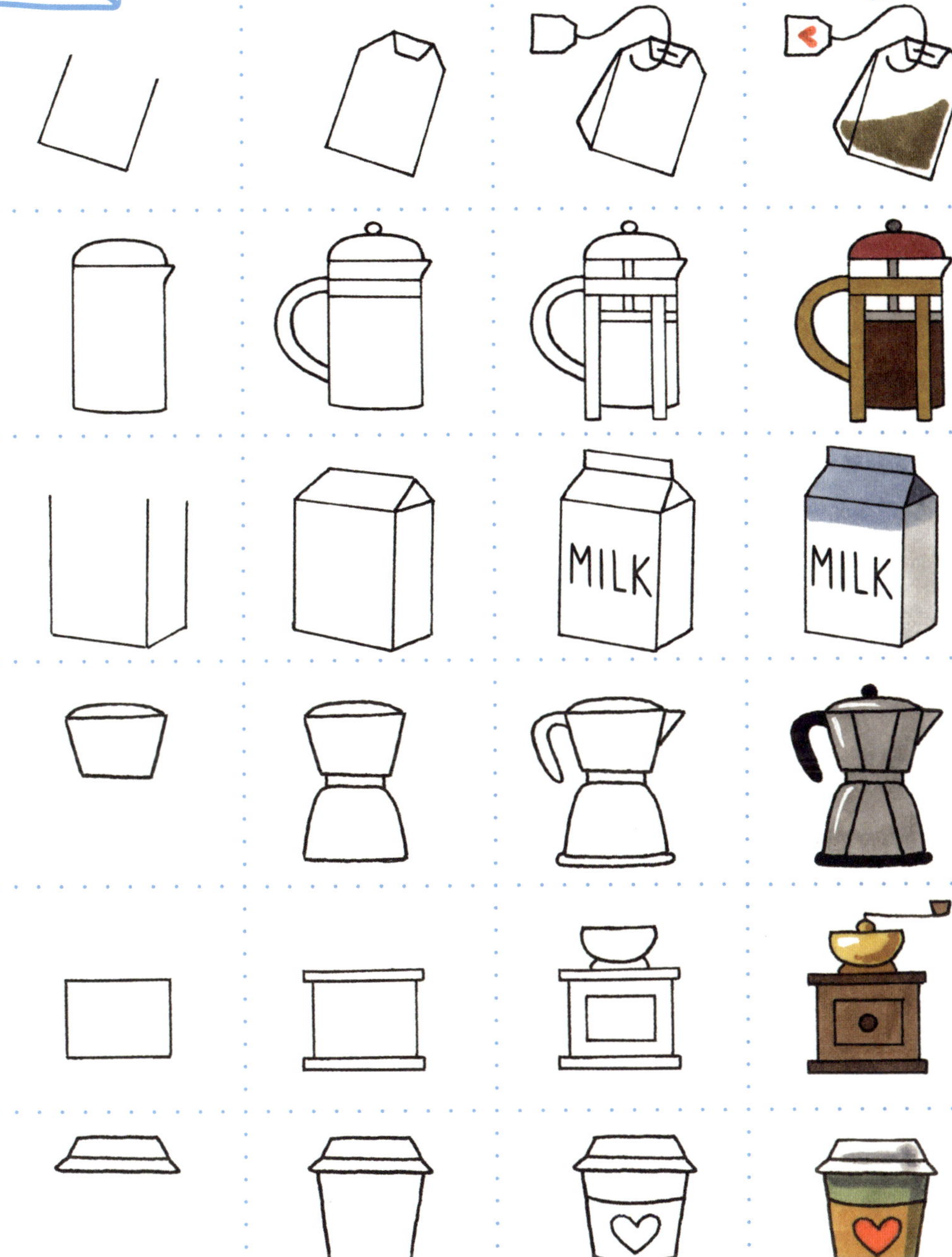

At the Beach

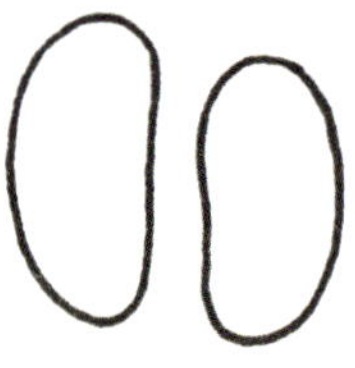 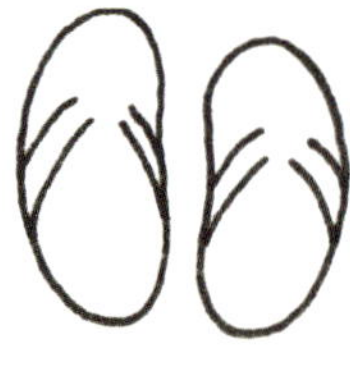 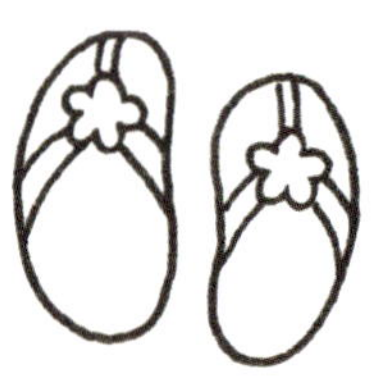 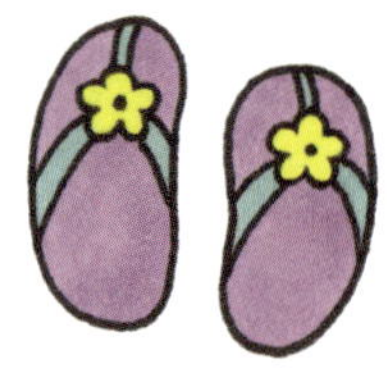

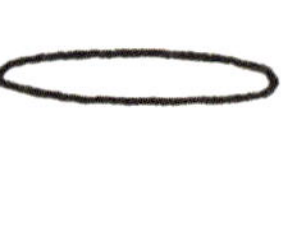 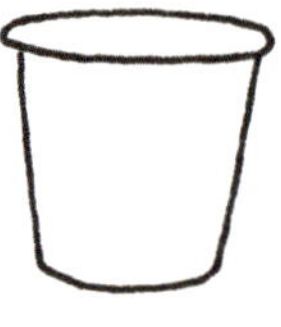 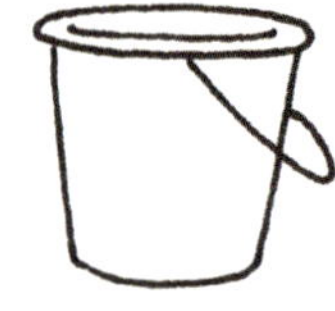 

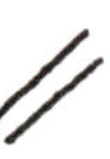 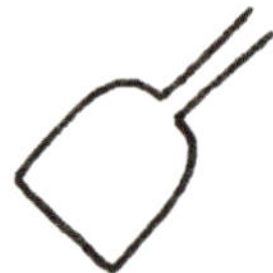 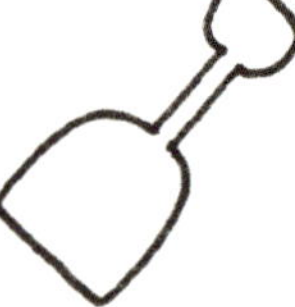 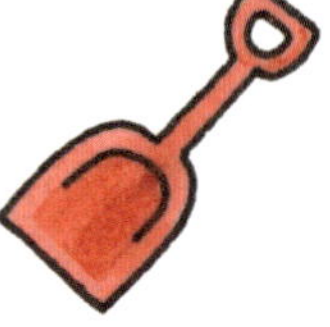

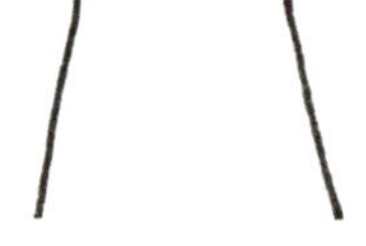 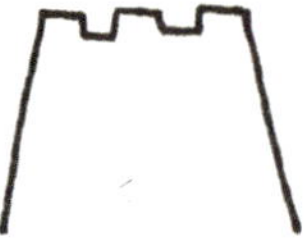 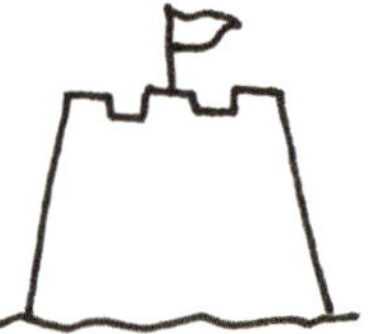 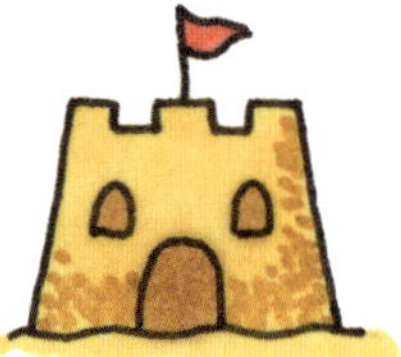

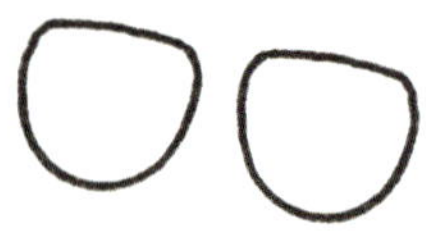 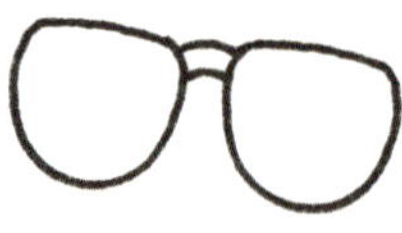 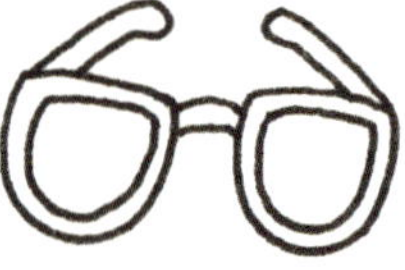 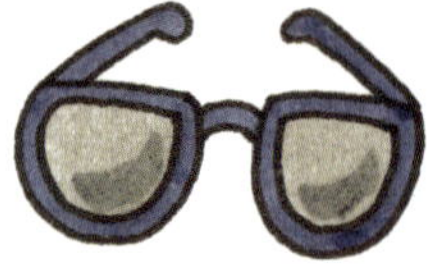

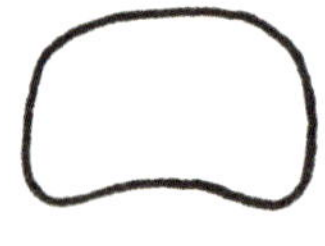 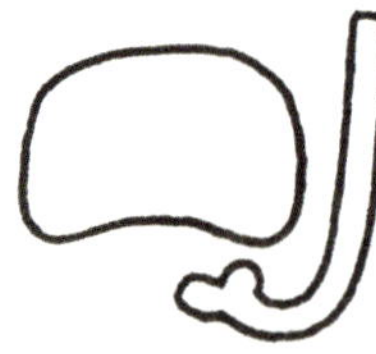 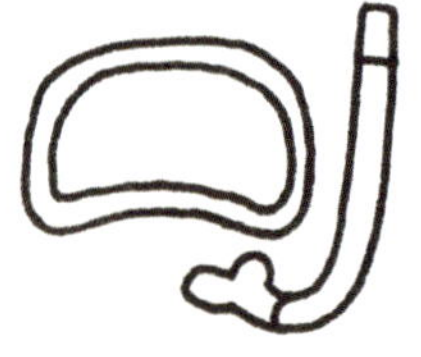 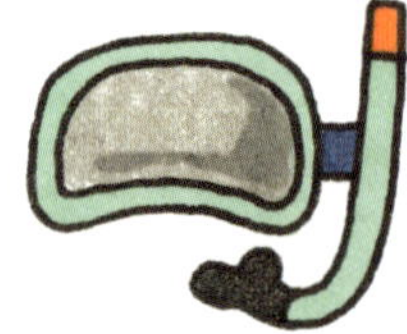

Draw Here

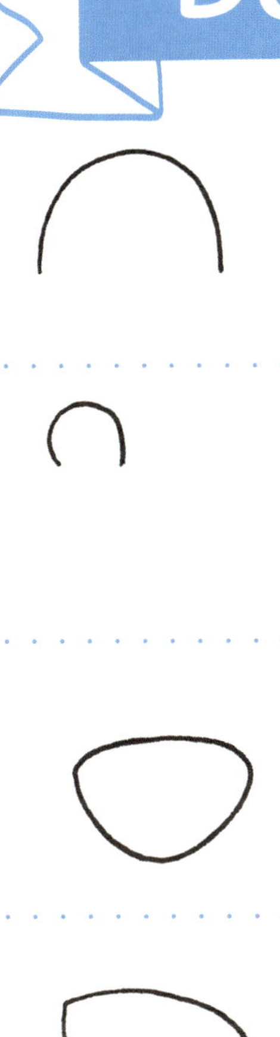
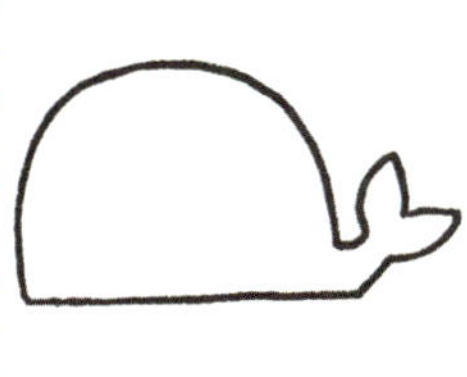
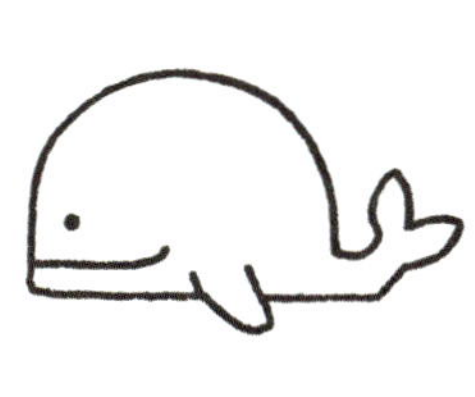
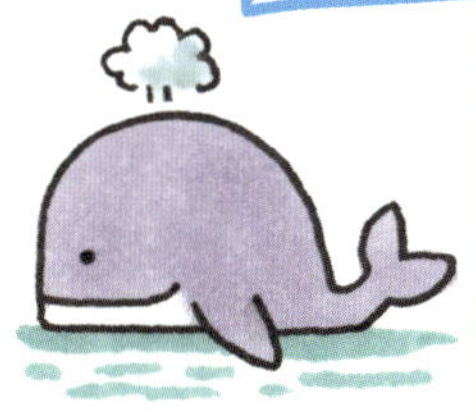
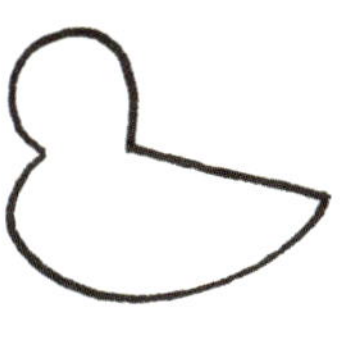
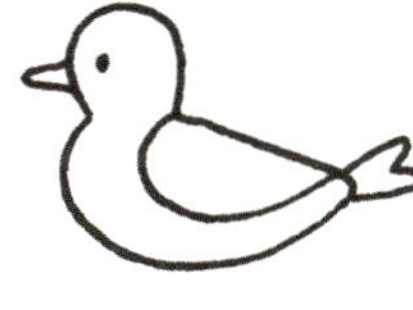
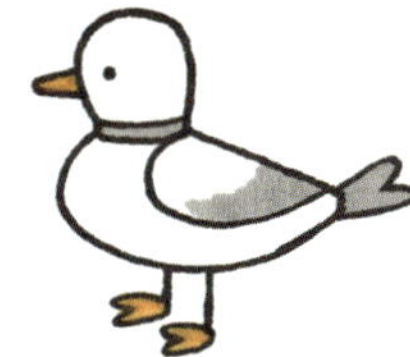
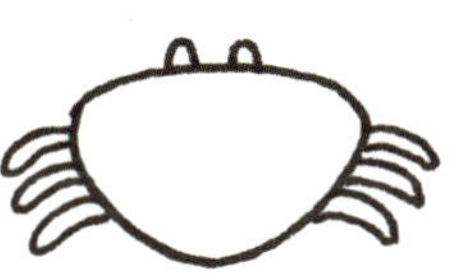
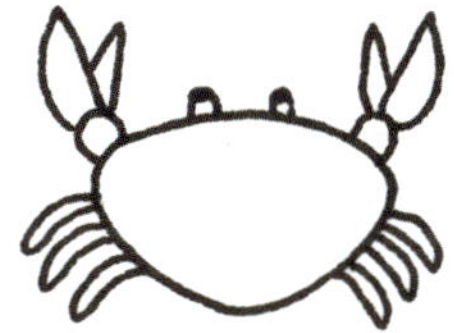
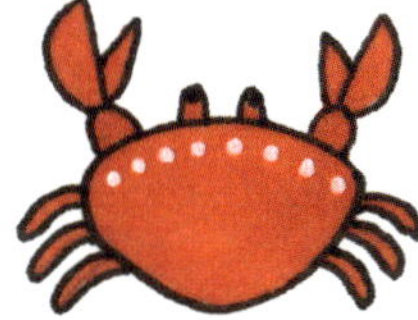
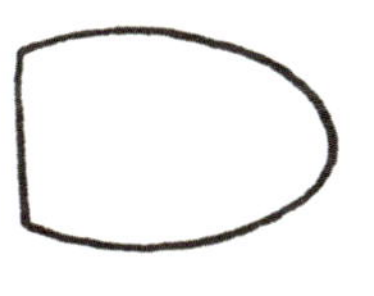
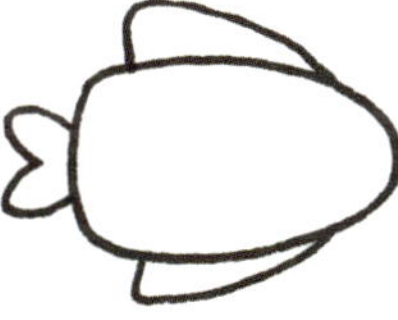
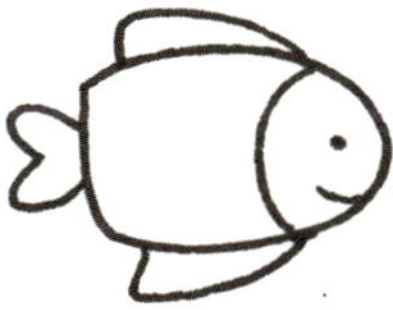
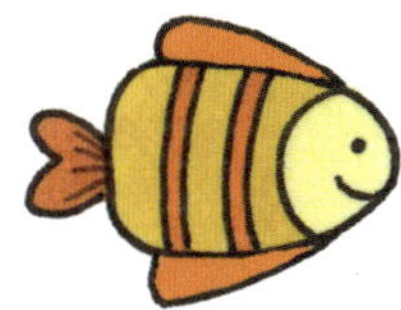
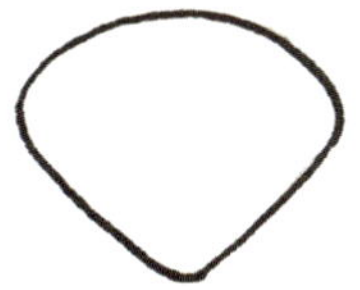
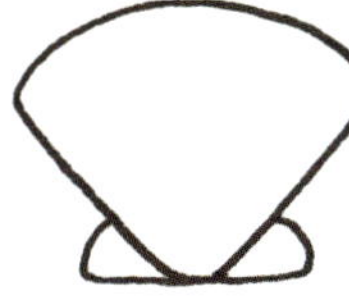
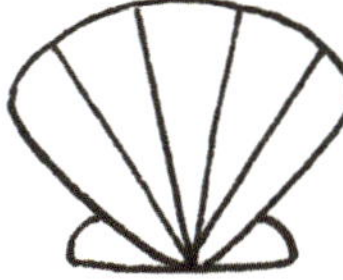
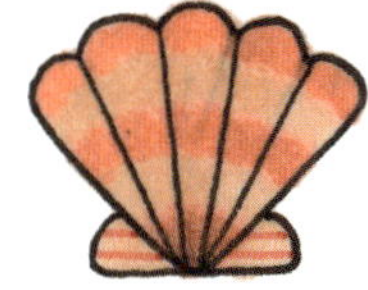
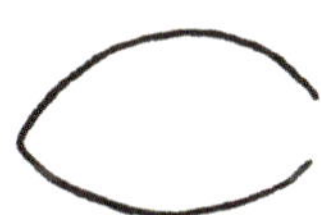
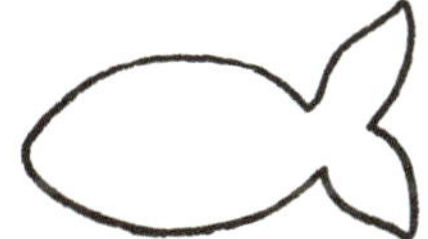
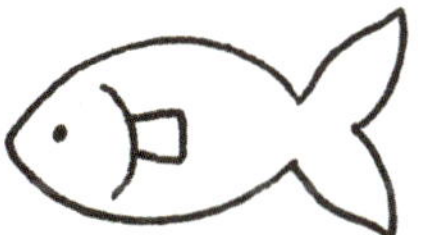
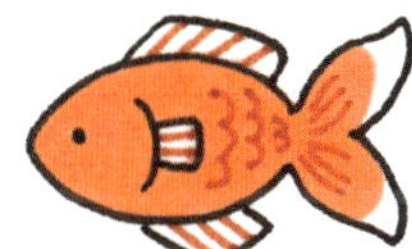

School Days

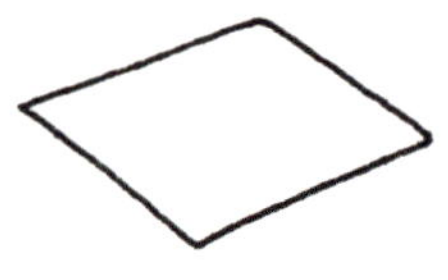 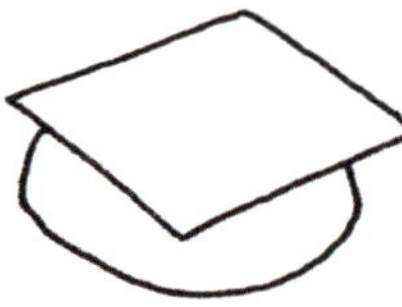 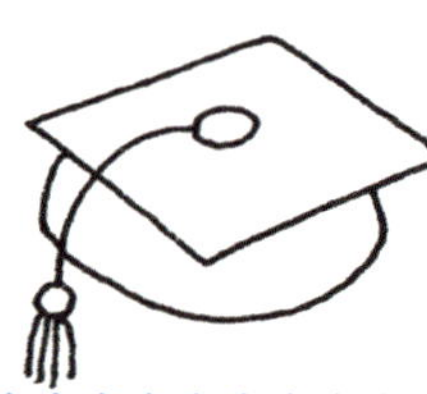 

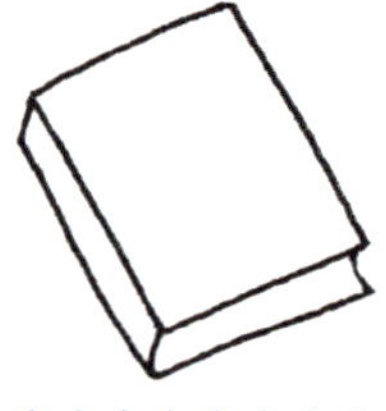 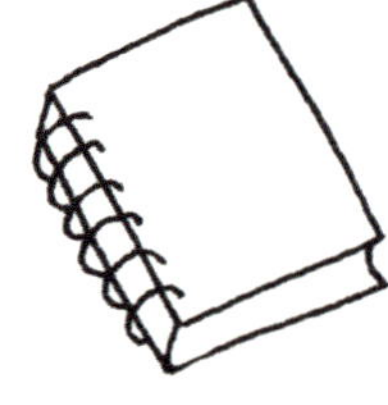 

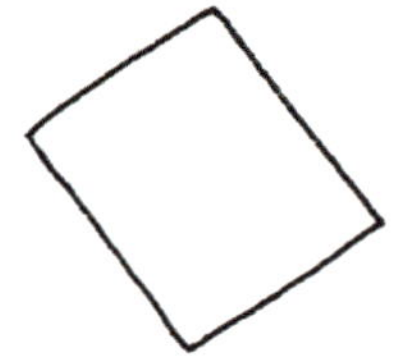 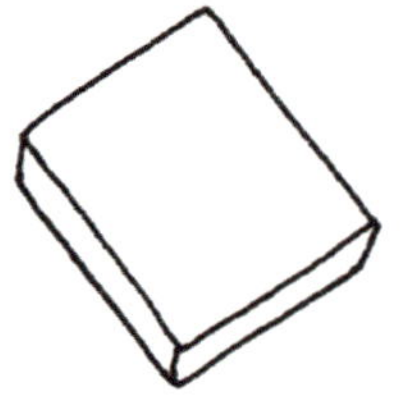 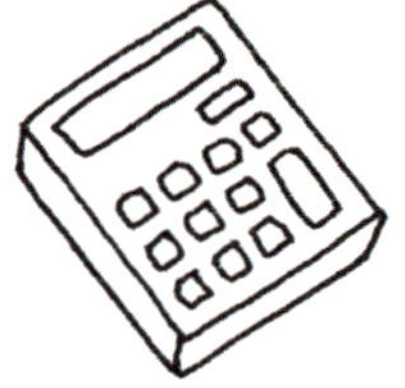 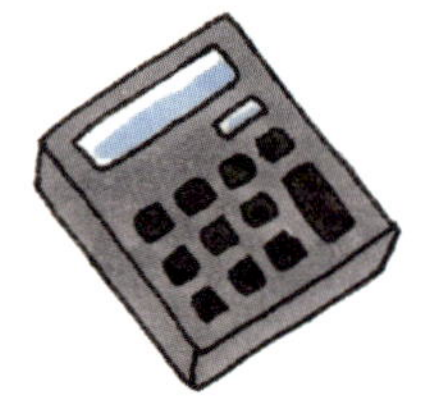

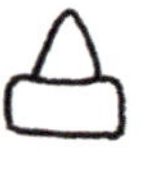 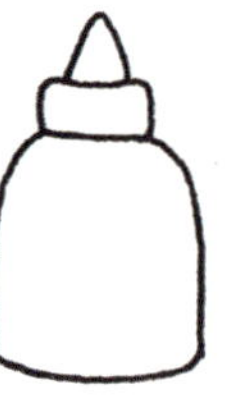 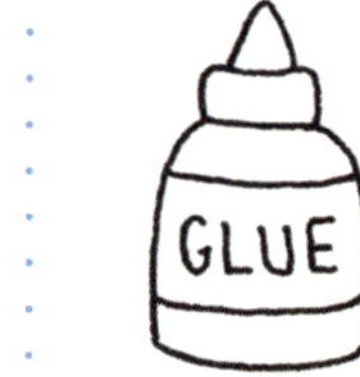

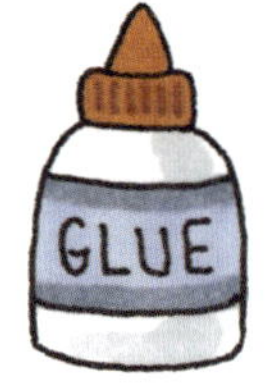

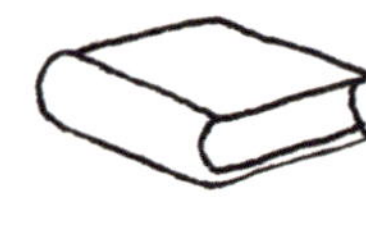   

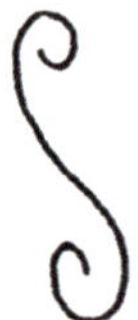 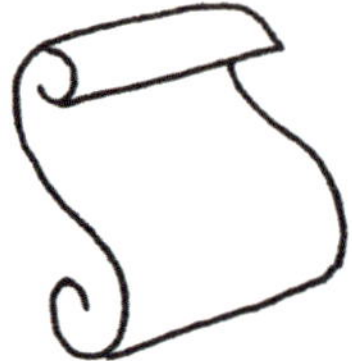  

Roughing It

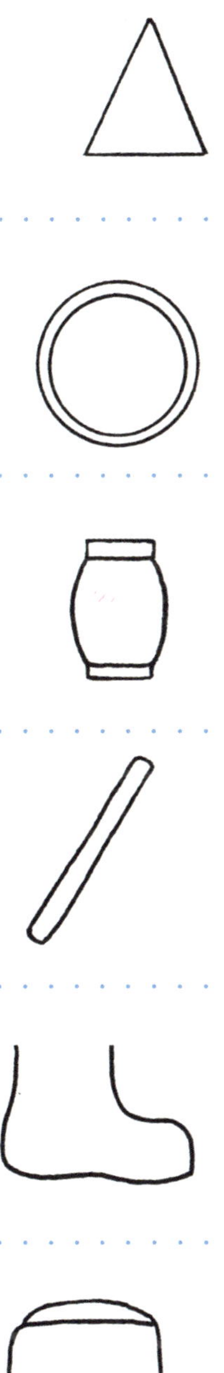
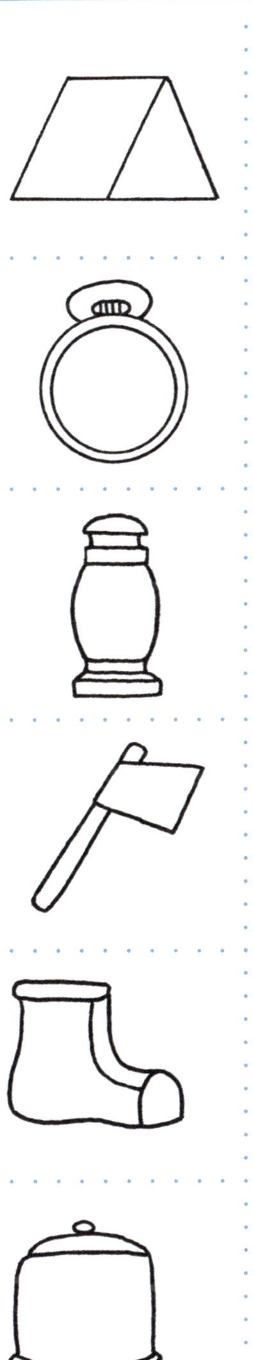
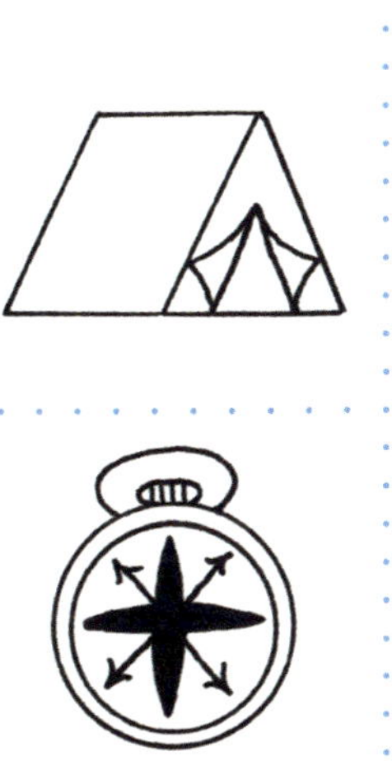
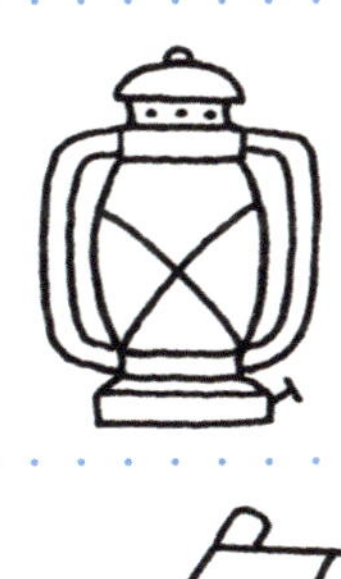
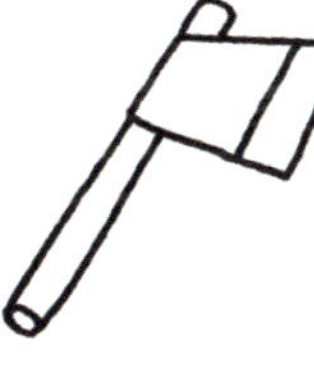
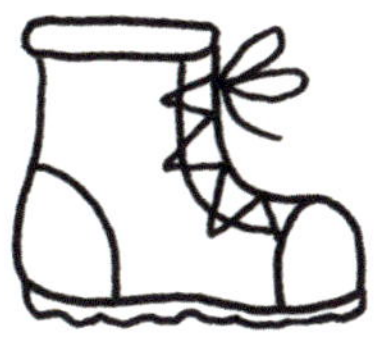

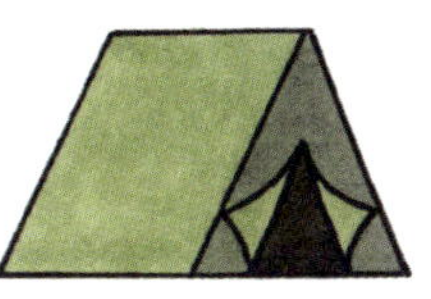
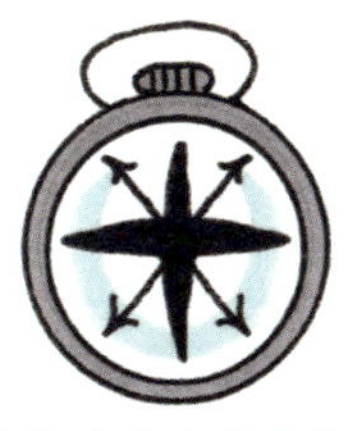
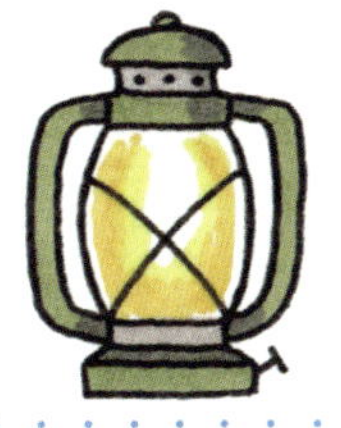
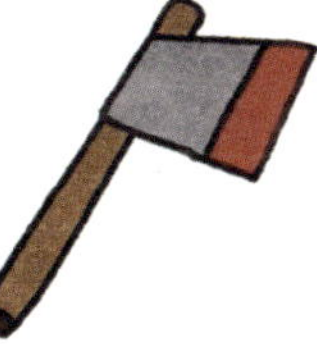
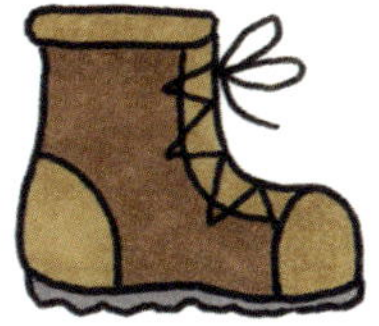
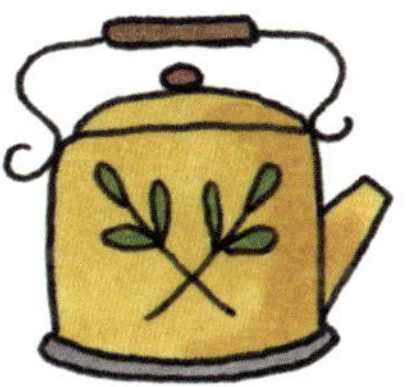

Draw Here

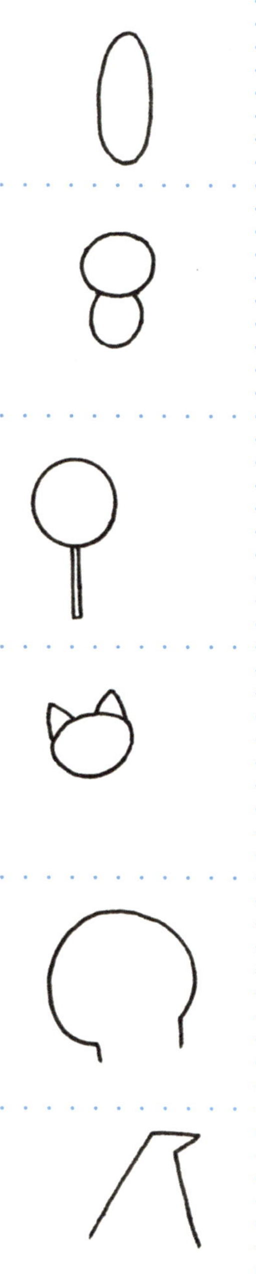
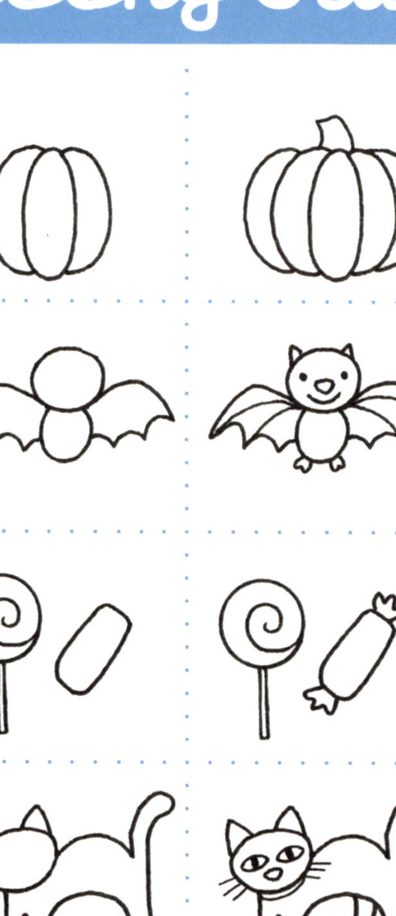
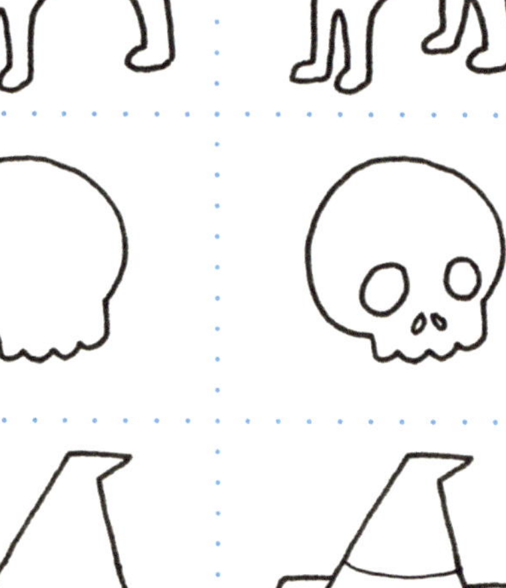

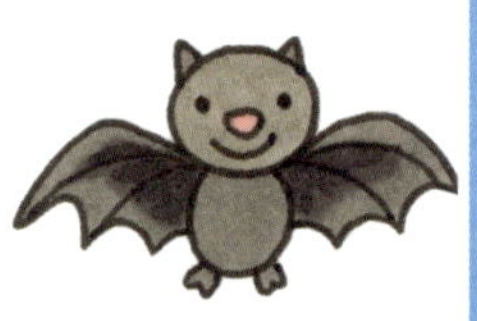
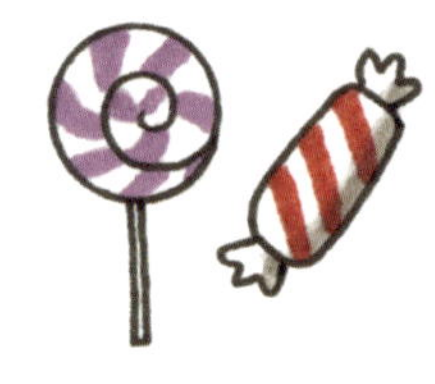

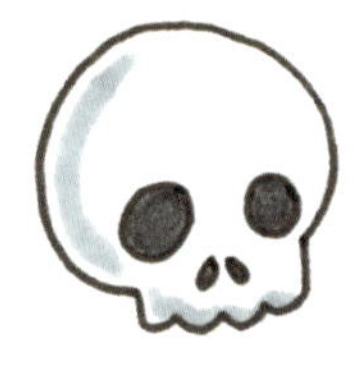

Autumn Things

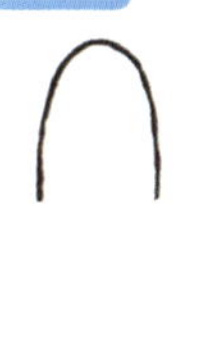 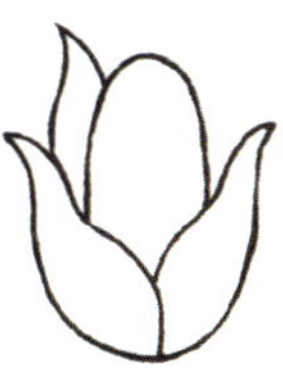 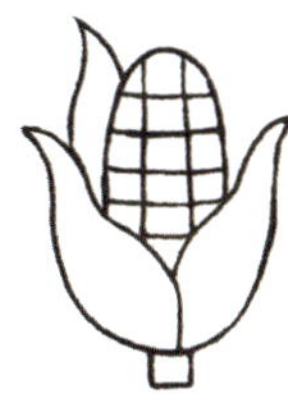 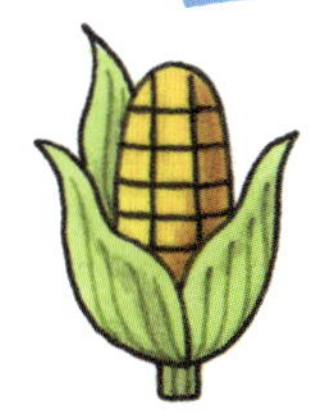

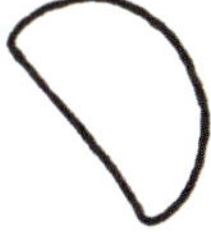 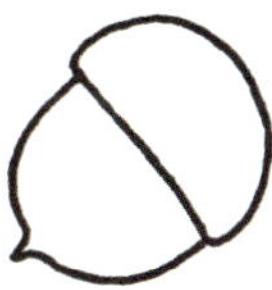 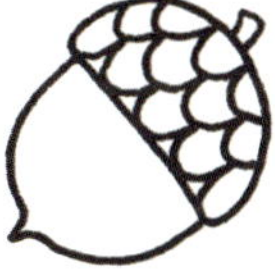 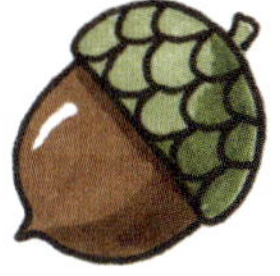

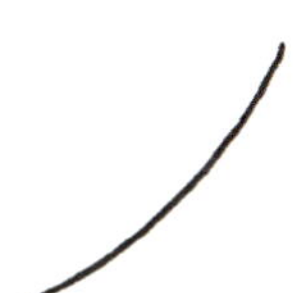 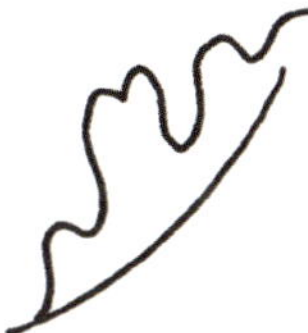 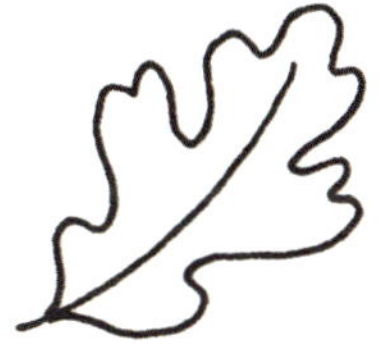 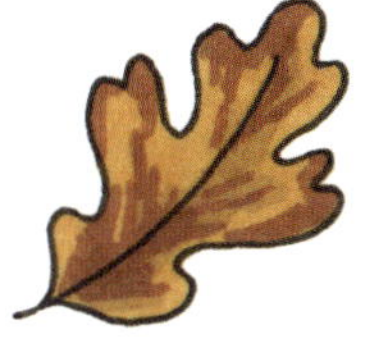

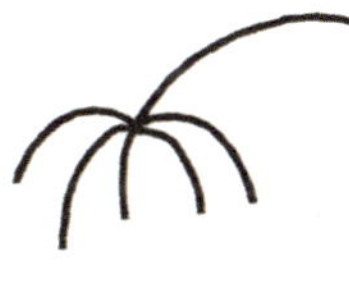 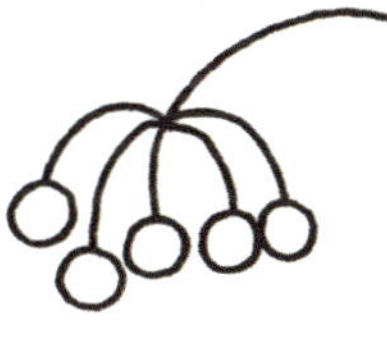 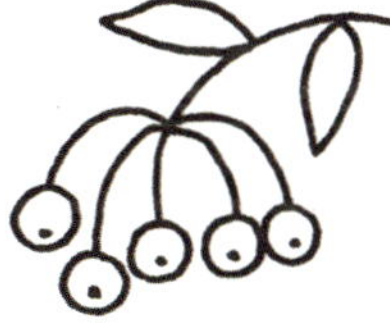 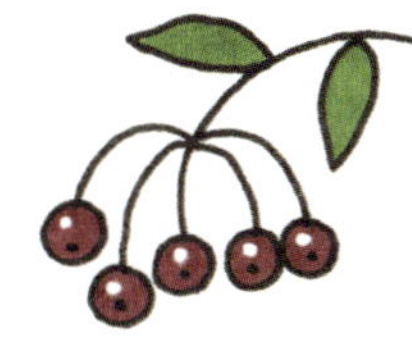

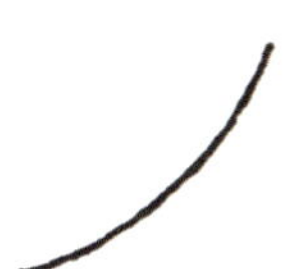 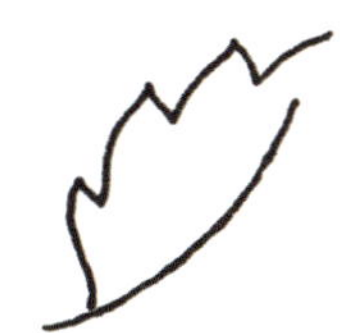 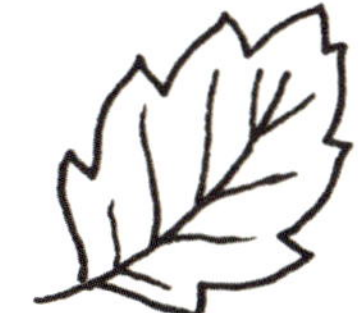 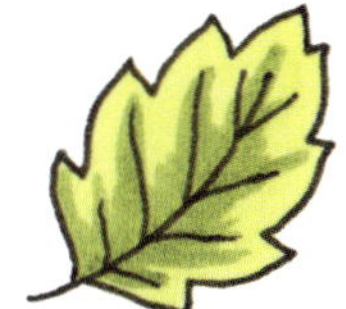

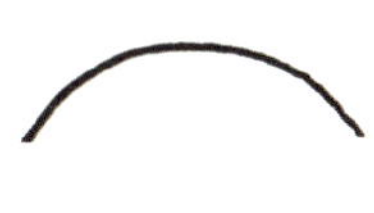 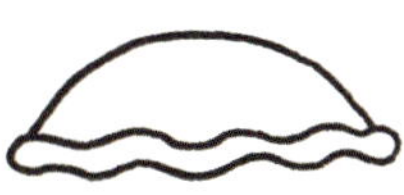 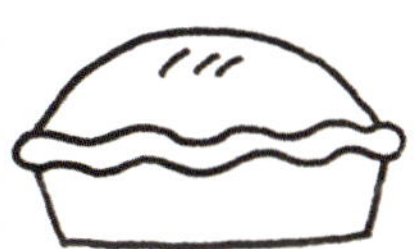 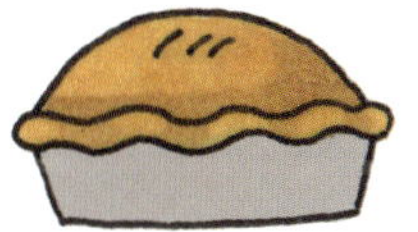

Bundle Up!

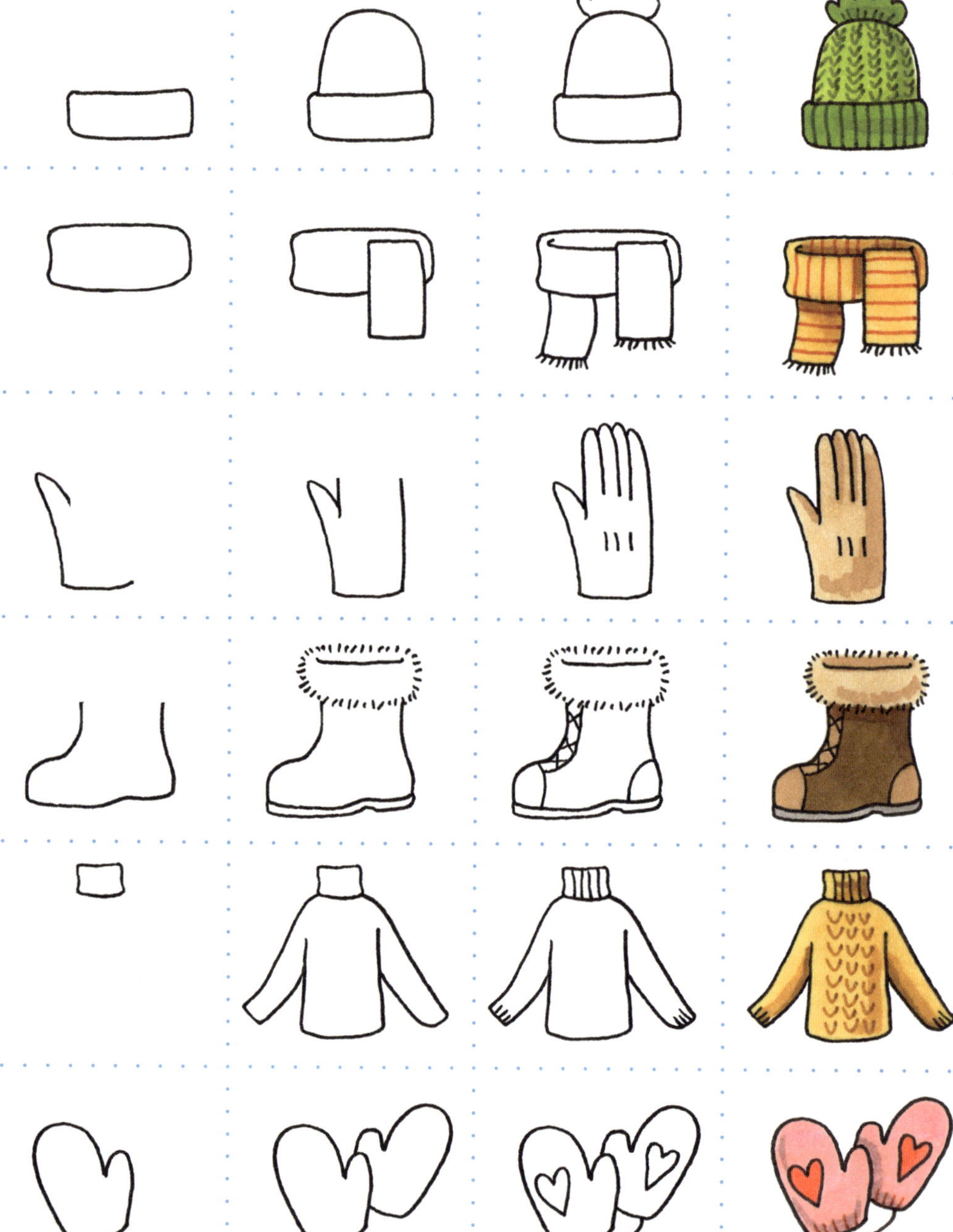

Happy Holidays!

Draw Here

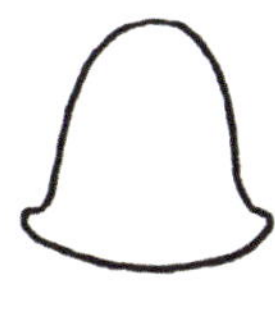 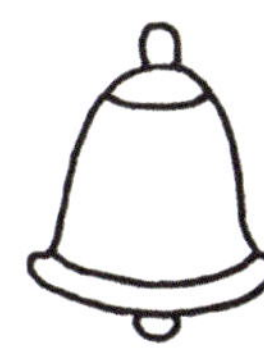  

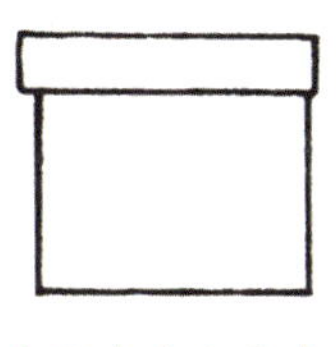 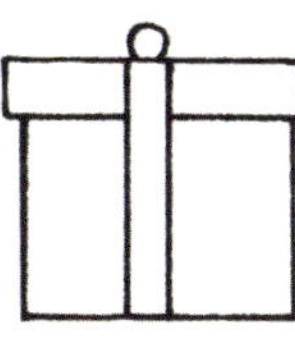 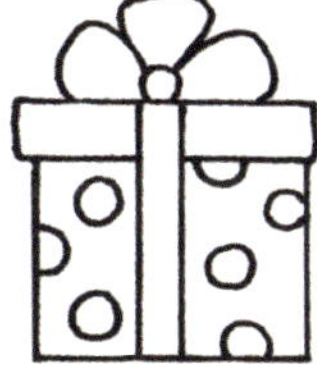 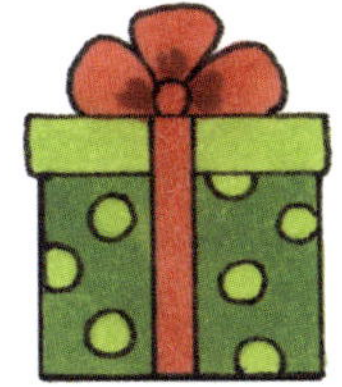

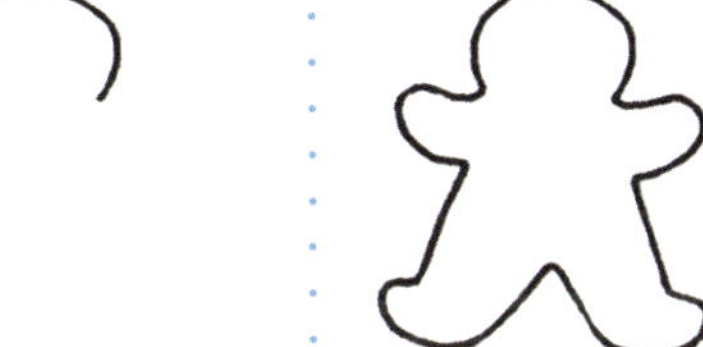  

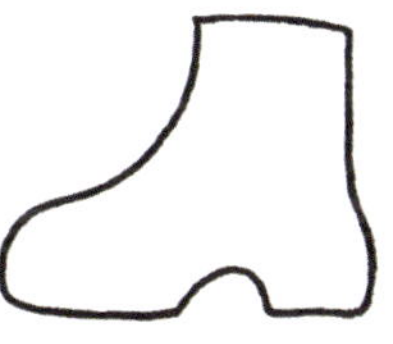 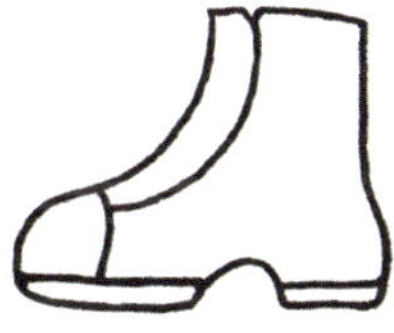 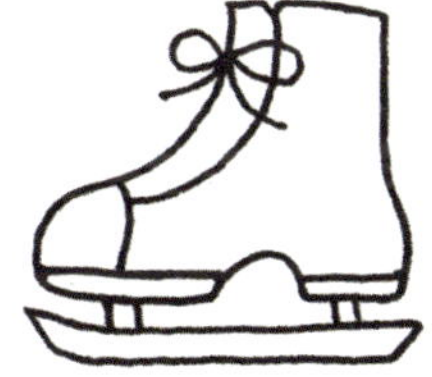 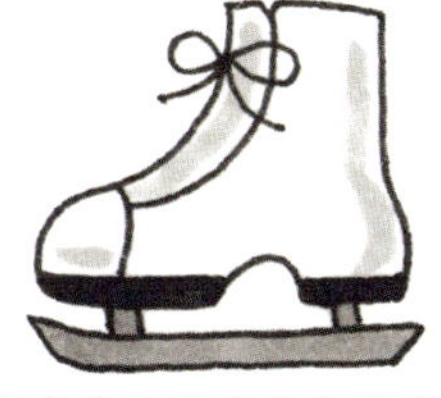

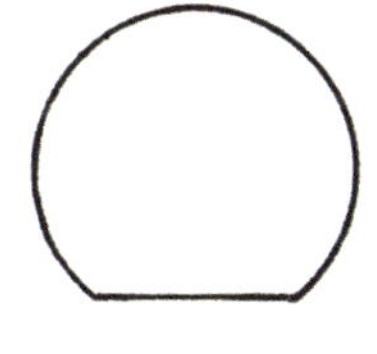 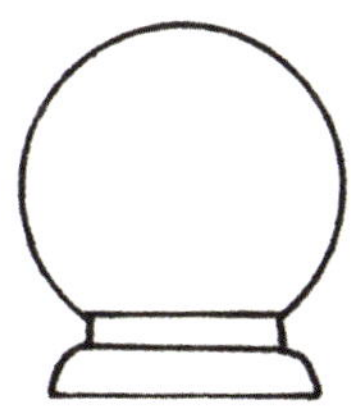  

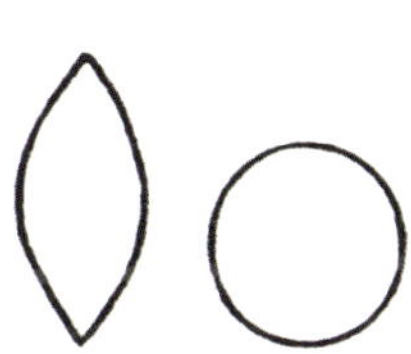 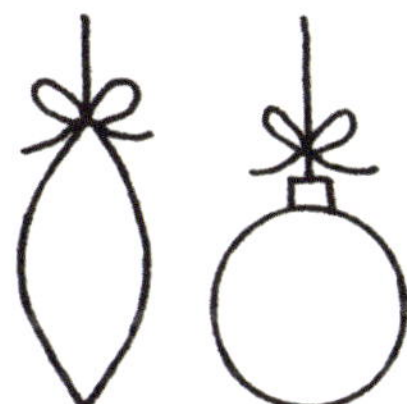 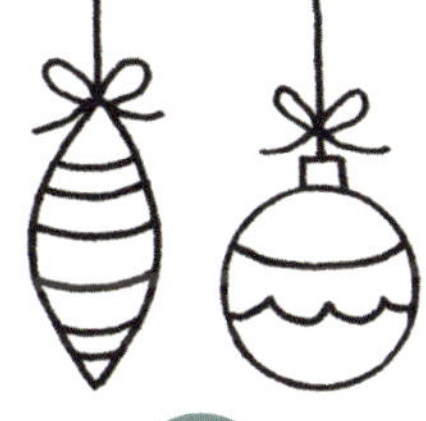 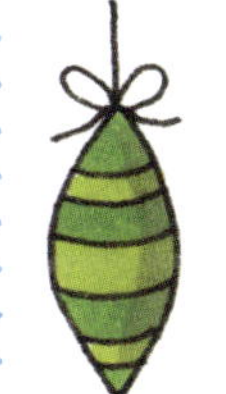 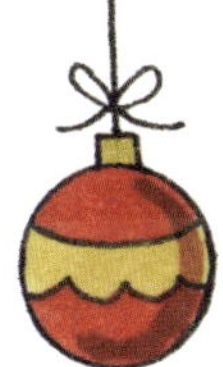

Everything Baby

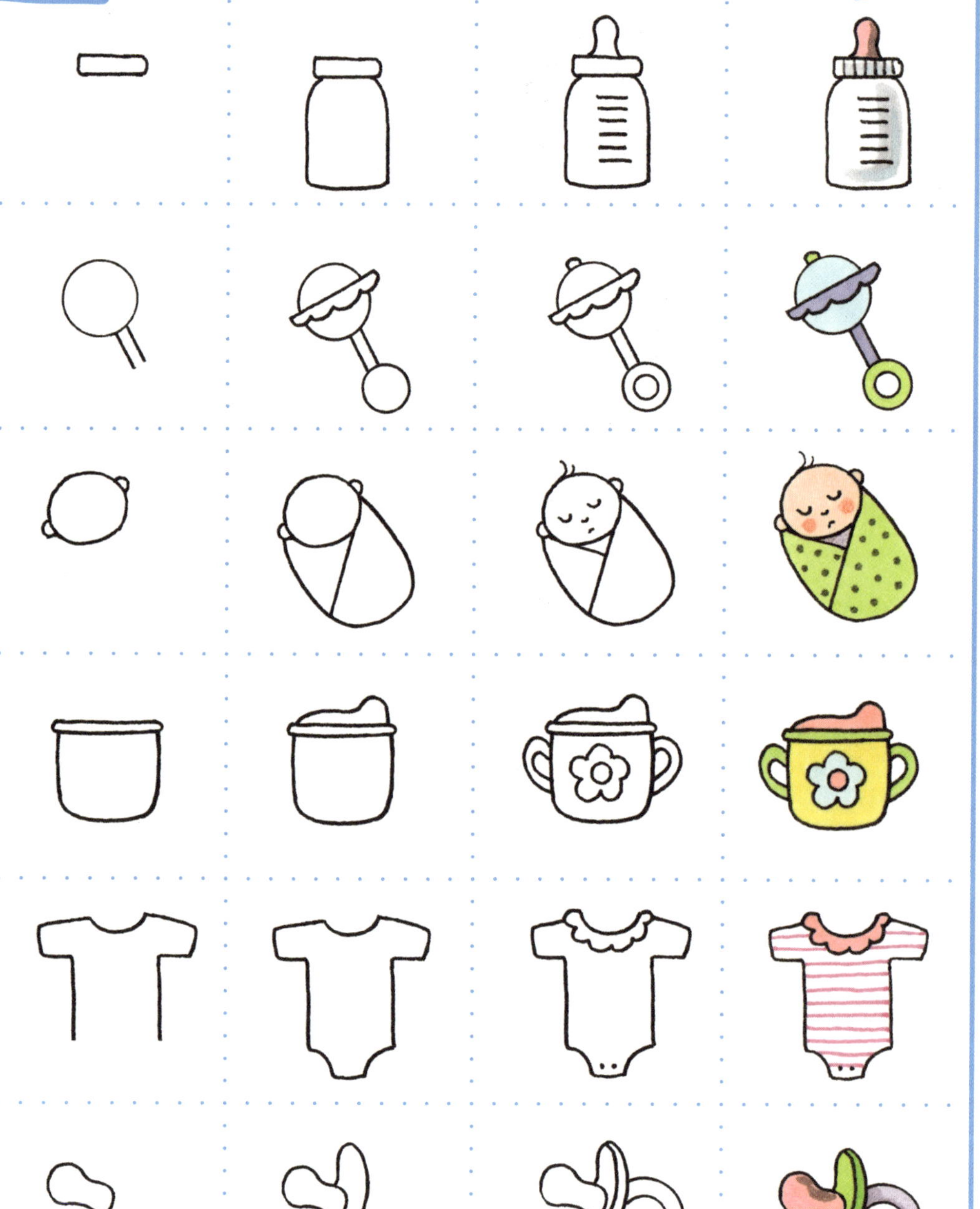

Dearest Reader & Fellow Super Cute Artist,

I hope you have enjoyed this book and that it has inspired in you a love of drawing cute things! As you continue practicing, you'll gain confidence and your skills will grow. Remember, this is a process for YOU, to help you relax and have fun with drawing. Take these lessons and let your creativity flow. Your journal or sketchbook can be a place of exploration and comfort. I draw in my journal every day for self-care and relaxation. Drawing is a great way to unwind!

Yours in Super Cuteness,
Jane Maday

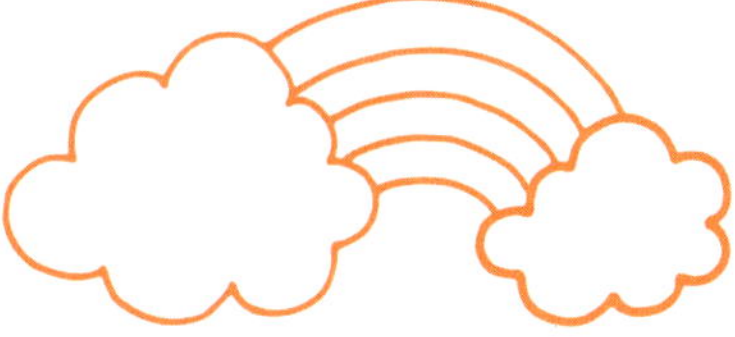

P.S. Come and visit me on Instagram, @janemaday, where I post pages from my journal. I'd love to hear from you!

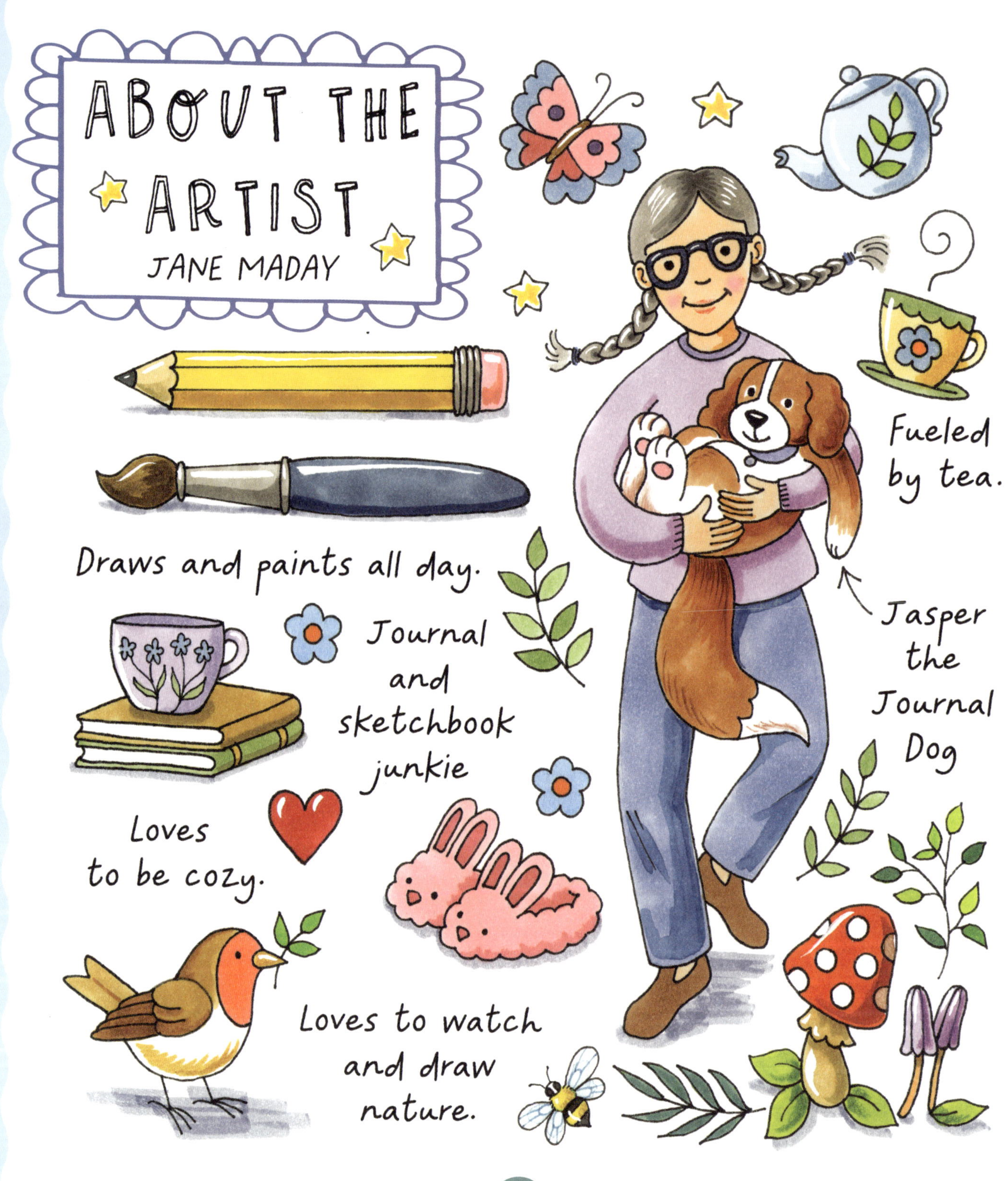

ABOUT THE ARTIST
JANE MADAY
Draws and paints all day.
Journal and sketchbook junkie
Loves to be cozy.
Loves to watch and draw nature.
Fueled by tea.
Jasper the Journal Dog